MANK

Also by Richard Meryman

ANDREW WYETH

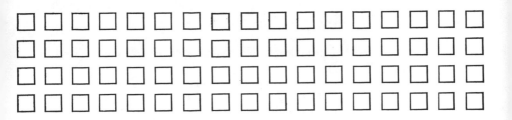

MANK

THE WIT, WORLD, AND LIFE OF HERMAN MANKIEWICZ

by RICHARD MERYMAN

WILLIAM MORROW AND COMPANY, INC.

NEW YORK   1978

Grateful acknowledgment is made for permission to quote from the following:

Excerpts from *Diary of Our Own Samuel Pepys* by Franklin P. Adams quoted with permission of the Estate of Franklin P. Adams and its attorney Jacob I. Charney. All rights reserved.

"Good creatures, do you love your lives" from *The Collected Poems of A. E. Housman*. Copyright 1936 by Barclays Bank Ltd. Copyright © 1964 by Robert E. Symons. Reprinted by permission of Holt, Rinehart and Winston, Publishers; the Society of Authors as the literary representative of the Estate of A. E. Housman; and Jonathan Cape, Ltd., publishers of A. E. Housman's *Collected Poems*.

PHOTO CREDITS

The following photographs are from the Museum of Modern Art collection:
p. 217 (MGM executives); p. 299, center (Orson Welles); p. 300, bottom ("rosebud" sled from *Citizen Kane*); p. 301, lower left (paperweight from *Citizen Kane*); p. 303, bottom (from *Pride of the Yankees*)
From the New York Public Library Theater collection:
p. 109 (Isadora Duncan and Sergei Essenin)

Library of Congress Cataloging in Publication Data

Meryman, Richard (date)
    Mank: the wit, world, and life of Herman Mankiewicz.

    Bibliography: p.
    1. Mankiewicz, Herman Jacob, 1897-1953.
2. Screen writers—United States—Biography. I. Title.
PN1998.A3M31955   812'.5'2   78-8276
ISBN 0-688-03356-3

BOOK DESIGN   CARL WEISS

Printed in the United States of America.

First Edition

1 2 3 4 5 6 7 8 9 10

TO HOPIE

ACKNOWLEDGMENTS

THE TASK OF ENCOMPASSING AND DEFINING A MAN'S LIFE IS
awesome. Then when the great problems and anxieties are
at last surmounted and there is actually a book, you feel
extraordinary affection and gratitude toward those who gave
help and sustained your faith.

My profound thanks, therefore, to Judy and John Mc-
Cusker, who transcribed miles of tape recordings, and to
Maggie Wells and Joan Stillman, who mined invaluable research material. Steve Gelman reacted to chapters as they
were produced. Elizabeth Aldrich read each of the many
rewrites and contributed the prod of her searching mind.
Finally, to see clearly the image I had created and discover
further weaknesses, I turned to the fresh eyes of still more
friends who contributed impressive time and intelligence. I
am enormously indebted to Peter Davis, Timothy Foote,
Ralph Graves, Peter Hansen, Harriet Hyman, Edward Kern,
James Lipscomb, James Watters.

There would, of course, be no book without the Mankiewicz family—Frank, Don, Erna, Joe, and especially Sara.
In supplying their recollections and memorabilia, they were
unstintingly generous and gracious. But like Charles Foster
Kane in *Citizen Kane*, the portrait of "Mank" is a composite.
It includes the recollections of more than 150 of Herman's
friends and acquaintances who worked hard to summon up
the past. They did this out of kindness, and because Herman

Mankiewicz in some way had mattered to them. My thanks
to:

Rita Alexander
Emanuel Aaronson
Eleanor D'Arrast
Brooks Atkinson
Herbert Baker
Richard Barr
Nathaniel Benchley
Irving Berlin
B. A. Bergman
Judge and Mrs. John Biggs
Albert Boni
Lewis Buckman
Bernhard F. Burgunder
Val Burton
John Byram
James M. Cain
Bent Cardan
Kitty Carlisle
Ruth Chase
William Chase
Ina Claire
Joe Cohn
Marc Connelly
Mr. and Mrs.
   Sheldon Coons
Joseph Cotten
Robert Coughlan
John Cromwell
George Cukor
Nat Curtis
Frank Davis
Isabelle Davis
Howard Dietz

Rebecca Drucker
Florence Eldridge
William Fadiman
Geraldine Fitzgerald
John Fox
Mattie Fox
Saul Fox
Sidney Freeman
Louis Gensler
Gail Gifford
Max Gordon
Bert Granet
Gerald Greene
John Groth
Fred Hacker
Francis Hackett
Jack Haley
Adrienne Hall
Maurice Hall
Jed Harris
Helen Hayes
Rose Hecht
Jo Hennessey
Dr. Maurice Herzmark
Brooke Hayward Hopper
Arthur Hornblow, Jr.
Harry Horner
John Houseman
Felix Jackson
Paul Jacobs
Mildred Jaffe
Sam Jaffe
George Jessel

Nunnally Johnson
Pauline Kael
Bronislau Kaper
Joe Kastner
Edwin Knopf
Mildred Knopf
Arthur Kober
Jennings Lang
Charles Lederer
Sammy Leve
Isaac Don Levine
Charles Levy
Robert G. Levy
Rachel Linden
Clinton M. Long
Simon Long
John Lee Mahin
Tom Mankiewicz
Harold Mankawitz
Fredric March
Lester Markel
Rear Admiral G. Markey,
  USNR (Ret.)
Sam Marx
Pamela Mason
Phil McAniff
Roddy McDowall
Harold Meryman
Louis Milestone
Henry Myers
George Oppenheimer
Murdock Pemberton
Nat Perrin
Ralph R. Perry
Ada Persoff
Tommy Phipps

Robert Pirosch
Eileen Pringle
Marcella Rabwin
Decla Dunning Radin
Sam Raefelson
Gottfried Reinhardt
Alan Rivkin
Jill Robinson
Yosal Rogat
Lin Root
Welles Root
Arthur Ross
Harry Ruby
Morrie Ryskind
Dore Schary
George Schaefer
Ad Schulberg
Bud Schulberg
Stuart Schulberg
Sigrid Schultz
Si Seadler
George Seaton
George Seldes
Danny Selznick
Irene Selznick
Sonia Shaplin
Arthur Sheekman
Madeline Sherwood
Estherlea Silverman
Jonathan Silverman
Murray Silverman
Pearl Sindel
Bella Spewack
Mrs. Dorothy Steiner
Erna Stenbuck
Donald Ogden Stewart

James Stewart
Ann Marlow Strauss
Frank Sullivan
Blanche Sweet
Princess Tournin Taxi
Irma May Templar
Marian Spitzer Thompson
Judy Tolmach
Marietta Tree
Mr. and Mrs. Hawley Truax
Henry Tuck
King Vidor
Richard Watts

Arnold Weissberger
Orson Welles
William Wellman
Katharine White
Richard Wilson
Robert Wise
Abel Wolman
Gordon Wolman
Peggy Wood
Bill Wright
Collier Young
Arthur L. Zerbey
Sam Zolotow

CHAPTER 1

IN THAT LIMITLESS GRID OF HOUSES BORDERING THE PACIFIC, there is inside a West Los Angeles home a closet shelf which holds two battered flat boxes. One is from Bonwit Teller, the other from Saks. They are the reliquaries of the life of Herman Mankiewicz. His widow, Sara, takes them down each year on the anniversary of his death in 1953.

The Bonwit box contains two mementos retrieved from his casket—a white linen handkerchief and a blue necktie on which his daughter, Johanna, painted a gold Oscar celebrating his Academy Award for writing the film *Citizen Kane*. Also wrapped in tissue paper are Johanna's baby dress, scuffed blue party shoes, and her first rabbit doll. Mankiewicz wanted her to be the perfection of himself, the child who would perpetuate the best he could be. But in 1974 in New York City she was struck and killed by a taxicab.

In the Saks box are Sara's love letters from Mankiewicz and her notes of condolence from his friends. "At the thought that I might lose you," he wrote her in 1920, "I've gone completely out of my head. I could no more tell you what I've done the past few days than I could tell you what sunlight is made of." And Sara rereads the words of George S. Kaufman, David Selznick, John Houseman, George Jessel, Robert Sherwood. "Deep influence on my life." "Bloodcurdling perceptiveness." "Fight he did from beginning to end." Ben Hecht wrote:

"What a troublesome fellow Herman must be in heaven."
Margaret Sullavan wrote: "Oh, poor Sara—poor me, too."

It is the residue of Herman Mankiewicz's struggle to experience love and, in spite of weaknesses, fulfill his talents.

Herman J. Mankiewicz was a man of only medium height, square build, but was often recollected as tall and impressive. His voice was loud, assertive, broadcasting confidence. Above a flexible, Beefeater face, his brow was broad and Beethovian. His hair was brownish. His blue eyes carried the mischievous look a friend called "the celebrated Mankiewicz leer." At his mouth a puckish, one-sided grin came and went. When he coughed, it was an explosion. When he slurped a glass of water, it was the suction sound of a drain emptying. When he poured cream into his coffee, the cup always overflowed. He never carried his money in a wallet; he simply stuffed bills into his pockets like crumpled Kleenex. He gulped his liquor. He smoked constantly, the pack of Camels always mangled, the cigarettes crushed. He would smoke the first quarter inch, nervously mash out the cigarette as he talked, then light another. The moment he grew excited—and that was often—he would sweat and mop his face till his handkerchief was soaking wet. His right thumb constantly rose to wipe the wetness from his chin.

The word that best attaches itself to Herman Mankiewicz is "more": He was more truthful, more kindly, more serious, more fun, more hurtful, more magnetic, more outrageous, more loyal, more tortured, more complex. And he was more witty—perhaps more than any man of his day, the 1920's into the 1950's. Ben Hecht once wrote:

> Most of Manky's utterances, including his deepest philosophic ones, stirred laughter. Even his enemies laughed. He could puncture egos, draw blood from pretenses—and his victims, with souls abashed, still sat and laughed. The swiftness of his thoughts was by itself a sort of comedy. Never have I known a man with so quick an eye and ear—and tongue—for the strut of fools.

In one sense Mankiewicz's story is a wit's progress, the overwhelming impact of sardonic humor in a man's life. His friends considered his companionship an enrichment of their lives. But with a cynic's awful clarity, he saw the ridiculous and the hypocritical—the whole game. And he had the compulsion and the mastery of the language to spear it with his contempt. During the last twenty-five years of his life his derision was directed at Hollywood. He was a scriptwriter, occasionally a producer, and eventually, even in that capital of idiosyncrasy, a legend.

Mankiewicz was part of a generation of newspaper expatriates who went west to get the big Hollywood money. But more than that, he was one of a special breed. Like Charles Mac-Arthur and Ben Hecht, he was an adventurer-wit. These men entered movie writing like self-serving Robin Hoods, bent on taking from the rich studios and giving to themselves. Like many others, Mankiewicz stayed on, always planning an august literary career and never reconciled to making movies. He once said:

> The best thing that can happen to a man working in this petal factory is that he makes ten thousand dollars a week and only spends twelve thousand—before taxes—and that he's buried in a gold-plated, rhinestone encrusted coffin, the cost of which is divided equally among a large number of sentimental, sixty-five dollar a week stenographers. And while he sleeps beneath the sod, his life's work is occasionally projected on the walls of converted grocery stores—and then the film is cut up into mandolin picks.

A self-mocking Till Eulenspiegel, Herman could be the ultimate companion—a fascinating stream of erudition, warmth, and wit. His joy was conversation, and friends flocked to hear what Hecht called "Mankie's ironic recitation of the joys of living." Helen Hayes remembers him as "an extraordinarily pleasing man." She says, "He made you feel relaxed—remarkable for a total debunker. He even made me feel amusing, which was an accomplishment." Says Geraldine Fitzgerald, "I unequivocally loved Mankiewicz."

But Mankiewicz also used his wit as an all-purpose weapon for survival. His bosses paid him large salaries for writing hard-edged comic dialogue. But to employ Mankiewicz was to become his tormentor. By turning his satiric tongue against those same bosses—and against his own destructive self—he preserved his soul. "From my father," said his daughter, Johanna, "I got the knowledge that you can live with anything, no matter how awful, if you make it comic. All those hostile feelings—including your own toward yourself—are tolerable if you make them funny."

Two examples of the Mankiewicz counterattack are famous Hollywood classics. In the mid-1940's, friends wangled Mankiewicz a badly needed job at Columbia Pictures, headed by the crude bully Harry Cohn, a former Tin Pan Alley song plugger. Fearing a confrontation with Cohn, they made Mankiewicz promise never to enter the executive dining room where Cohn tyrannized the producers and writers who sat around at the single, long table. After three uneventful weeks Cohn suddenly commanded Mankiewicz to attend a screening of the latest Columbia movie—and to be at lunch to talk about it the next day. Midway through the meal Harry Cohn hunched toward him, glowered, and demanded to know what he thought of the movie. The entire table was silent. Mankiewicz opened his mouth, shut it, then said, hedging, "I think it will make money."

"You're full of horse shit," shouted Cohn down the table.

"I'm sure I am, Harry," said Mankiewicz, conciliatory, perhaps mindful of all his gambling IOUs.

"That picture stinks!" said Cohn, bearing down. "I don't just *think* it stinks. I don't just say *the audience* will think it stinks! I *know* it stinks!"

"And how do you know when a picture stinks?" asked Mankiewicz with dangerous geniality.

"It's very simple," said Cohn, plunging ahead. "If a picture is great, see, I don't move at all. If a picture is good, I just move a little. If a picture stinks, my ass wiggles all over the chair." Cohn, triumphant at this irrefutable logic, beamed at his minions down the table.

Mankiewicz started to speak. One of his screenwriter friends called out, "Don't say it, Mank."

But with such a target in his sights, with his own self-disgust pumping in his veins—and with such an audience—he could not help himself. "What makes you think," said Mankiewicz, "that your ass is wired to a hundred and forty million other American asses? Where is it written that you've got the monitor ass of the world?"

Everybody laughed. Harry Cohn, apoplectically red, bellowed, "Get the son of a bitch out of here!" That night, as was his custom when fired, Mankiewicz arrived home lugging a bagful of studio pencils, envelopes, and letter paper.

For Herman there was a form of self-preservation in snatching Pyrrhic victory from disaster. At least his wisecrack comeback would be the talk of Hollywood the next day. Though it is denied by Arthur Hornblow, Jr., the story of Herman at one of the producer's elegant parties remains part of Hollywood lore. Hornblow was a wine and food snob, a man to whom "correctness" counted. Herman fortified himself against such behavior with preparty drinks. There were more drinks at dinner—plus several wines. Suddenly Herman rushed from the table and was audibly sick in a nearby powder room. He emerged pale and perspiring. In the room there was silence—broken by Herman. "Don't worry, Arthur," he said. "The white wine came up with the fish."

Like many humorists, Mankiewicz was a man charged with private anguish. Part of the pain was his sense of waste. He possessed a scholar's mind, a sort of Smithsonian crammed with an extraordinary collection of both odd and classically important knowledge. He owned one of the few distinguished libraries in Hollywood—literature, history, politics, Americana, humor, biography; limited editions, signed editions, first editions. He read them all. His enduring wife, Sara, summoned by the alarmed butler, once hustled upstairs to Mankiewicz's bedroom. But Mankiewicz was not drunk. He was reading *Finnegans Wake* aloud.

Mankiewicz lived with the knowledge that his intellectual life was irrelevant—that he was an integral part of the Hollywood trash scene, a hired pencil doing what he was told. In Hollywood, dubbed by Mankiewicz "this Athens by the sea," the assembling of a political library was like collecting everything he knew about the girl he loved—and could never be with.

Herman's strong critical opinions were backed by a preternatural memory. He could remember chapter titles, the page on which a character first appeared. He could paraphrase whole passages and recite poetry endlessly—Heine, Shakespeare—including the differences between folios. This quiet side of Mankiewicz specialized in the obscure. In 1937 he received a grudging note from Alexander Woollcott: "It is only when you hold your conversations with me in solitude that you have all the answers, but it seems you were right about that poem. It was by Bunner."

Mankiewicz's true specialty, however, was political history, mastered in freakish detail. Perhaps the happiest hours in his life were spent reading such books from his own library as *The Origin of the Republican Form of Government; The Mississippi Valley in British Politics; Congress, the Constitution and the Supreme Court.* A compulsive gambler renowned for his colossal bad luck, Mankiewicz once wagered $100 that a stranger in a bar could not name Theodore Roosevelt's opponent for the presidency in 1904. "Judge Parker," said the man. "I nominated him."

Twice in his life Mankiewicz did try to merge his shelved and authentic self with his professional self. In the mid-1930's he attempted a movie damning Hitler. But it was blocked by studio executives fearful of jeopardizing their German markets. Then in 1940 he succeeded spectacularly. Drawing on his knowledge of journalism, twentieth century, American wealth, and most specifically of William Randolph Hearst—both from his reading and personal acquaintance—Mankiewicz wrote the script for *Citizen Kane*, the Orson Welles triumph. This masterpiece, still exhibited constantly throughout the world, remains the most important and seminal American movie ever made. Filmed in 1940, it was a synthesis and extension of everything innovative in film to that date. As a totality, *Kane* was so revolutionary in its techniques, so devoid of sentimentality, so advanced in its use of psychology that the movie became a springboard for future motion pictures—and eventually a landmark in cinema history. Perhaps no other script has provided a movie with a structure at once so complex and so perfectly machined. Its central plot device, the search for the meaning of "rosebud," cinema history's most famous symbol, was invented by Herman Mankiewicz.

It is difficult to gauge Mankiewicz's potential as an artist, particularly above and beyond movie writing. The broad and powerful mind, the fluent precision of language behind his erudition and wit were evidence of extraordinary ability. At times in the movie studios he achieved importance, while exerting himself only casually. Many of his contemporaries believed he had genius. *Kane* seems to confirm this judgment. But whatever the degree of his gifts, he was hounded and handicapped by self-doubts bred in his childhood. And many of the decisions and temptations he faced are universal in creative careers. How he met them becomes, in part, a study in the handling and mishandling of talent.

But the importance of Herman Mankiewicz does not lie in his accomplishments. He is significant because of what he was and where he was. His life dramatizes three historic eras, so special they are almost mythical. As a freebooting young newspaper correspondent he explored apocalyptic, post World War I Berlin, a city feverish with hopelessness, considered the "sin capital" of Europe. He was part of the excitement of Prohibition New York in the 1920's, that carefree time lived at full throttle when eccentricity was enshrined—especially at the Algonquin where Herman traded ripostes on an equal footing with the celebrated wits of the Round Table. One of them, George S. Kaufman, employed him as a reporter/critic in *The New York Times* theater department. Another, Harold Ross, drafted Herman to help start *The New Yorker* magazine. In the late twenties Herman settled in Hollywood, the American Babylon. For twenty-five years he moved among its biggest names during its delirious mogul period—that swim of glamour and absurdity.

However, those episodes in social history—and their values —had a special capacity for distorting men personally and professionally. Mankiewicz became the paradigm of their effect on vulnerable talents and sensitive souls. The novelistic saga of Herman Mankiewicz—the creation of that prodigal, prodigious personality—is a cold-eyed portrait of those eras and the romanticized names that peopled them.

During his hectic life Mankiewicz inspired all combinations of fear, dislike, loyalty, and love. But no matter if his company was Isadora Duncan or Charles MacArthur or Groucho Marx or Greta Garbo or Marion Davies, he was always the object of amazement. His friend Orson Welles once said, "Mankiewicz was some sort of tremendous performer in a Hieronymus Bosch landscape of his own. There was always the feeling that you were in the presence of thwarted violence. It was this thrashing of some great creature, some beached creature. Some magnificent creature. You didn't know what it was because you had never seen one of those before. None of us ever had. It was Mank."

CHAPTER

2

□ □ □

It does something to you, if from the time
you're old enough to see, you get standards
set for you, and ideals, and ambitions, that
you . . . well, you know you aren't up to
them.

—HERMAN MANKIEWICZ,
Script for *Christmas Holiday*

IN EARLY 1940 HERMAN MANKIEWICZ BEGAN THE FIRST
draft of *Citizen Kane*. He dictated it to a secretary, as was his
habit. Rita Alexander remembers: "He began with the title,
the description of the scene, the indications of the camera
movement, the dialogue, and so on. It was really extraordinary.
It all came out not fast, not slow—at a continued pace as
though he had it all in his mind."

When Herman first mentioned "rosebud," she asked, "Who
is rosebud?"

"It isn't a who, it's an it," said Herman.

"What is rosebud?" asked Rita Alexander.

"It's a sled," said Herman.

Citizen Kane is the imaginary biography of a newspaper
tycoon and American sultan, Charles Foster Kane. The movie
begins with his death, virtually alone, in his vast, self-created
castle, Xanadu. Kane's lips, filling the movie screen, mouth
his last word: "rosebud." A newsreel company, putting together an obituary on Kane, dispatches a reporter to find the
meaning of "rosebud." In the process the reporter learns the
details of Kane's life, including the fact that his parents ran a

boardinghouse in Colorado. A lodger absconded leaving Mrs. Kane apparently worthless stock in a gold mine, which became the fabulous Colorado Lode. Mrs. Kane, feeling unequal to raising a child destined for a king's wealth, signs her five-year-old son over to a bank which will rear him and manage his inheritance. The boy's future guardian, Thatcher, an officer of the bank, arrives to take him away to New York. There is a snowstorm, and the child Kane is happily playing with a sled and a snowman. When young Kane is told he will leave with Thatcher, the boy hits him in the stomach with the sled.

The reporter searching for "rosebud" reads Thatcher's memoirs and interviews four people who were close to Kane: his oldest friend, his office manager, his butler, and his second wife. None of them can explain "rosebud." But their memories show Kane as a man destroyed by wealth and the inability to love. Then, after Kane's death, while his vast accumulation of art treasures is catalogued, the valueless relics of his life are burned. The boyhood sled is flung into a furnace, and the consuming flames light up the rosebud painted on its wooden top—Kane's symbol of the childhood and the parental love that was denied him.

Herman Mankiewicz must have identified powerfully with Kane and with "rosebud." He, too, had deeply bitter feelings about his boyhood in Wilkes-Barre, Pennsylvania. Those years created a youth and man of resilient ambition but riddled with self-doubts—and almost immune to normal restraints. He approached life as a prolonged escapade. Even the wife he loved, the redoubtable Sara, was only a sometime brake. Eager for adventure, he took her as a bride to 1920's Berlin, claiming he had a foreign correspondent job with the Chicago *Tribune*. Soon he had to confess the job did not exist. Then, to refuel his self-esteem, he pretended that the *Tribune*, after all, had hired him on the spot.

Rosebud, the symbol of Herman's damaging childhood, was not a sled. It was a bicycle. When he was ten, a bike, that vehicle intrinsic to childhood freedom, was promised to Herman for Christmas. In a thrill of anticipation, he came downstairs on Christmas morning. There was no bike. His father, perhaps short of money, perhaps blind to its importance, had not yet bought it. Weeks later Herman got his bike and careened with his friends, feet on handlebars, down the tree-shaded streets.

Herman was a mischievous child. One day after some misdemeanor, Herman was confined to the house by his mother. To keep him there during her absence, she hid the long stockings he needed for his knickers. Herman went to his mother's room, put on a pair of her stockings, got on his bike, and rode off to the Wilkes-Barre public library, where he loved to browse among the shelves and to read for hours. When he came out, the precious bike was gone—stolen. Herman's punishment was permanent. His father never bought him another bike. His mother answered Herman's pleas by telling him it was all his own fault. Kane's deathbed cry for "rosebud" and his unlived boyhood was also Herman's call to fate, "Where is my bike?"

Herman's bike meant freedom both from his father, the primary cause of his early scars, and from his home, where he did not get enough love. Herman's father, Franz Mankiewicz, was born in Berlin in 1872. After attending the University of Berlin, he arrived destitute in New York in 1892. He became a reporter and editorial writer on a German-language paper. In 1896, at age twenty-four, he married a pretty, lighthearted dressmaker named Johanna Blumenau, who had emigrated from German-speaking Kurland. On November 7, 1897, their first son was born. In honor of Johanna's brother, he was named Herman Jacob Mankiewicz. A daughter, Erna, was born in 1901. In 1904, hired as editor and manager of the Wilkes-Barre newspaper the *Demokratischer Wachter*, Franz moved his family to the medium-sized city in southeastern Pennsylvania. There, in 1909, a second son, Joseph Leo, was born.

Franz Mankiewicz considered himself a failure. He knew German-language journalism held no future. He was constantly short of money. He felt within himself potent gifts, undefined, undirected. He wanted to be a teacher but was deemed unqualified. Unhappy, frustrated, he drank quantities of beer, and there were bellowing battles with Hanna at home, terrifying to Herman as he grew up.

During those early years when Herman's traits and needs were shaped and misshaped, Franz imposed on his son his own aspirations and Teutonic standards of perfection. Herman could be schooled for a professorship: Herr Doktor Herman J. Mankiewicz. The ultimate!

Throughout his life in Wilkes-Barre, when Herman came home with perhaps a 92 in a test, Franz would immediately demand, "What happened to the other eight points?"

Herman was usually truculent or argumentative. "I only made one mistake," he would say.

"That doesn't impress me at all," the unsmiling professor would say. "Why didn't you get a hundred? Ninety-two is not the best you can do."

"I was the best in the class!"

"Don't tell me you were the best in the class," his father would shout. "There were plenty of boys who deserved that grade much more than you because you didn't do any work. You're just telling me you're in a class with a lot of inferior minds."

In the German schools that had educated Franz Mankiewicz, a mistake in homework or recitation meant a grade of zero, and whipping was a routine punishment. According to Herman, who had an acute sense of injustice, his father spanked him several nights a week, whether he deserved it or not, for something he had done or failed to do at school. When Herman performed up to his father's standards, Franz never praised him.

"Those years," says Joe Mankiewicz, Herman's younger

brother, "must have been terrifying and destructive beyond description."

Then, in 1906, Herman endured an additional turn of the screw. In Wilkes-Barre Franz made a slight entrance into teaching by tutoring boys from the snobbish Harry Hillman Academy in German and French. When the modern-language teacher fell ill, Franz took his place, though the salary was meager. Thus, at the age of thirty-four he began his born profession. To everybody he soon was Professor Mankiewicz.

This Prussian, powerful personality attacked teaching and self-education, said Herman later, "like an earth-moving machine." Franz began a life of night school, summer school, home courses, while working to support the family. He tutored and took Harry Hillman boys on local field trips and summer tours of Europe. He could be heavily genial, and he became a personage in the community—recording secretary of the Concordia-Männer-Chor, Democratic county chairman.

As Franz's immersion in education deepened, his beer consumption diminished. Now his fights with Hanna were provoked, not by his anger and frustration, but by her resentment of his truancy from the family. He had become, in fact, a stock absentminded professor. At dinner Franz Mankiewicz once said, "Hanna, you will be very proud of me. I met two ladies today coming toward me. I concentrated very hard and remembered the name and said, 'How do you do, Mrs. Neuschatz.' "

"Who was the other one?" asked Hanna.

"I didn't notice."

"That was me," said Hanna.

The intellectual pressure on Herman was not counterbalanced by tenderness from Franz. One side of Herman always loved his father deeply—hungered to be cherished and forgiven and encouraged by the superior mind of the professor. It was that side which idolized the professor, which worshipped the world of the intellect, which was the son of

the father. But as Joe Mankiewicz says, "Herman's love became transformed by confusion into fear and defiance—and
then finally into a love/hate for his father. He could never
control or change that, and it left him never at peace. This
must have been a cause of Herman's most self-destructive and
anguished experiences, as if he himself *had* to be both the
punished and the punisher."

Herman's mother was not an alternative to his father,
though Herman needed her love and attention. But, born to
be a lower-middle-class hausfrau, Hanna found herself in an
impossible predicament. She was not equipped to be the wife
of a brilliant, violent, obsessed man she herself loved and
feared, while coping with a brilliant, hypersensitive, equally
complex and violent boy. Herman once dismissed his mother
as "a round little woman who was uneducated in four lan-
guages. She spoke mangled German, mangled Russian,
mangled Yiddish, and mangled English."

In the inevitable competition for Hanna's attention, it was
the son who lost to the father. Moreover, she had a daughter
to bring up. Then the symptoms she thought were menopause
turned out to be a second son. She sewed the children's
clothes, crocheted the curtains, made the feather beds. She
stalled the creditors. Though she had a servant girl, Hanna
was a slave to the household, running it on a small, fixed
allowance for a husband who expected all things ready when
he wanted them.

Hanna had a genuine humor and provided laughter in
the house. She gave Herman his wit. She also gave him
what love her life permitted. It was not enough. But it was
all he had. Years later he often wept when he resurrected
the little German prayer she recited nightly at his bedside:
"*Ich bin klein.* . . . I am little, my heart is pure. Let no one
enter there but God alone."

His father's presence pervaded Herman's life, even at
school. Herman was enrolled on a scholarship at Harry Hill-

man Academy. Each morning father and son crossed the wooden porch of their house and set off for Harry Hillman. Herman was a thin figure with a pale, square face, blondish hair, big ears, and a slight round-shouldered hunch. He wore a white shirt, necktie, brown corduroy jacket and knickers, high button shoes, and long brown stockings which ended the day down around his ankles. By then he could insist on "store" clothes like the other boys, not the ones his mother made. Nevertheless, Herman's classmates remember him as "shabby," "cheap clothes," "never presentable."

Socially Wilkes-Barre was sharply stratified. At the top were the old families able to trace their lineage back to the time of William Penn. At the bottom was the large immigrant population working the anthracite coal mines. "Herman was too new," says a classmate at the Harry Hillman Academy. "You couldn't come into Wilkes-Barre and be somebody until you demonstrated your worth. We lived in a very closed caste society. And so for Hermie to make the grade, he had so many strikes against him, it wasn't funny. He was not athletic. He was literary. He was introspective. He was small. And he was rather embarrassed."

But Herman learned in those years to get recognition with his facility and wit. "Everything always came quickly for Hermie," a classmate remembers. For a dime he would translate anybody's Latin homework, reading it off as easily as English. But in his father's language classes, Herman's best was barely good enough. A fellow student remembers that the professor "used to bulldog Herman as though he wished Herman wasn't around. He wanted Herman to equal or excel everyone else, and he hated it when Herman showed up badly in front of us. It was a prickly relationship. I always felt sorry for Herman. I felt he didn't have a very happy boyhood."

There was a slice of Herman's Wilkes-Barre youth, away from the stern eye of his father, that was classically happy. He swam with friends in the river under the Market Street bridge and rode open trolleys to Harvey's Lake or to the Sans Souci amusement park they pronounced "San Suzy." They played baseball—Herman was catcher—in a field near his house where the middle-class neighborhood thinned out into open land and truck gardens growing asparagus and celery. They played pool at the house of Phil McAniff, Herman's inseparable friend.

After school Herman would take off his coat and tie, unbutton his collar, tuck it back underneath his shirt, roll up his sleeves—and go looking for Phil. They talked Latin to each other, and Herman could always stump Phil, who, as the best athlete in the neighborhood, always picked Herman, the worst, for his teams.

The two boys got jobs selling peanuts and popcorn at the Wilkes-Barre baseball park—until they were fired for sitting down to watch the games. And each spring, when the circus came, Herman and Phil were up at dawn to watch the animals unload down planks from flatcars.

Together the two boys discovered the escape world of fantasy—in the theaters of Wilkes-Barre, where Herman began his permanent romance with the stage. In the delicious darkness of the Bijou Dream Theater, he and Phil reveled in the burlesque rituals of that day—the "Parade of Nations," and the bathing number, the skit in which the soubrette hides her money in her stocking, and the scene in which two men, out with other girls, pretend to be waiters to fool their wives who have just entered the restaurant. At the Grand Opera House the two friends sneaked up the back fire escape to sit in "nigger heaven"—the third balcony—and watch such shows as *The Chocolate Soldier*. At the Poli Theater they even got jobs as walk-on "supers"—two shows a day, fifty cents a show.

Always in Herman's life, the theater, even vaudeville, was eternally touched by nostalgia. In the 1920's, when he was a reviewer on *The New York Times*, Herman wrote:

> This notice is written by one whose first and last recollection of Weber and Fields is of a wintry matinee—as to both weather

and audience—in Wilkes-Barre in 1912. I have kept with me the memory of that great moment in which Joe Weber—calmly crediting himself in a pool game with seven of eight balls which he had whisked to their pockets by a broadside sweep of his cue —is coldly advised by Fields that he must name his ball. Whereupon he promptly says, "I name him Rudolph," and goes on about his game.

Finally, geography permanently separated the two companions. Phil went away to college at Holy Cross in 1912. Though they wrote each other, Herman that year essentially lost his friendship with Phil and in a sense his childhood.

At the age of thirteen Herman passed the entrance examinations for Columbia College. He was graduated from Harry Hillman Academy at fourteen, but a Columbia rule prevented him from entering until he was fifteen. To fill the intervening year, he worked in a coal mine as a surveyor's assistant.

Traveling to the mine at dawn, Herman carried his lunch pail and proudly wore on his head the miner's gas lamp. His duties of fetching and carrying included "rushing the growler" —going to the saloon for a tin pail of beer, foaming up white and dripping in crazy tracks down the cold bucket sides.

Herman's brief stint as a coal miner taught him the social pleasures of both alcohol and a rapt audience. The miners nicknamed him Mike and taught him to smoke cigarettes and to drink the beer he fetched. To the other boys, Herman was suddenly a man—and a raconteur able to enthrall. He embroidered his adventures in the rough worker's world, and he repeated the miners' dirty jokes: There was a pretty young girl walking down the street, and a man came up to her and said, "You have a hair on your lollipop." "I should have," answered the girl. "I'm fifteen years old." Herman's friends laughed at that till their sides ached.

Both father and son were fixed on horizons far beyond Wilkes-Barre. The professor had taken qualifying examinations for the New York City public school system. Herman had been harking to the distant whistle of the Black Diamond, the evening express train to Harrisburg. Like the theater, it sounded an invitation to a glamorized world of freedom. Sometimes at night—taking his baby brother, Joe, with him— Herman stood by the tracks where the Black Diamond stopped in Wilkes-Barre. He looked up into the lighted dining car at the vision of white tablecloths and elegantly dressed people, like actors on a stage, eating unimaginable food on their way to exhilarating destinations.

In 1913 the Mankiewicz family moved to New York, forty-one-year-old Franz to take a job at the prestigious Stuyvesant High School, fifteen-year-old Herman to enter Columbia College and major in philosophy. All his Wilkes-Barre problems accompanied Herman to New York, but now his defenses were solidly in place.

Doubting his capacity for *real* achievement in his father's terms, Herman substituted mental agility for effort. Part of Herman's arsenal was a spontaneous talent which, even unstretched, was enough to bring success. The great professor of English and author John Erskine was hugely impressed, and Herman became his protégé. The Columbia dean, Frederick Keppel, was also admiring. In 1916, his senior year, Herman achieved a campus triumph; he and a songwriting friend, Ray Perkins, wrote the annual Varsity Show. Their script for a musical called *The Peace Pirates* was chosen over eighteen competitors and was the first political satire ever selected. Acting in the show were Lorenz Hart and Oscar Hammerstein II. The musical received good reviews—"a notable triumph" —and was sold out for a week at a theater in the Hotel Astor. Herman was graduated with honors in English and German, and in September 1916 he entered graduate school as an English major.

Though Herman regarded himself as an apprentice litterateur and potential playwright, his immediate ambition was journalism. In his sophomore year he edited "The Off Hour," the

Columbia Spectator's humor column, a sometimes strenuous collection of verse, comment, and contributions. At Columbia his passionate interest in politics was ignited. In 1915 the nation—and the campus—were in turmoil over the question of whether to join the war in Europe. Civilian soldiers were training in camps at Plattsburgh. Anti-German feeling was building. Herman was a pacifist. Disposing of one prointervention organization, Herman said, "Why, after all, should there be any sense in the Common Sense League? One doesn't as a rule get a cottage with cottage cheese." He believed that America was being maneuvered into the war by Britain, and he wrote in his "Off Hour" column:

> If England was what England seems
> And not the England of our dreams
> But only putty, brass, and paint . . .
> 'Ow quick we'd chuck 'er.
> Well, who says she ain't?

By now the professor and Herman had become intellectual rivals. Father and son had entered Columbia simultaneously, Herman for his B.A. and Franz for his M.A. The professor could not endure Herman's knowing something he did not know. And Herman could not bear his father's telling him something he *should* know. "Herman and Pop," says Joe Mankiewicz, "approached learning at about the same time. Who knows what became a matter of jealousy? My father cut down Herman at every possible moment." The winning of a Mankiewicz argument had little to do with who was right. The winner was the one who ended up in command. The professor always finished dominant in voice and choler.

Herman's drinking increased. He was notorious even beyond the Columbia campus as "Mank the Tank." Lorenz Hart, the future songwriter, was a drinking pal. Sometimes Hart's father, another Prussian, would telephone the professor and the two men would go out at night searching for their errant sons.

Hanna Mankiewicz, too, found a route to escape. At home, despite her angry entreaties, Franz continued to shut himself away in his study, reading, tutoring, counseling students— wooing education like a transcendent mistress. At dinner, his primary time with his family, the professor kept propped beside his plate an Ingersoll watch that sent him hurrying away at seven-thirty to teach at Harlem Evening High School. Franz's books became to Hanna the intruding rival. One lonely, rainy Sunday afternoon, in a fury, she ripped them from the shelves and flung them about the living room. Finally, she gave up on Franz, played bridge, won cut-glass prizes, and devoted her heart to a receptive subject. She helped found the New York Philanthropic League, which cared for crippled children, and remained a trustee for decades.

As the professor's status and security in education increased, his public personality underwent a remarkable change. Outside the family the Prussian disciplinarian became charming and benign. The world considered him a paragon as a man and a teacher. Boys and girls, young men and women teachers streamed through the Mankiewicz apartment for conferences and advice. He was a fountain of moral homilies for every situation.

Studying at night, he received his master's degree from Columbia in 1915, and still at Stuyvesant High, he achieved his doctorate in 1924. Finally, in 1931, he became a genuine *Herr Professor* in the Department of Education at City College. He wrote and edited a series of German and French grammars, edited the *Modern Language Quarterly*, published by Indiana University, and gave erudite and published lectures at universities. He was a friend to German critics and writers. He founded a luncheon round table at Columbia for German intellectuals, and Albert Einstein became a member. In 1936 Professor Mankiewicz was honored by 350 friends and colleagues at a testimonial dinner whose sponsors included Einstein and the mayor of New York City, Fiorello LaGuardia.

"Pop was a tremendously industrious, brilliant, vital man," Herman once said. "A father like that could make you very ambitious or very despairing. You could end up by saying, 'Stick it. I'll never live up to that, and I'm not going to try.' That's what happened eventually with me."

Franz's stipend from Stuyvesant and Harlem Evening High and tutoring was small. His meager earnings now had to pay for Herman's tuition at Columbia. Franz put cardboard inside his worn-out shoes to save the extravagance of new soles. He hired himself out to translate German travel brochures and laxative ads. The suits Herman wore at Columbia were shabby and cheap. They changed color, classmate Frank Perry remembers, "depending on whether they had been rained on or not."

Conspicuous poverty continued to be a controlling fact of Herman's life, forcing him into the humiliating role of artful cadger. His classmate Julian Rosenberg says, "I don't know how he subsisted other than by sponging." In the Columbia humor magazine *The Jester*, his friend Morrie Ryskind wrote:

> I'll say this much for H. J. Mank,
> When anybody blew, he drank.

A second way Herman dealt with poverty was gambling. It was one way to get a large sum quickly and easily. He occasionally earned money by typing other people's theses, and he worked one summer in a city playground—prosaic jobs he felt were beneath him. He was happier with schemes that somehow beat the system through superior ingenuity and brainpower. At Columbia he ran a hip-pocket lending library of pornography. *Fanny Hill* cost a dollar an hour; *The Memoirs of Josephine Mutzenbacker* fifty cents. But betting was Herman's avocation. His classmate Howard Dietz remembers

Herman darting into dark entryways for quick transactions with bookies.

At Columbia Herman was seen as a furiously proud loner. He still felt socially inferior. His home had never been a place that cultivated the social graces, refinement, the expression of soft emotions. Herman had basic good looks, innate warmth, and at his core an appealing teddy bear gentleness. He was fun. He was exciting. He was vehement of voice, adroit of tongue, passionate with ideas, possessed of charm. Says Marion Spitzer, a friend of a few years later, "At his core he was a decent, honest human being whom I always respected."

But Herman was strong medicine. One of the bastions of his self-defenses was the exaggeration of his faults. By flaunting his weaknesses, they somehow became rebellious badges of individuality. "Mank hated himself," says Dorothy Kahn, a student friend of Herman's. "And if you'd been Mank in those days, you'd have hated yourself, too. Before he was somebody, people were pretty rude to him because he really was a boor. He'd push his food on his fork with his fingers, would belch, used words forbidden then, like 'half-assed.' He wanted to be known as an eccentric, and he enjoyed shocking people. It was the business of 'you don't judge a book by its cover.' He scoffed at good breeding, but he wished that he had it."

His uncertainties with girls and polite society—anything threatening—Herman sublimated with satire. He pretended to scorn the evening phonograph record dances that girls gave at their homes, where Herman either was not invited or felt uncomfortable. "As a method for killing time," he said, "dancing can be favorably compared to drinking sodas or taking Comparative Literature three-four."

Herman sometimes invited a girl to ride, inexpensively, on an open-topped double-decker bus from Columbia down Riverside Drive, across to Fifth Avenue, and down to Washington Square and back. In an "Off Hour" column he re-created one of these trips as a study in deflation:

He calls for her about eight o'clock and leads her to the nearest bus-line. After a wait of thirty minutes, during which it seems to him that the bus-company has suspended services, they secure a seat on top of a Washington Square bus.

HE: What beautiful oak trees along the drive!

SHE: They're lombardy poplars.

Silence. He is busy thinking up a poem and trying to find a rhyme for lombardy poplar; decides it can't be done.

HE: Here's the Soldier's and Sailor's Monument.

SHE: Really?

Silence. They pass a grocery store bearing a sign that a certain Dinkelspiel is the proprietor. He tells her the Dinkelspiel joke Series 8, number 40. She reminds him that he told it to her on the last bus ride. The cold is beginning to tell on him and as modestly as possible he tells her he once knew a feller who died of tuberculosis following a bus ride. She wants to know the feller's name; he has forgotten it.

When the ride ends back at Columbia, Herman heads alone for the Lion, the local saloon.

Herman dropped out of Columbia graduate school in February 1917, eager to begin his life. In terms of intellect, ambition, and ability to impress, he was a formidable fellow. But at twenty-one the essential Herman was still a slender boy, courting manhood and romance, seeking a strength to match his facade. Bedeviled by self-doubts, he was most comfortable in the freewheeling, slightly raffish society of newspaper reporters and Broadway press agents and critics. It was a cosmos that valued the wit and the child in a person, and it was utterly removed from his father's disciplined, high-minded world.

The United States had entered the war against Germany. Though he expected to be drafted, Herman went to work as a cub reporter on the *Tribune* and secretly held a simultaneous job on the staff of the *American Jewish Chronicle*. This bit of banditry was possible, explained Herman, because of "the extreme laxity of their enforced hours of work." He wrote articles, book reviews, and under the title *Society Sphere* he did short, introductory essays before the social notes. These essays were oddly but typically polemical. One on coming out parties struck back at the polite society that had scorned him: "The elders of the debutantes fold their hands complacently, and, smiling benevolently, approve the gauche young man who is at the moment paying attention to their darling daughter: 'Such a *nice* young man! So good-hearted and everything.' What the 'and everything' means is matter for conjecture; but one thing is certain; it does not mean intelligence."

The *Chronicle*, for which he did theater reviews, was also an entree into the Broadway world he loved. And Sam Hoffenstein, who had grown up next door to Herman in Wilkes-Barre, was now a theater press agent. He was also on his way to becoming a light-verse poet of international reputation, author of *Poems in Praise of Practically Nothing*. Hoffenstein supplied Herman with free tickets and introductions to such powerful figures as George S. Kaufman and Alexander Woollcott, respectively *The New York Times* theater editor and critic. They were delighted and impressed by this quick-witted young man. Woollcott, a collector of original personalities, in particular drew Herman into his social orbit. For a twenty-one-year-old trying to build a sense of self-worth, that was powerful reassurance.

Then, in February 1918, Herman struck a Comstock lode of reinforcement, a lifelong vein of forgiveness and belief. He met a young Jewish beauty named Shulamith Sara Aaronson. The boy who disliked his private vision of himself saw in the eyes of Sara the idealized Herman Mankiewicz he longed to be.

The *Chronicle* editor, Dr. Samuel Melamed, traveled to Washington, D.C., to read a paper on *A Panorama of Ancient Judaism* at a meeting of the Menorah Society at George Washington University. Herman went along to report on the speech for the *Chronicle*. In the audience were twenty-one-year-old Sara—oval-faced, huge brown eyes, full figure—and her older sister Naomi—beautiful with a cameo delicacy. "I'm not boasting," says Sara, "but it was known around the city that if you wanted to hold onto your beau, don't introduce him to the Aaronson girls."

Naomi was studying to be a teacher. Sara worked for her father, Reuben Aaronson, at his small factory, the Columbia Specialty Paper Box Company, "Manufacturers of Paper Boxes of Every Size and Description." She was the bookkeeper, general manager, floor sweeper, and emergency machine operator.

During the speech Herman edged toward the rear of the hall "to escape Melamed's trisyllabic dogma." Sara and Naomi took long, approving looks at the slender, "nice-looking" young man. A mutual friend introduced Herman, who was allowed to come along to a soda fountain for raspberry tonics. Herman, on his best behavior, got himself invited to dinner. He walked with Sara to the Aaronson home, talking about New York and the theater and the production of *The Doll's House* he had just seen—"a fat, elocuting Nora who, in a self-respecting household, would have been munching poisoned macaroons ten minutes after the curtain went up."

"By the time we got home," says Sara, "I was absolutely in a dreamworld. I'd never heard anything like such talk."

The Aaronson home at 1107 Fairmont Street, in the northern part of Washington, was part of a block-long row of small, connected two-story brick houses. There were five Aaronson girls and one boy. Their mother, Olga, ran an open house for their friends. "I don't know what we ate at that first dinner," Herman once reminisced. "But I'll bet it was herring and schnapps and cream cheese and sour cream—and chicken. And 'you should get sick, Herman, but you must have another piece.'"

Ritualistically after dinner the girls and their guests gathered around Naomi at the upright piano in the living room. Everybody sang, and Sara was tremendously impressed that Herman knew not only all the refrains of the songs, but the first verses, and never started at the chorus.

Herman once wrote about that evening to "Schnutz," one of

his pet names for Sara. "Either I pretended to be statuary and stood around," he punned, "or I was a prairie fire and rolled around the room until somebody put me out. I don't remember. But I do remember that my Schnutz's eyes were so wonderfully sweet and all of my Schnutz was so clean and gentle and good."

Herman landed in Sara's life like a stone in a placid pool. Sara—and the Aaronson family—appeared in Herman's life like a doorway to a warm room. "I know when he came to our house that first time in Washington," says Sara, "there was a great need of love in him. Nobody had ever made a fuss over any success he'd had. His family's attitude was, 'Well, you *should*. That's expected of you. You're brilliant. You are your father's son.' Guilt! Guilt is what that gave him—and guilt is what ran through his whole life."

The Aaronson household was totally beyond Herman's knowledge. That evening after the lecture he bathed in the family's embracing affection and unassuming gaiety. He soaked up the admiration of that covey of innocent, pretty sisters, girls whose horizons of revelry were picnics in Rock Creek Park and Saturday afternoon band concerts on the White House lawn.

And there was Olga Aaronson, a round, all-loving woman less than five feet tall. Herman called her "a perfect person" and sometimes said longingly to Sara, "If only your mother had married my father." Once, when her children heard Olga upstairs laughing, they asked her why. "I don't know," she replied. "I just hear my girls laughing downstairs." Her precepts to her daughters included no word about sex ("Your husbands will instruct you in all of that"). Her message to Sara was: "When your husband comes home in the evening, you should be rested, you should be dressed, your house should be warm, your dinner ready, your children should be clean and quiet—and then you will have a happy marriage."

Sara's father, Reuben Aaronson, a short, finely made man, was an immigrant from Russia and a learned Hebrew scholar. The paper box factory he founded supplied black file boxes to the U.S. government. A former mathematics teacher in Russia, he could figure expenses to the penny and outbid his competition. But he was an impractical businessman. The summer before Sara was to go to college, she helped her father in the office. He became so dependent on her, she had to forgo further schooling. Much of his life Reuben was a man beset, helpless against his daughters who adored him. Years later Sara found written on one of her father's check stubs his silent outcry: "I say no. They buy. I pay."

The morning after that first visit to the Aaronsons, Herman borrowed a nickel from a friend, phoned Sara, and invited her to see a musical comedy starring Justine Johnstone. Herman had ripped his everyday pants, but he did have his tuxedo. Suddenly, dressing in formal clothes was a marvelous idea. But his brown shoes had to be blackened with a preparation that stayed wet and smelly. In the theater people moved away from them. "Oh, he was so dear," says Sara. "I just laughed and giggled at everything he did. And I was so impressed by the fact that he had already seen this musical we were going to. I was absolutely smitten."

Leaving before the final curtain so that Herman could catch his train back to New York, they plunged into a bitter cold night. A glaze of ice covered the pavement. Three blocks from the house on Fairmont Street, at the top of the rise, Herman suddenly pulled Sara out of the trolley. And down the hill, hand in hand, they slid and ran and slid.

At the box factory the following morning, Sara went into the little toilet closet where she kept, penciled on the wall, a list of her beaux in the order of their current favor. It was much erased because the rankings constantly changed. With her pencil she wrote "Herman Mankiewicz" at the top—and drew an X through all the other names.

* * *

In February 1918, a few weeks after he met Sara, Herman, always patriotic, joined the Army Air Service. He was sent to aviation training school at Cornell University in Ithaca, New York. There he exhibited zero flying aptitude. When whirled in a flight simulator, he was instantly airsick. Eventually he was washed out, and he enlisted in the Marines.

Herman and Sara had exchanged a few letters, and in August 1918 he wrote that he would be passing through Washington on his way to training camp at Parris Island, South Carolina. Would she see him? Olga Aaronson took her to Union Station at five o'clock on a broiling hot afternoon. Sara and Herman strolled about the station while Olga waited on a bench.

At Parris Island, Herman, now a Marine private, had his first taste of mass military life and the rigors of basic training. "This word 'private' is a joke," he wrote Sara. "I have no more privacy than a goldfish. I live in an open tent and my every action takes place in sight of hundreds of frankly admiring strangers. No man, runs the adage, is a hero to his valet—surely no man is a hero to the men who go swimming with him."

Two and a half months after Herman enlisted—and after Union Station—he was at Quantico, Virginia, expecting to be shipped to France. Herman was also corresponding with a girl he had known at Columbia. He received at Quantico an impassioned letter from her renouncing him for the salvation of the Republic. "Go, my darling," the letter ended, "go, and if need be, die."

Herman landed at Brest on November 3, a part of the 4th Brigade, 2nd Division, AEF, which was pursuing the retreating Germans as the Armistice was signed on November 11, 1918. Herman continued to march across northern France, Belgium, and Luxembourg, entering what he called "Heinieland" at Wallendorf. He tramped through sodden ground and freezing weather, "going through little villages he found fascinating," says Sara, "especially if they had wine." He also entertained himself by telling the girls he met fanciful lies about America—that all children there are born with tortoise-shell glasses.

Once in Germany, Herman's fluency in the language brought him sudden importance. He and a pal named McCoy volunteered to reconnoiter ahead to discover the reception the troops could expect. The two adventurers aimed straight for Cologne, and Herman always claimed they were the first two Allied soldiers in the city. "I saw the German army enter Cologne in retreat," he wrote his father, "and reviewed them in front of the Cathedral with Cardinal Hartman."

Herman escaped his leatherneck drudgery when his English professor at Columbia, John Erskine, offered him an assignment teaching English and journalism at a military college set up in bleak temporary barracks buildings at Beaune in France. In the mail Sara received a group picture of the faculty, on the back of which he wrote, "My other faculties will follow in due course."

From Beaune, Herman asked his family to pull every string and trick to get him released from the Marines. And he begged for letters from them. "Why don't you write?" Herman pleaded in a letter to his mother. "Do you realize that I've been here over six months now and haven't received a line from you. The only unacknowledged letter I have is one from Joseph, received yesterday. Exactly how much are you all writing to me? I wonder."

In June 1919 Herman returned to Quantico, Virginia, for demobilization. He went directly from Quantico to Washington and his Shulamith Sara Aaronson. It was only the third time they had ever met. In Sara's eyes, "he was so brawny and strong and wonderful." They took a trolley that afternoon to Rock Creek Park. They strolled its shady paths—Herman in his Marine private's uniform, Sara in a long beige dress, skirt demurely covering her high shoes, a bow at the waist, leg-of-mutton sleeves. Much later he wrote Sara his lampoon version of this moment in their lives:

> H.J.M. (just returned from the wars) "Have you ever thought seriously of getting married?"
>
> S.A. "Oh, Mr. Mankiewicz, how you carry on."
>
> Silence. Mr. Mankiewicz realizes that something is wrong and inwardly curses Moses, whom he suspects to be responsible for his not being allowed to smoke on Shabbos [the Sabbath].
>
> H.J.M. (swallowing several times and remembering rather humorously that he is a Marine.) "Could you learn to love me?"
>
> S.A. "Probably. I learned Hebrew once."
>
> Silence. Mr. Mankiewicz suspects that all is not going well. The suspicion dawns on him that the quarter he paid for "Advice To Young Gentlemen and Young Gentlewoman on how to propose and how to receive proposals including three specimen letters and a cure for boils" is a dead loss. He swallows again and looks fervently at the calm, majestic brow of his beloved idol.
>
> H.J.M. (suddenly and with the voice of a sick calf) "Shulamith!"
>
> S.A. "Mank!"
>
> Clinch.

In actuality, as soon as they were alone in Rock Creek Park, Herman tried to kiss Sara. She pushed him away, announcing that she would never kiss anybody unless she were going to marry him. "Honestly," says Sara, "I think I forced him to propose. I was just too pure for words."

Once their troth was plighted and kissing was permitted, they took a carriage all the way home. Herman suddenly told the cabdriver to stop. He leaped from the cab, ran to an astonished man on a street corner, and half shouted, "She accepted! She accepted! She's going to marry me!"

At the doorstep Herman said good-night and disappeared into the night. Sara went inside and announced that she was marrying Herman. "Marry him!" exploded Reuben Aaronson. "You don't even know him. You don't know anything about his father, his family."

"Poppa, *you* can investigate the family," answered Sara. "*I'm* going to marry Herman." Her sister Mattie excitedly rushed into her bedroom and pulled a picture of the First Zionist Congress in Basel, Switzerland away from the wall. On the wall behind it, she wrote, "Sara engaged to Herman Mankiewicz. July 3, 1919."

From Washington, twenty-one-year-old Herman went to Sharon, Connecticut, where his family was spending the summer. He was concerned about his eleven-year-old brother, Joe, who had very nearly died of pulmonary pneumonia. Joe can still remember his joy as he ran pell-mell to meet his worshiped brother and to receive a present of a German soldier's canvas belt.

Back in New York that summer, Herman settled in a $5-a-week room on 116th Street, $2 of which came from his father. Herman was rehired on the *Tribune*. His Broadway connections promoted a side-line job with the Famous Players Film Company to write publicity in German for films sold in Germany.

Loving letters traveled north and south. "Serene and sheltered in the midst of your family," wrote Herman to Sara in Washington, "you write that you have a sensation that you believe to be homesickness. There's more poetry and beauty in that concept, dear, than in a million poems. And truth. For it's the sensation I feel."

Chill voices from cool heads intruded on this rapture. Olga had become immediately fond of Herman. But Reuben and Herman regarded each other with wary disfavor. Herman would not forgive Reuben for the narrowness that had deprived Sara of a college education. Reuben considered Herman irresponsible. Efficient Naomi, who actually ran the house, had questions. They began counseling Sara against marrying a man who seemed to "lack solidity, sobriety, maturity, and Jewishness." Other beaux were held up as marvels of substance and stability.

Sara was unmoved and determined. Herman promised the dubious Aaronsons that he would follow all the outward symbols of Judaism if only out of respect for Sara. And he argued that "the problem arises from my unwillingness to take unimportant things seriously and my desire to avoid appearing sentimental by making bad jokes. The fact is that I am the most serious man in the world, even when I'm joking."

But Herman himself questioned his fitness for Sara. To him she personified the qualities he guiltily believed he lacked. Perhaps he hoped that in marriage she would remake him into what he wanted to be. "It's almost an axiom," he wrote to her, "that in the presence of cleanness and goodness and sweetness a superficial cleverness shrivels up and dies, recognizing its own unworthiness. You are so far above me in all that amounts to anything in this life that I can only marvel at the love that has come into my life. I can only close my eyes to my unworthiness and pray that I may prove worthy of your love."

Not the least of Sara's virtues was her strength, which attracted Herman and daunted him. He wrote to his beloved: "Again that terrible vision creeps over me, of me in my old age washing dishes while my wife blows cigar smoke into the lace curtains and tells me I can swab the floor when I'm through. Please, please my little sweetheart, don't write to me so determinedly. You frighten me. Are you by any chance related to Jess Willard?"

In the fall of 1919 Sara traveled to New York to meet Father and Mother Mankiewicz. The Mankiewicz apartment was then on St. Mark's Square on the Lower East Side. Herman was waiting nervously in front of the Mankiewicz brownstone to usher Sara and her escorting uncle up the three flights of stairs. Herman, not without irony, had already coached Sara on what to say to his parents: "Just tell them what a great guy I am, how wonderful."

The apartment was small. And, Sara says, "there was this stout, big bosomed woman and this big powerful man with a booming voice: 'Hello, hello, hello!' In all my life I'd never been in a room with such enormous people—all bellowing at me. I was scared out of my wits. I almost fainted."

The professor and Hanna Mankiewicz were delighted with and incredulous over Sara. Hanna had one of her precious heirloom earrings made into an engagement ring for her. "I'm sure," says Sara, "that Herman's father thought he would marry some chorus girl or get involved with something terrible. And then this sweet, little, inexperienced girl shows up. They loved me."

At one point in the afternoon the professor drew Sara aside into his study. "Herman is a good boy," he said to her gently. "But you'll find he has many faults."

"I don't know any faults," Sara said, astonished.

"Oh, my girl," said the professor, "you'll find out. He is not perfect."

"I looked at him," Sara remembers, and "I wondered *what* kind of faults he could possibly be talking about. Since that day I've thought of that conversation many, many times."

An actual marriage date remained vague. Herman got a job in the press department of the Red Cross, collecting and processing material for its newsletter. He was transferred to the national headquarters in Washington, lived near Sara, and came to dinner every night. And every night he and Reuben had at least one argument, "painstakingly debating," Herman said, "whether the grass is black or yellow, he saying black and I yellow." And Herman would awe the adoring Aaronson girls with his comments. "They should shove an umbrella down the Kaiser's throat," he told them, "and then open it."

After dinner the lovers were left alone in semidarkness on

the Mission couch. Sometimes they played records on the standing, windup Victrola. One of their favorite songs was "Come On and Baby Me."

In December, after six months of formal engagement, Herman was offered a job in the Red Cross press office in Paris with the rank of captain. He eagerly accepted. In Paris Herman gregariously drank at the Dome and browsed at Sylvia Beach's bookstore, the legendary gathering places of the expatriate American writers. He took side trips to Nice and Monte Carlo. He lay in his small hotel room and looked out the window at the Eiffel Tower in the moonlight and thought of Sara.

Not until March did Sara finally have a photograph of herself she was willing to send Herman. He wrote back:

> I'm greatly afraid you've caught cold, for I placed you on a writing table near a window that's always open, and this morning when I awoke you were sniffling and your nose was red. When I turned my head away you struggled frantically to get out of your glass frame so you could at least powder your nose. And I let you struggle heartlessly. In fact, I shook my can of talcum powder in front of you. Tonight I'm going to watch carefully to see what you do if one of your hairpins falls out. Will you abandon that aggravating pose—one hand supporting your chin, the other wandering off into the air—and stoop to pick up the fallen pin?

Then in late June 1920, after a trip to Berlin to see his father's relatives, Herman boarded the boat train for his journey home to "Schnutz." He had been gone six months.

Herman married Sara on July 1, 1920. He did not arrive from France until the day before the wedding. The reunion between the lovers had been predescribed by Herman in one of his last letters from Paris:

> The sun will be shining and the birds singing and I'll walk down Fairmont Street and climb the steps and ask for "Miss Sara" and Mattie will say, "What name please?" and I'll tell her and she'll say, "How do you spell it?" and I'll wait twenty

minutes and grumble terribly at the delay. And then my sweetheart will come down languidly to greet me. Oh, Schnutz, you will be all bathed and napped and pink dressed, won't you darling. And shamefacedly we'll kiss right in front of everybody, won't we? We will, you know.

The Orthodox wedding was held in the parlor on the Axminster rug, surrounded by the Four Seasons prints, the piano, and the windup Victrola. Only family were invited, but even distant cousins came. Professor Mankiewicz was embarrassed by his ignorance of the ritual and his grotesque attempts to speak Yiddish. All the guests stood. Two rabbis officiated, one of them with a fly on his nose throughout the ceremony.

After the wedding the guests sifted to the relative cool of the outdoors. They leaned on the pipe railing that ran down the terraced front steps in front of the house and against the picket fence encircling the backyard, where the wedding pictures were taken. Herman, with one arm around Sara, the other around Naomi, called out, "Which one is the bride?"

By seven o'clock Sara was exhausted, and her uncle drove the newlyweds to the Harrington Hotel, an ordinary room-and-bath commercial hostelry. When they pulled up in front of the Harrington, Sara appealed to Uncle Meyer, "Won't you come up with us for just a little while?" He politely refused. In their rather worn room, no flowers or champagne awaited. When the time came for Sara to get undressed, she made Herman go into the closet. "Everybody had lectured him about being careful with me," she says. "He didn't come anywhere near me. And that was fine because, boy, was I tired and scared."

The next day, a Friday, the couple had to leave Washington in time to get to New York before nightfall. Sara could not travel on the Sabbath. Both families came to the station, and all the Aaronson women cried.

"Herman and I got onto the train," Sara recalls, "and it was as though I didn't exist. Herman got his newspapers, and he read them—once in a while touching my hand. It was an old marriage by then. It was twenty-four hours." In New York Sara had to get to their nearby hotel, the Herald Square, before dark. So they ate their first dinner together in Pennsylvania Station, sitting at a counter. Sara could not eat non-kosher meat. She did not like fish, so she ordered Grape-nuts. Herman had a full-course dinner. "I watched it brought and taken, plate after plate," she says. "And he got an evening paper, and he folded it in that long, thin way newspapermen do—he did it to the end of his days—and he sat there at the counter reading his paper. And I thought, 'My heavens above! Is this what being married means? No Sabbath dinner? No candles? No nothing?'

"I felt so sorry for myself, so bereft—until I took a look at him. He was so intent on this newspaper. And all my pride in him came back in a minute. I thought, 'You've just married the greatest guy in the world. He's not just a ninny who's going to make love to you in the railroad station. And I felt so full of love.' "

CHAPTER

3

□ □ □

Within Germany the war is still regarded by the better classes as a sort of world mutiny.

—HERMAN MANKIEWICZ

HERMAN AND SARA SET SAIL FOR EUROPE AND BERLIN IN August 1920, as he once romantically wrote her: "My Schnutz and I will stand on deck, arm in arm, and watch the Statue of Liberty fade gently into the night." They both were twenty-two. Sara was senior by two months, which allowed Herman to say, "I married an older woman."

On the deck of the SS *Kroonland*, bound for Holland, they posed side by side for a photograph. On Sara's smooth face was a smile of pride and unshadowed delight. She was holding onto Herman, one hand resting behind his shoulder, the other clasping his forearm, almost as though she were holding Herman back with one hand and pushing him forward with the other—an involuntary forecast of her future role in his life.

Beneath Herman's shock of hair, rumpled as a cub's fur, his smile was not quite as blissful as Sara's. He carried the knowledge that no Chicago *Tribune* job awaited him in Berlin. His only prospects were vague offers of help from newspaper correspondents he had met in Paris. But he had taken immediate charge of Sara's dowry, approximately $2,500. On the *Kroonland* they were traveling first-class, their luxury paid for, says Sara, with indulgent affection, "by my rich husband —with my money."

One evening they went to their cabin early, and Herman asked, "Where's that wine you got?" Sara produced one of the two bottles of her sacramental port. He insisted she join him in a glass, which she gingerly sipped, barely wetting her tongue. In her experience the good people, like her father, drank only a bit of schnapps on the Sabbath and used a little wine to make the Kiddush prayer. Heavy drinkers, never Jews, were poor, low-class people who had nothing else to enjoy.

Soon the first bottle of sacramental wine was empty—and then the other. "That was my first inkling," Sara remembers, "of what those faults might be that Father Mankiewicz had talked about. I added to that list as time went on."

From Holland they journeyed by train to Berlin and began the first lap of the marriage that Herman imagined as "Just you and I, sweetheart, with all the world our playground. I thrill when I think of the wonderful future we'll have, sweetheart—not so many automobiles and yachts and fur coats, perhaps, but all the love and faith and joy in the world—with maybe a plate of kreplach on Sunday."

Their "honeymoon hotel" in Berlin did not exactly fit this dream. From the station the two walked to the small kosher pension picked out for them by Herman's Tante Anna, to whom, like the rest of the Mankiewicz family, kosher was almost as foreign as fish on Fridays. "It was a fleabag such as you have never seen," says Sara. "I mean actual bugs in the bed. A dirty, *filthy* bed. But we didn't care much. There was a great deal of laughter."

That first night, exhilarated with a sense of adventure, Herman and Sara went to a Victor Herbert type of sentimental operetta. And the next day the two explored Berlin. Kaiser Wilhelm's capital had grown by four times in the past fifty years. There was a freshness in its crisp air, in its ample avenues elegant with trees, in its constant parks. And there was even a kind of exuberance in the grotesque splendor of the public buildings: the domed, pillared, and statue-encrusted Reichstag, the uninspired, many-spired cathedral, the palaces of the kaisers like neoclassic fortresses. Everywhere were columns and cornices, porticoes, and pilasters. To the two young tourists the upper air seemed to throng with cherubs and eagles, winged lions, thoughtful Goethes, and stone Valkyries breasting silent winds.

In the midst of these monuments to dead glories, Berlin was living through its post World War I convulsions. The same revolutionary mix of disillusion, despair, and excitement that had deposed the Kaiser, that had triggered the bloody street battles between leftist irregulars and rightist troops, that had created the shaky Weimar Republic was also overturning the old rules in painting, music, architecture, theater, and sex.

During the years they lived there, 1920 to 1922, Herman and Sara saw the beginning of the decade in which Berlin became the most electric city in the world. But its energy was a delirium of rebellion and permissiveness which Berlin literally did not survive. Germany would eventually welcome Adolf Hitler, and by the end of World War II the city would be the target of 363 Allied air raids and 22,000 Russian artillery guns. The Berlin of the twenties was like some Atlantis that flowered and then disappeared utterly beneath waves of flame.

In their Friedrichstrasse hotel the newlyweds laughed about the extraordinary amount of foot traffic tramping up past their door from the restaurant below. In retrospect, Sara says, "It was a house of prostitution." Outside, on the street, bizarrely rouged prostitutes patrolled in tall boots and tiny skirts, their handbags swinging from fingers lurid with brilliantly lacquered nails. They would come up to Herman as though Sara did not exist and, as she puts it, "make a swift proposition." "*Nacht?*" they would say. "*Kleine?*" "Night?" "Quick one?" "*Ein bisschen Vergnügen?*" "A little bit of pleasure?"

Sara also remembers men peddling contraceptives. The brand name was Glück Auf. "Today with my dirty mind," says Sara, "I realize it might have meant 'Happy Erection.'"

Herman, the young reporter and political savant, knew the implications of what they saw. For Sara, naive, happy, in love, the signs of upheaval were too subtle to read. Most Berliners continued their daily business as usual. The enormity of the calamity was camouflaged, but even the facades were ersatz. Herman and Sara saw pink and blue dickeys displayed in shop-windows and thought they were the latest fashion. But the Berliners bought and wore them next to the skin because they could not afford shirts. On sale were "genuine leather" suit-cases which disintegrated in the first rain. Cigars had Havana bands, but Herman soon discovered that some of them were made of cabbage leaves soaked in nicotine. "Fourteen-jewel" watches stopped running in a few weeks. Sweet cakes were for sale—made from frostbitten potatoes. Shops had angry signs "No French Goods Sold Here," and inside, Sara bought gloves from Paris for fifty American cents.

Beggars were nicknamed shakers because they quivered and quaked when foreigners passed. Herman and Sara stopped for coffee and drank what the Berliners called *Blümchenkaffee*— "coffee of the little flowers"—because through the weak liquid the flower pattern was visible on the bottoms of the little Saxon cups. Attracted by the sounds of gaiety, Sara would peer into the small dance halls, called *Dielen*. The couples inside conscientiously jigged up and down to songs with such lines as "Tomorrow's the end of the world" or "Why should I cry when time comes apart? Around the corner there's another sweetheart."

Sara efficiently began finding an apartment, and Herman went through the motions of reporting to his "job" at the Berlin office of the Chicago *Tribune*. Each morning, dressed in one of his two suits and proudly kissed by Sara, he would issue forth, a scared twenty-two-year-old with no prospects, no connections, and magniloquent promises to the two families back home.

In a panic he took the first job that came his way, unloading cartons from trucks at a department store. But he was paid in marks, which constantly shrank in value. So Herman, with his normal aplomb and Sara's dowry, set about getting the job he had claimed to have had already, which would pay him in U.S. dollars.

He went alone to scout the terrain. He stood in the center island of Unter den Linden and inspected his target, a doorway and a window across the street in the granite five-story Hotel Adlon. On the window was inscribed "The Chicago Tribune, The World's Greatest Newspaper." Reconnoitering, Herman crossed to the *Tribune* office and looked into its narrow interior, where a secretary sat at a desk in front of a rear cubicle for the Berlin bureau chief. Then he entered the Adlon lobby.

If the *Tribune* was the goal, the way to get there turned out to be via the splendiferous Adlon. The hotel's ground floor consisted of an enormous space divided into the reception and dining areas by three rows of square yellow onyx pillars whose capitals were inlaid with precious metals. On the marble floor were carpets from Constantinople. Down from the coffered ceiling hung an enormous bronze chandelier depicting the sun and all the planets. And upward rose a polished white Carrara marble staircase. Marble figures gleamed in the corners.

It was to the Adlon bar, just off the dining area, that Herman inevitably went. He knew that if his problems of survival were to be solved, it would be within this mirrored room, where a drink cost less than ten American cents. In laughing, pontificating groups at the polished hookshaped bar, or assembled at the dozen small tables, were the American newspaper correspondents. In other clusters were the movers in the Berlin theater world, gathered to warm themselves with gossip and business deals. Herman knew how to shine in that setting. Soon he began reporting to the Adlon bar as though to his office.

Once acclimated, Herman felt able to approach the *Tribune* bureau chief, George Seldes, for help. He spotted Seldes sitting at an outdoor café with another man, who turned out to be Albert Boni. Boni had recently sold out his share in the publishing firm, Boni and Liveright, creators of the Modern Library. The former publisher was now in Berlin negotiating for the memoirs of the deposed Kaiser.

Herman marched up to Seldes, introduced himself as a young newspaperman in serious trouble, and plunged into a woeful, semispurious tale. It involved a New York *World* job in Paris that had fallen through, his arrival in Germany with a new bride and no money, and a Berlin bank president uncle whom Herman was too proud to approach. Seldes was sympathetic and said he would try to help.

In the meantime, there was still money from Sara's dowry and those side deals Herman was forever finagling. While taking a political science course at the University of Berlin, he noticed there were no flower carts such as those he had seen outside the Sorbonne in Paris. He set up a cart and hired a *Fräulein* to tend it. He had intense and fruitless huddles with an unsavory Pole to whom Herman wanted to sell German war planes. He dabbled in foreign currency exchange manipulations. For a small percentage, young Herman helped tourists at the Adlon buy their German marks in Berlin's flourishing black market. And Charles Boni remembers a visitor exclaiming to him about that remarkable fellow Mankiewicz. Herman, again for a percentage, was investing tourists' hard currency in the German stock market, where the numbers constantly rose as the result of inflation. At the end of the week he returned to his clients handsome increases in marks. But those innocents did not realize that these inflated marks were worth the same as or perhaps less than their original investment.

Herman's most fruitful energies were expended at the Adlon bar. Though nobody would give him a job, he simply anointed himself a foreign correspondent by playing the role. The brash kid who had posed on the SS *Kroonland* took on the look of a grown man of substance. He adopted bow ties, fawn leather gloves, a black cane, and an air of authoritative maturity. Soon he was a fixture in the group that gathered in the correspondents' corner at the bar. He stood there, one foot on the brass rail, chiming in on their embroidered war stories, delivering his own political dictums. He denounced the peace treaty written by "the Vultures and the Messiah" at Versailles. "That treaty," he said, "was signed with the blood of generations to come, and not, as it should be, by the blood of the past generation."

In that bar talk Herman absorbed inside gossip from the employees of William Randolph Hearst, the eventual model for Charles Foster Kane. Hearst correspondent Karl von Wiegand was already buying medieval treasure for the castle his publisher was building in California.

A young part-time reporter for the New York *Tribune,* Rebecca Drucker, arrived with stern instructions from Alexander Woollcott to look up Herman Mankiewicz. She easily found Herman, "nearly always too close to the bar," and remembers his clique of correspondents as men who "aimed at toughness." "And toughness," she continues, "was what Herman aimed for, no question. By toughness, I mean you couldn't be caught off guard, couldn't be surprised at anything. You never sounded like an intellectual. You knew where the best food and drink could be found and what things cost and how to manipulate money. You gambled. And you could bull your way into any place, and you had no illusions. And you were an American, and that meant that you were the cream of the earth."

Herman, almost a boy, was accepted into this fraternity because he was bright and good company. To Sigrid Schultz, the secretary in the *Tribune* office, Herman was "somebody you liked to talk to, somebody who was alert. He had a way of looking at you from under the eyelids—a look of observing very, very closely whenever you said anything. He knew a lot." To Rebecca Drucker, he was "a quick, sharp debunker, and strictly a natural—really great fun. His father was a professor, and I think he was determined to be as little like a professor as possible." When a group of newspapermen were discussing one of the many Berlin workers' strikes, Herman, "to spread an increased knowledge of English in Germany," offered anybody at the bar a thousand marks for a good German translation of Ed Wynn's line "It will never get well if you picket."

Journalism suited Herman almost too well. Reporters have always risked the occupational hazard of becoming professional spectators: watching, analyzing, distant, immune, untouched. At the same time, moving from drama to drama, they enjoy a repeated adrenaline rush of vicarious excitement. The correspondents' existence—escaping the clocked commonplaces of life, being in the midst of the news, having pronouncements canonized in print, keeping the adventure alive with drinks, with gambling, with manly camaraderie—Herman loved all of it.

In Berlin Herman believed he would soon take charge of his life. And his ambitions were still ripe. "Herman was very idealistic and full of dreams of glory for himself and all of us," Sara recalls. "He was going to write the great American play and a great novel. And I had no doubt."

However, that mix of excitement and detachment can become a way of hiding from reality. It was a world in which Herman could subdue his self-doubts with laughter—while suppressing the deep emotions he needed to be an artist.

The here-today, anywhere-tomorrow liberation of journalism was ideal for the Herman who compartmentalized his life so no person would see him plain. Sara had no vision of him with his Broadway friends. His father could only imagine his college pleasures. The Berlin correspondents never guessed he had taken honors in German literature. Nobody, including Sara, ever knew all the gambits that filled Herman's days. Pumping as much excitement as possible into life, he lived it like a balancing act. He needed that adventure of suspense: how far he could push his luck, how long before he would be found out.

There was, for example, Herman's "job" with the Chicago *Tribune*. After a month in Berlin he confessed his courtship lie. But now, he told Sara, George Seldes had hired him as an assistant, so he was a full-fledged foreign correspondent. And Sara, who often rendezvoused with Herman at the *Tribune* office and found him at the typewriter, has never doubted the story was true.

However, both Seldes and Sigrid Schultz insist that Herman was only on the staff for a brief time in the winter of 1922. Nobody else in Berlin in those years remembers differently. Herman simply did not dare let Sara know the truth. One of his strongest supports was her idealized image of him. He needed to see himself as she saw him.

Herman, with extraordinary ingenuity—and perhaps mischievous zest—must have arranged circumstances to deceive her, parlaying his contacts at the Adlon bar into work as a free-lance legman, hired one job at a time. Though Seldes denies it, the evidence is that Herman did *Tribune* reporting assignments and wrote his reports in the office. Then Seldes, following the common practice of those times, rewrote Herman and filed to Chicago under his own by-line.

Eventually, however, in January 1921, Herman did actually get a job. For $15 a week he became a Berlin stringer for *Women's Wear Daily,* which then included both fashion and business reporting. The job was arranged by Sigrid Schultz. "I did it partly for his wife," says Sigrid. "I liked her, and I thought she had a problem with that husband."

The *Women's Wear* job was heaven-sent. Now Herman was an accredited correspondent. He could interview anybody, go anywhere as a member of the American press corps. At the press luncheon given by German Chancellor Josef Wirth, who was secretly allowing the German Army to be rebuilt in Russian training camps and factories, Herman was seated next to the chancellor.

Herman enjoyed the reporting, the swashbuckle, far more than the discipline of writing. He was expected to submit a weekly file to Bertram Perkins, the Berlin correspondent for *Women's Wear* who spoke no German. Saturday was the deadline. More and more Herman began waiting till the last minute. Then he began missing deadlines. He would simply disappear. Sigrid Schultz felt responsible and would hunt Herman down and lead him into the inner *Tribune* office. She locked him inside until he had finished.

Her wisdom was proved the day Karl von Wiegand, looking for a victim for a poker game, came storming into the office, demanding, "Where is Mankiewicz?" These poker games took place in the luxurious Adlon bridal suite, supplied free when it was available. Betting was already in Herman's blood, but the Adlon games had new ingredients that helped make him a compulsive gambler. Cards were one of the ways that men like Herman kept their lives racing on a perpetual jag. In Berlin, in New York, in Hollywood poker was almost a matter of manhood. There was that subtle romantic image of the hard-bitten he-man winning or losing great sums, the stuff of folklore.

Though he usually lost at cards and was then living by his wits, Herman's genuine talent and intelligence gave him earning power as a free-lance journalist. And of course, he patronized the black market. "If you buy your marks right," he told the new-arrival tourists, "bock beer comes to two cents a glass." In 1922 Herman and Sara's comfortable standard of living required perhaps twenty American dollars a week.

Their apartment was in an upper-class neighborhood, and Sara always had a maid. When Herman came home at night —throughout his life his adventures were mainly confined to the daytime—Sara often hid when she heard him at the door. He called out, "Shnooks, where are you? Come out." Then, laughing, he searched through the high-ceilinged, dark-paneled rooms. Finally, Sara would jump out at him. "I always thought I scared him," says Sara.

Sometimes Herman jokingly pretended to box with her,

dancing around, ducking, weaving, throwing mock punches. Occasionally a blow landed by mistake, bringing tears and wonderful comforting. Then Herman sometimes stepped out to the local *Stube* and brought back a pitcher of beer to drink along with handfuls of hazelnuts while he boasted of his day's exploits. "He got not only drunk," Sara says with nostalgic tolerance, "but fat."

During the day Sara sometimes went on cultural excursions with Herman's Tante Anna, who taught art history in a Berlin high school. She often gave Sara guided tours through the classical museums. In one they paused at a copy of the Roman statue the "Apollo Belvedere." Sara examined the heroic nude figure from head to toe. "Well," said Sara, "my Herman is much more beautiful."

With wifely thrift, Sara was taking advantage of the inflation to stock her future. She bought a sealskin coat, and she used her linens from Berlin for the rest of her life. After her shopping excursions Sara would come by the Chicago *Tribune* office and go on to dinner with Herman. Then they had their choice of some eighty legitimate theaters, and they went regularly. If news reporting was adventure to Herman, the theater world of "let's pretend" was romance. He added freelance theater criticism to his other enterprises. His contacts at *The New York Times* were receptive, and early in 1921 he began filing a periodic column called "News of the Berlin Stage."

According to popular history, Berlin of the 1920's enjoyed a creative binge in the theater. But not according to Herman. Brecht's *Threepenny Opera* did not yet exist. Herman considered the reputation of the other celebrated innovator Max Reinhardt inflated. A wealthy theater majesty, Reinhardt moved through his realm of three theaters with an entourage of satellite aides and society women streaming behind him. His success was built on the philosophy that spectacle is the essence of theater. But Herman called Reinhardt's production of *Orpheus in der Unterwelt* "Orpheus in Underwear" and wrote that "Reinhardt's attempts at novel scenic effects are the subject of innocent merriment to those who have seen the work of Ziegfeld. Robert Edmond Jones is superior to Reinhardt in every way except the possession of an apartment in Berlin."

According to Herman, "The myth of the Berlin theater originates with the loudmouthed veneration by foreign critics tired of the offerings in their own country." And he complained of the strain of "having to learn fifty times on one Berlin season that Fifi didn't sleep in the same bed with Rudolph, but that Mimi did—and of having to wax merry fifty times over plays by Oscar Wilde, sometimes with German authors."

After the first four columns had been printed, Herman received a check from *Times* drama editor George Kaufman, paying him $8 a column "with deductions for dashes, as is the benevolent custom of the office." "Your stuff is great," continued Kaufman. "Woollcott thinks so, too. I have liked everything, uniformly, except the long piece that you wrote, and the chief reason I didn't like that is that we haven't room for long pieces."

After the theater Herman and Sara often went on to a cabaret, the phenomenon which Herman called "Germany's version of vaudeville." Sometimes they went to the enormous balconied beer hall, the Romanische Café, that sat a thousand customers. It was the haunt of artists, writers, prostitutes, revolutionaries, small-time speculators, chess players at rows of little tables in the balcony, and black marketeers in wide "tango trousers" and nipped-in jackets with garish colors and loud checks. Sara remembers the Romanische as "crowded; a great deal of hilarious 'Ho, Ho, Ho' laughter; big fat necks. Lots of toasts. *Hoch,* and you stood up and drank your beer or wine. *Prosit.*"

By the summer of 1921 the mark had inflated from 4.20 to 75 to the dollar. By the summer of 1922, when Herman returned to America, it had reached 400. That year a Berlin widow, who had earlier inherited a fortune of 800,000 marks, used her last 65,000 to buy a typewriter to get work typing university students' theses. In the summer of 1923, when Herman came back to Berlin on a brief business trip, the mark was millions to the dollar.

No German in Berlin could escape that sense of hovering catastrophe. The Russian poet Ilya Ehrenburg wrote: "I felt as though I was at the front and the brief hour when the guns fell silent was dragging on." Berliners were simultaneously weighed down and released into desperate permissiveness. Despair and self-preservation fueled a feverish *joie de vivre* and desolate corruptions.

When Ben Hecht came to Berlin in 1919 as a correspondent for the Chicago *Daily News,* one of his chief sources for military gossip was a group of homosexual aviators he met at an officers' club. Hecht wrote:

These were elegant fellows, perfumed and monocled and usually full of heroin or cocaine. They made love to one another openly, kissing in the cafe booths and skipping off around two A.M. to a mansion owned by one of them. One or two women were usually in the party—wide mouthed, dark-eyed nymphomaniacs with titles to their names but unroyal burns and cuts on their flanks. At times little girls of ten and eleven, recruited from the pavements of Friedrichstrasse, where they paraded after midnight with rouged faces and in shiny boots and in short baby dresses, were added to the mansion parties.

Berlin's emergence as the public "sin capital" of European tourism exactly paralleled the rate of inflation. At the beginning, in 1921, Herman wrote in *Women's Wear:*

They have been getting Berlin ready for the American tourist and his money, and trying to revive the city's pre-war gaiety to divert the tourist dollars from Paris and Brussels. Several new and tinseled resorts have been opened featuring American 'jazz' which is believed here to be as essential to the visiting American as grape juice. One Original American Jazz Band was even said to contain an American. After sputtering for a few weeks, they are gone. Berlin remains unsmiling, and her night life is an insomnia cure.

By 1922, as the inflation raced into insanity, the network of streets around the Friedrichstrasse and Kurfürstendamm had become an erotic theater of the absurd. The distance of years has romanticized Berlin sin. The playwright Carl Zuckmayer was for a time one of the army of touts that lurked on side streets to get business for the *nacktballetts* run illegally in private homes after the much flaunted 11 P.M. official closing time. Zuckmayer wrote: "A muted phonograph whined and a few girls of indeterminate age—janitors' or generals' daughters—wearily and unimaginatively performed 'nude dances.' The whole thing might easily have been considered as a social-welfare association."

Herman explored this world. But, says Sara, "Herman protected me from all that degenerate stuff." She did not even get to see the woman boxers at the Metropole Cabaret.

In the spring of 1921 Sara discovered she was pregnant. That July her sister Naomi arrived, in company with the full Mankiewicz family: the professor, Hanna, Erna, Joe. They settled down for the month at the Baltic Sea resort of Herringsdorf with Sara, and Herman came on weekends. While the others swam, pregnant Sara stayed demurely in her dress.

From Berlin the still boyishly loving Herman wrote Sara a postcard: "This being a sealed letter, I have no hesitation in telling you that I just love my little cockles. It's a first rate cockles, and I don't care if it is enjoying itself in Herringsdorf with its poor husband sweltering here. I love her. My cockles. (It's not so hot, cookie, and anyhow, I'm going to hell soon.)"

Alexander Woollcott, Edna Ferber, and her elderly mother arrived in Berlin, and Sara returned long enough to give them a party. And one night at the Adlon bar Herman joined in a crap game with the three tourists. The ritual of the game called for the player throwing the dice to put down money and say, "Will you have some?"—meaning some of the betting action. But each time, Edna Ferber's mother would nod graciously and say, "Certainly. I'll just take a few," and help herself to part of the pot, stuffing the marks into her handbag.

Sara's pregnancy ended on January 20, 1922. She was at the *Tribune* office waiting for Herman when her labor pains began. They went home, packed a suitcase, notified her doctor, and took a cab to the clinic in the Charlottenburg section.

At the hospital there was no heat and no elevator service. It was routine in postwar Berlin for at least one utilities union to be striking in political protest. The doctor refused to appear until the moment of delivery. It was so cold Sara slipped into bed wearing her fur coat. There was a hot-water bottle, but the midwife begged it away from Sara to keep her own feet warm.

Herman hurried back to their apartment, picked up the two chickens cooked for the Sabbath the next day, and went directly to the Adlon bar. Setting the chickens on the bar, he announced his news to the assembled correspondents. All night, while she shivered, they toasted the incomparable Sara —and ate her chickens.

The next morning Don Martin Mankiewicz, named after the professor's cousin, was born. The circumcision ceremony touched a softheartedness always part of Herman. As he described the event to Sigrid Schultz, tears streamed down his face. "Why do they have to do that to a tiny baby?" he wailed.

But Herman had a second reason to be upset. He had retained a high-priced doctor and a live-in nurse for the first two weeks at home. Despite the inflation and Herman's miscellanea of jobs and schemes, he had spent and gambled away all his money. He could not get Sara out of the hospital until he paid the bill.

Somewhere Herman did get the money, and oblivious Sara came home "full of love and joy and thankfulness." But after Don was born, says her sister Ruth, "we wanted to get them home." And Herman was ready. He had used up Berlin. It had been a phantasmagoric lark, but it was leading nowhere. He was ready for a new world to conquer, a new set of people to impress as a brilliant charmer, going places. The new world he had in mind was New York, but Herman's finances could barely transport him beyond Germany.

In May 1922 a possible solution checked into the Adlon Hotel—Isadora Duncan and Sergei Essenin, one of the most bizarre couples in the history of the arts. Isadora, along with Sarah Bernhardt and Eleonora Duse, was one of the great female stage personalities the half century produced. She virtually invented modern dance. The first famous apostle for the liberation of the female body, Isadora evoked the artistic purity of classic Greece by dancing unfettered in a gauzy robe. When she performed in America, after years in Russia, the evangelist Billy Sunday screamed, "That Bolshevik hussy doesn't wear enough clothes to pad a crutch."

Now the pioneer dancer was forty-four and overweight. In Moscow she had just married her alcoholic, combative lover, Essenin, a Russian poet fifteen years her junior, who had already been married twice but never divorced. Neither one knew the other's language, and they could speak together only in a babyish patois of pidgin English and Russian.

Isadora was embarking on a concert tour of Europe and America to raise money for her Moscow school of dance, which the Russian government refused to finance. She needed a publicity man. One of Herman's side jobs had been in publicity, including work for the Moscow Art Theater and Jack Dempsey's visit to Berlin. Isadora hired him. He planned to travel to America with her and remain there when the tour was finished.

That afternoon Sara received a phone call from Herman, telling her he was bringing Isadora and Essenin home to dinner that night. "Look," he said, "don't be surprised at Essenin. He's crazy. And he eats nothing but cucumbers and sour cream."

When the two arrived, Isadora wore her usual loose Grecian robe. The five-foot-five dancer had curly red hair and sentimental eyes. Her mouth was beautiful but cruel, and she spoke with a short, clipped accent. The golden-haired Essenin was dolled up like a Berlin boulevardier.

"They were loving," Sara remembers, "but both sort of out of control. This mad poet was getting more and more drunk, and he was spouting Russian poetry. And she started to dance. She'd had a lot of wine. She wore a very low neckline, and her robe kept slipping off her shoulders. It made no difference if her bosoms were exposed. You felt she would just as easily have taken off all her clothes if anyone had said. . . . Lots of laughter. And that madman—nobody could understand him. She would tell him things in English, and he would pretend to understand—laugh boisterously and start quoting Russian poetry—and she would stamp her feet and get up and do a revolutionary dance. It was terribly exciting and funny. Herman would talk about her right at the table. By that time she was so drunk it didn't matter."

Isadora was booked to dance in Berlin at one of the music halls but canceled in a fury when she discovered she would share the program with a trained dog act. Her tour actually began in July in Brussels, and Herman had his first confrontation about pay. Isadora's finances were in a customary dishevelment. Her house in Berlin had been sold by her attorney for only a fraction of its value. Much of her property—library, furniture—had simply disappeared. Her Berlin bank account had been impounded because of her Communist allegiance. In addition, Herman wrote to Sara: "There were some checks in Russia that Isadora 'forgot about.' It seems she gave blank checks to the director of her Moscow school with which to buy food, and he's been indelicate enough to use them."

Herman agreed to accept less pay. "But," he wrote Sara, "by charging deluxe in Europe while traveling second class —a thoroughly fair and equitable procedure—I can schlag out a little more. Our recent disagreements have cleared the air and we're getting along like two cooing doves."

During the three concerts in Brussels, with an advance sale of a remarkable $12,000, Herman was unimpressed by what he saw. "The diva has danced twice," he told Sara by letter, "and she ain't so good. It's true that every one of her movements, her poses, calls to mind one's general impression of Greek art and even the faint memory of some vase or column somewhere, but on the whole there's a fleshiness and a lack of fire that makes it impossible to keep up any illusion."

From Brussels the entourage, including Herman, journeyed on to Paris, where Isadora was to do a series of recitals at the Trocadéro. While Herman was promoting publicity for that engagement and another in London, the Russian government refused to allow her dance chorus to leave Russia. Isadora, furious, canceled both concerts, though she badly needed the money. "Isadora wants to go to Venice to rest," Herman wrote to Sara disgustedly. He was again having problems. When he pestered Isadora for his pay, she would fly into a rage and fling a random handful of cash at his feet. While he picked it up from the floor, she railed at him for his disloyalty.

In early August, Herman gave up. As a ticket to America, Isadora had proved a disaster. He quit and departed for Berlin to find a new stratagem. Isadora went with Essenin to Venice, sublimely sure that the money would turn up to pay for her "vacation" at the Hotel Excelsior on the Lido.

Oddly, Isadora was an early and perverse object lesson to Herman. She proved that a person with nerve and magnetism and talent could live irresponsibly by impulse, floating like a cork on top of circumstance. Isadora, who spent millions of dollars—only some of them her own—lived sublimely certain that somehow she would always be saved. And somebody always did rescue Isadora—and Herman.

A boundless optimist, Herman turned any hope into an accomplished fact. The second half of his problem, employment in New York, seemed solved. He received a letter from George Kaufman, who had been publishing Herman's Berlin columns in the *Times*. "I'm interested in your prospective return," Kaufman wrote. "I think you would be a wonderful man for my job here. I'll be giving it up in about a year, I think. It doesn't pay a million dollars, but I'll do all I can if you say the word."

Sara recalls: "To Herman that was already money in the pocket. I said, 'Herman, it isn't really a job, you know.' But he said, 'Don't worry.' "

Professor Mankiewicz came to Germany with his family again that summer of 1922 and took Sara and baby Don home to America, ending what Sara looks back on as "two years of utter happiness—glorious, beautiful, young, happy years." For his own passage, Herman applied to his poker pals. They took up a collection, so much out of every poker pot, and bought his ticket. As Herman sailed cheerfully off into the sunset, one of the correspondents around the Adlon poker table asked, "By the way, besides what we just gave him, does Herman owe you money?" Every man raised his hand.

CHAPTER

4

☐ ☐ ☐

Damn it! It was the twenties, and we had to
be smarty. That's the terrible thing. I should
have had more sense.

—DOROTHY PARKER

HERMAN IN 1922 RETURNED HOME TO AN AMERICA IN THE
throes of its own postwar hysteria. But where Germany had
been redolent with despair, the 1920's were the last euphoric
decade in America, those years when an adult could comfortably treat life as an extension of collegiate good times.
Putting quick distance between itself and the war, America
was rushing back to normality in a holiday mood. Crazes
swept the country: flagpole sitting; six-day bicycle races; dance
marathons. Housewives, including Hanna Mankiewicz, played
Mah-Jongg, shouting "pung" and "chow." Coué Institute dis-
ciples repeated over and over, "Day by day, in every way, I am
getting better and better." Beauty pageants were born. Then
came crossword puzzles, and anybody on the street could
name the Egyptian sun-god. Commercial radio was a sudden
reality and an instant fad. And what was playing in every home
was "Yes, We Have No Bananas."

America wanted heroes, and the decade was blessed with
prodigious ones in sports: Babe Ruth, Bobby Jones, Red
Grange, Bill Tilden, Jack Dempsey. The glory of Lindbergh
was unrivaled, even by the remarkable Model A Ford. The
newspapers, feeding the romance-struck country what it
wanted, treated life like a three-ring circus. The New York
World had such headlines as "Soubrette, 19, Dies by Poison

Doubting Sweetheart's Love. She Failed to See Him Though He Waited, as Usual, During Rehearsal." The historic Scopes heredity trial was turned into show business, and the Hall-Mills choir singer murder was kept a national topic for nearly a year. The decade was a dizzy pendulum swing away from *Main Street* Babbittry, away from Bible Beltism, away from a whole litany of Victorian taboos, away from sobriety in anything. Prohibition and the speakeasy made lawbreaking and booze into national pastimes.

In this collegiate era it was the rage to be witty. The epicenter of humor and sophistication was the Algonquin Round Table, the clique of newspaper columnists, playwrights, producers, actresses, press agents, theater critics who assembled daily at lunch at the Algonquin Hotel to have at each other with wisecracks. Herman soon became a member. New York in the 1920's was made to order for him.

However, when Herman arrived in New York from Berlin, the vaguely promised job in the *Times* drama section was not wide-open and waiting. And George Kaufman, though cordial, had changed his mind about leaving. He recommended Herman to his friend Herbert Bayard Swope, executive editor of Pulitzer's New York *World*, the city's premier newspaper.

"Swope of the World. Herbert Bayard Swope," as he always announced himself on the telephone, was a prodigious personality in a period that specialized in originality and extravagance. A member of the Algonquin Hotel set, Swope had the energy of a Gatling gun. Westbrook Pegler summed him up as "all gall, divided into three parts—Herbert, Bayard, and Swope." When Oscar Levant remained seated, lounging on his spine, Swope said, "Goddamn it, when I come into the room, you should stand on your feet." Herman told friends, "Never Swope until you are Swopen to."

Herman was hired for $25 a week. Top reporters received $100. In those first months back in America he was still boyish about his ambition. And soon, when Sara went to Washington to see her family, Herman was writing to "dear Schnuggles": "I believe that I'm doing even a little better than making good—for example, they've just assigned me a desk all of my own which they won't do if they don't expect you to stay."

Clustered on Park Row with the *Tribune, Sun, American, Journal,* and *Post* near City Hall, the *World* was in the Pulitzer Building, a conglomeration of neoclassic columns, Gothic arched windows, and a skinny gold dome—"gilded from within," said Herman, "by the exhalations of the Messrs. Pulitzer." And Herman relished constituency in those city room groups of reporters lounging on chairs or one haunch up on a desk, swapping stories and "jokes that would make a 156-year-old Turk look like a tot."

Herman covered fires, murders, a luncheon address by steel magnate Judge Elbert H. Gary, whom Herman idealistically despised as an exploiter of helpless workers, a graft investigation in Atlantic City, a will challenge in court, the New York repercussions of the burning of Smyrna by the Turks, charity foundation lunches, and so on. He was one of two reporters who infiltrated the Ku Klux Klan to document its presence in the Northeast.

"I've been getting almost star assignments," Herman boasted to Sara. "I may be fooling myself, but I think they like my work very much." He always took pains to impress Sara. For Herman, Sara's admiration was a kind of putty filling in between what he wanted to be and reality. When he covered the surprise marriage of the daughter of the former president of the Singer Sewing Machine Company, he told her this bit of inconsequence would run in the *World* for two days. "I'll be able to talk salary to Swope when it's finished," he said. The story ended up a three-quarter column on a back page.

On Herman's salary, they could just afford a second-floor apartment of a two-family house in Flatbush, Brooklyn, a stark neighborhood dotted with open lots like a half-finished development. Each night, after an hour or two of conviviality at a speakeasy, Herman arrived home around 1 A.M., his fedora slightly on one side of his head, the press card stuck in his hatband. Herman did not carry a door key. He would only have lost it. Each night he roused Sara with a whistle from the street as she dozed upstairs. "It was a kind of warble—like a love call—a little off key, and I never got over it," says Sara. "I'd buzz him in, and he would come bounding up the steps so full of excitement and bursting with the story that he'd discovered and everything that had happened. And then he'd have to go in and see Don, wake him up sometimes.

"In the morning he'd show me in the paper the stories he'd covered. And he would be very angry if they hadn't got into the paper. But all I wanted to know—was he in danger? Those were the most marvelous nights and days. I was so proud of him. He had a real job. He was a real husband."

But there was a cloud, still small, on the horizon of Sara's contentment. Her version of bliss was not Herman's. He did have strong feelings for family and fatherhood. But his social hunger was more intense. Herman was a circulator, particularly among the celebrated and the powerful. And in New York he was soon cultivating the Algonquin Round Table group. Shy homebody Sara was proud of those companionships for Herman's sake. But confronted by their raillery and theater gossip, she suffered.

A few weeks after Herman and Sara returned from Berlin, they attended one of George Kaufman's celebrated parties. "I can still get a cold chill when I think of it," says Sara. She stuck close to Herman, constantly hurrying to his side whenever he circulated away from her, until he began joking, "You go play over there. Get a coloring book and color something." Around eleven o'clock Marc Connelly and his wife, Madeline, started saying their good-nights, and Sara, in a voice louder than she intended, said, "Look, Herman, people are going home."

"That caused quite a sensation," Sara remembers. "For a

long time afterward they all referred to me as 'People are going home, Herman.' "

Within Herman was a worshiping boy, but he moved among this clique with the assurance of an equal, though many of them, like Alexander Woollcott, Heywood Broun, and Franklin P. Adams, were the famous voices of their time. Indeed, he was their peer in wit and knowledge, if not in accomplishment. They were his natural galaxy.

At the *World* Herman had easy access to Heywood Broun, his longtime idol, who was the theater critic and author of a discursive, personal column "It Seems to Me." The genial Broun was six feet four inches tall, weighed 250 pounds, and was utterly indifferent to his appearance. He arrived at the paper in a huge racoon coat he himself had shortened with a razor blade. Though his person was immaculately clean and his clothes were expensive, his shirttails constantly ballooned out of rump-sprung, knee-sprung, worn-thin pants. And his size thirteen feet were jammed into broken-backed shoes, worn unlaced to accommodate huge ankles. In his bottom desk drawer was a wadded-up tuxedo jacket which Broun would take out, shake free of paper clips, and wear to theater first nights.

Herman, at the *World*, could also cultivate Franklin P. Adams, the irascible, perfectionist architect of "The Conning Tower," to which Herman had contributed while a student at Columbia. F. P. A. was spectacularly ugly. The *World* editor, Irvin Cobb, on seeing a stuffed moose head, exclaimed, "My God, they've shot Frank Adams."

Always able to make Adams laugh, Herman dared penetrate F. P. A.'s relentless privacy. Adams kept a pile of mail on the floor in front of his closed office door, a stratagem to convince interrupters that he was not inside. But it never worked. From inside came the familiar sound of F. P. A. screaming at hapless phone callers. When a contributor asked for the return of an unused poem, Adams would shout, "I never asked for it in the first place," and slam down the receiver.

Herman also sought out the political reporters who kept him privy to behind-the-scenes gossip. And perhaps the biggest political story at that time was William Randolph Hearst, who was again trying for the U.S. presidency, the obsession that dominated two decades of his life. As Hearst's father once said, "I notice that when my boy Bill wants cake, he wants cake; and he wants it *now*."

As a stepping-stone to the presidency, Hearst was maneuvering for the nomination for U.S. Senator from New York. He needed the backing of former Governor Al Smith, who was running for a second term as governor. Smith was offered the support of the Hearst newspaper chain, whose powerful circulation was built by exploiting crime news, violence, fear, envy, hate. Herman summed up: "The Hearst press is not mediocre. It's yellow ochre."

Al Smith refused to share any political ticket with Hearst. Writing a few years later in an early issue of *The New Yorker,* Herman explained why. He described how Hearst, during a long New York milk strike, had printed cartoons of Governor Smith as an ogre snatching milk from anemic babies and how Smith had found his mother in tears. "For William Randolph Hearst," wrote Herman, who would soon be eating at Hearst's dinner table, "the puzzle is probably Al Smith's possession of old-fashioned virtues."

The state Democratic convention in Syracuse was forced to choose between the two men. It voted almost unanimously for Smith. That was the end of the publisher's presidential dream, much to Herman's relief. "No wonder Hearst's views are distorted," he said. "It's no joke having to keep one eye on England and one on Japan while both of them are on Washington."

The Round Table's acceptance of Herman confirmed George Kaufman's original judgment of him. Although Kaufman often teased Sara, wondering aloud how she stood that husband of hers, he also told her in a moment of seriousness, "Herman is extraordinary and exceptional and will do great things."

Early in 1923 *The New York Times* expanded theater coverage in the Sunday edition to two pages. Since Kaufman's work was increasingly interrupted by his burgeoning career as a Broadway comedy playwright, he hired Herman away from the *World* to be his assistant.

The job was one of the plums of 1920's journalism. Radio and movies were infants, and the theater was a large part of New York's pull on the imagination of America. By the mid-twenties eighty theaters averaged 225 productions, every one of them reviewed in the city's fifteen newspapers. Frequently there were two and three openings on a single evening—eleven one Christmas weekend. "Ninety percent of all young men want to be drama critics on New York newspapers," Herman said. "The remaining ten percent are training for asparagus farming." For the daily paper he assembled minor items for a short department called "Theatrical Notes." For the Sunday *Times* he wrote profiles of actors, actresses, and producers and passed along gossip for Kaufman's regular column, "News on the Rialto," which Herman wrote when Kaufman was absent.

Those New York years were glorious for Herman because work combined logically with his kind of play. The *Times* theater critic in 1925, Brooks Atkinson, remembers: "Herman was always out someplace. He entertained the hell out of everybody, including me, and could always laugh himself out of any situation." At the slightest excuse Herman roamed what he called "the hot Broadway sands" in search of publishable gossip.

Broadway in the 1920's was a sensory delight. There was the dry chugging of the high cloth-topped cars, the a-ooo-gah horns, the jangling bells of the red and green trolley cars that rattled along the centers of the avenues. There was the clatter of elevated trains hurtling above Sixth Avenue and the clamor of pianos, cornets, saxophones, and banjos from upstairs rehearsal halls. On every corner were shabby young newsboys, cigarettes projecting from their pinched faces. "Read all about it! King Tut's tomb opened!"

Herman had his own explanation for the cheerful faces he encountered. "Those men smiling broadly as they pass by," said Herman, "are not, as you might suppose, happy on the receipt of good news from Geneva. They have not sat up all night with a friend who at dawn won his weary fight with death. Theirs is not the joy of cheery sunshine and the merry chirp of the birds. No! No, indeed. Those men are theatrical producers. They know that some fellow producer has staked his all on a new show the night before—and failed."

Herman, on his rounds, was circulating through a huge neighborhood of friends. For all the quickness of his tongue, he exuded a natural warmth and worked to amuse whoever he encountered. One day on the sidewalk he met Brock Pemberton, a producer and Algonquin member who had a play opening the following week. Pemberton had just bought a new shirt. "What did you do that for?" Herman said. "You'll only lose it next week." He constantly slipped into theaters to watch rehearsals from the dark at the back of the orchestra, including Kaufman directing the Marx Brothers in *The Cocoanuts* and creating the Groucho character, particularly the walk.

Herman would drop by the dressing room of his friend W. C. Fields, starring in *Poppy* in 1923. Fields had an innocent, conventional wardrobe trunk which, when opened, became a bar of bootleg booze. Herman arranged an interview with him for his brother, Joe. When it appeared in *Caliper*, the monthly magazine of Stuyvesant High School, Fields, a practicing curmudgeon, astonishingly wrote a thank-you note to Joe. It was evidence that to Fields—and many other people on Broadway —Herman was a man with power.

Herman himself often focused his self-mocking wit on the absurdities in his life. Describing his backstage interviews of actresses, he wrote:

> The hounded and unappreciated young theatrical reporter will be introduced to an icy and severely cold-creamed beauty, the

introduction being effected in the tone generally heard in a Baltimore lunchroom when a well-dressed burgher says, "Give this poor fellow a cup of coffee and put it on my check. There, my good man, that will buck you up."

The young woman, it always develops, met the Prince of Wales in London and more than met King Alfonso at Deauville. Oscar Hammerstein, moreover, heard her sing in a convent while still just a child—that is, the young woman—and prevailed upon her to take up the stage as a career—despite the fact that her family had vast estates in the South before the war. All young women of this type call the interviewer Mr. Markowitz, which is the unpardonable crime, and it is the absence of penalties for it that has really kept our Aryan civilization at best a half-baked thing.

Herman identified with the barefaced hokum of show business, and he wrote about it in his ironic, relishing style. There was, for example, Ziegfeld's creation of the star Anna Held:

> Miss Held was living at the Hotel Marlborough at the time. One day a milkman brought suit against Miss Held for an unpaid milk bill of a staggering amount—six large cansful daily. The court reporters set out for the Marlborough. It is recorded that one of the more cynical of them expressed thanks that at last he was now on a story free of the slightest suspicion of press-agentry.
>
> When they arrived at the Marlborough, they found Mr. Ziegfeld waiting for them. What use, they asked, could Miss Held possibly have for so much milk? Mr. Ziegfeld registered surprise. Had they never, he asked, heard of Poppaea, the wife of Nero? She believed that the loss of her complexion would mean the loss of his love. From an old Egyptian slave she learned that a milk bath daily would preserve this complexion—and there you are.
>
> Mr. Ziegfeld did not rest on this mere lesson in history. He asked the boys point blank if they would like to see Miss Held in her milk bath. The boys—schooled that a newspaperman must take the bitter with the sweet—said yes. Trailed by the newspapermen like so many panthers, Ziegfeld approached the

bathroom, flung open the door, and there lay Miss Held completely surrounded by milk.

The point of the story, it should perhaps be added, is that milk is only slightly less transparent than wood. Nevertheless, the front page publicity immediately placed Miss Held among the most famous women of the country.

Herman and Sara attended the theater almost nightly. And to be closer to Broadway and his new life, they moved from Brooklyn into an apartment on upper Central Park West. Soon Ben Hecht was calling Herman "The Central Park West Voltaire" and Harpo Marx was knocking on the door to ask, "Can Hoime come out and play?" In this apartment Sara was hostess to Herman's unsettling Round Table friends. One typical dinner party included Michael Arlen, Prince Bibesco, Robert Benchley, John V. A. Weaver, Peggy Wood, William Bolitho.

Herman was then the third-string *Times* theater critic, setting off to openings in his tuxedo, swinging his cane. He reviewed the less important plays, while, joked Herman, "the disgusting poses of the legitimate dramatic critic are cluttering up the drawing rooms of the town, and the dramatic editor is pouring shallow phrases into the pink ears of receptive ingenues."

Often Sara accompanied Herman back to the *Times* tower. While she waited on a chair in the hallway outside the small theater department cubicle, Herman and Kaufman inside pounded out their reviews. Herman, frowning, assaulted his big, square Remington with two fingers, jabbing out his sentences. "The play needs only the addition of a couple of nicely fried eggs to pass anywhere as America's favorite dish," he once wrote. On the attack, he said, "This is a cheap, rubber stamped, sniveling play that affronts the intelligence every moment of its existence." Dismissing a musical, he wrote, "With these summer shows, it isn't the heat, it's the bromidity."

George Kaufman, tall, lean, hair like a privet hedge above a high forehead, sat with legs wrapped around his chair legs.

He had a long, dour face, huge nose, heavy eyebrows, and his dark and melancholy eyes, peering over his horn-rim glasses, could be fearsome. It was a face and frame perfect for dressing up as Lincoln, which Kaufman liked to do at costume parties. When his friend actor Raymond Massey became a household image in the play *Abe Lincoln in Illinois*, Kaufman peevishly remarked, "Massey won't be satisfied until he's assassinated."

Kaufman wrote his reviews as fast as he could type. And surprisingly from a comedy playwright and a famous one-line wit, they were usually straightforward and somewhat prosaic. Herman's reviews were more original, more sparkling.

One October night in 1925 Herman was assigned to review an opening of *School for Scandal,* in which Lady Teazle was played by Gladys Wallis, described by Herman as "the wife of the mighty Samuel Insull of Chicago, in which city scarcely a wheel turns or a lamp glows except at his pleasure." After twenty-five years off the stage, she had used her husband's fortune to form her own acting company and to hire a Chicago theater. Herman later acidly explained: "The great wave of applause which shook Chicago last Spring when Mrs. Insull played Lady Teazle for charity swept that gratified veteran right onto Broadway where, after an opening night made notable by more floral tributes than have been flung across the local footlights in a generation, her production has been running at a staggering loss."

Herman returned from that opening to the *Times* full of fury and too many drinks. He was outraged by the spectacle of a fifty-six-year-old millionairess playing a gleeful eighteen-year-old, the whole production bought for her like a trinket by a man Herman knew to be an unscrupulous manipulator. Herman began to write: "Miss Gladys Wallis, an aging, hopelessly incompetent amateur, opened last night in. . . ." The paragraph continued briefly, mentioning Miss Wallis's "mincing steps." Then Herman passed out, slumped over the top of his typewriter.

Sara, who had attended a different opening, came to the

Times and sat waiting patiently in her usual chair. Finally, hearing no typewriter at work, she gingerly opened the drama department door. As Sara was trying to rouse Herman, George Kaufman arrived. Sara, terrified, murmured, "I'm having a little trouble with Herman."

Kaufman, confronted by his dead-drunk assistant, who had stretched his patience before, and by an unprintably reckless review, openly lost his temper for the first and only time at the paper. When Herman was finally roused and sat drowning in black coffee and contrition, Kaufman excoriated him, then coldly said, "OK, Herman, go on home. Take him, Sara."

"We didn't have a very happy trip home," says Sara.

The next morning she got up early and bought a *Times*. There was a terse announcement that the play would be reviewed the following day. When Herman read that, he said, "That's it. I'm fired."

A few hours later he turned up at the *Times*, carrying, of all things, a bottle of bootleg scotch. He persuaded the drama copyboy, Sam Zolotow, to take the whiskey to the assistant managing editor, Frederick Birchall, and plead Herman's repentance. Zolotow remembers saying to Birchall, "I'm here on an errand of mercy. Mank realizes the offense he committed; he promises not to do it again if you'll restore him to your good graces." Then, as Birchall looked quizzically up at him, Zolotow said, "And as a testimonial of his promise, he asks you to accept this bottle of scotch."

Birchall did eventually relent. In the meantime, Herman had fatalistically cleaned out his desk and departed, loaded with *New York Times* stationery, pencils, and paper clips, wrapped in a newspaper. And at home Herman telephoned his friend Horace Liveright, the flamboyant head of the publishers Boni and Liveright, who had repeatedly tried to hire Herman as an editor. Liveright was delighted by Herman's fiasco and promised to double his salary. Sara stopped worrying.

By that time the incident had become *the* item of Broadway gossip. Woollcott arrived at the *World* full of the story. Herman's phone began to ring. Many of the calls were from press agents offering jobs: "We can use you over at the Shuberts'. Don't worry." "That," says Sara, "kind of took the steam out of the whole thing. He was pretty cocky after that." Herman began telling his friends, "As, without argument, the best Sir Benjamin Backbite the Wilkes-Barre of 1912 ever knew, I am particularly qualified to review any production of *The School for Scandal*. Similar qualifications apply to *The Importance of Being Earnest*."

The next day Kaufman called and told Herman to come on in and go back to work—and he did.

With that cast of characters, it was a memorable bit of drama, and Herman resurrected it for *Citizen Kane*. Jedediah Leland, played by Joseph Cotten, is Kane's oldest friend. On the night Kane's mistress debuts as an opera singer, Leland returns to Kane's Chicago paper drunk and begins his review, "Miss Susan Alexander, a pretty but hopelessly incompetent amateur . . ." and passes out. In the movie, however, Kane finishes the savage review himself—and then fires Leland.

Herman's social life, like the decade, was lubricated by bootleg booze. In Herman's world, a man who ordered a glass of soda with a squeeze of lemon, please, risked becoming an outcast. And if a Mankiewicz or a Benchley or a Parker had weakness for alcohol, the flaw was not only normal, but almost an asset. "In New York," says Sara, "the topic of conversation was drink—how to make it, how to get it, how to abuse it. Prohibition destroyed a whole era of young men."

Herman's perfect habitat was the speakeasy. Those were the sleepless, drop-in years when certain professions and groups could always find friends at their particular cozy, clubby, illicit "bar wombs," where the word "speakeasy" was what it implied. Never have so many brilliant minds expended so many hours on conversational binges. And the intoxication came from more than booze. In those basement bars Herman experienced the wild exhilaration of the mind racing and finding the anecdote, the wisecrack, the fact, the argument that was the topper, that got the big laugh, that seized the floor.

In the mid-twenties Police Commissioner Grover Whalen estimated the number of speakeasies at 32,000. Bootleg booze could be bought in New York at soda fountains, shoeshine parlors, barbershops, paint stores, malt shops, fruit stands, vegetable markets, smoke shops, laundries, confectionaries, delicatessens. One grocery store sold gin packaged as a can of tomatoes for $2 and whiskey as a can of beans for $4. While at the *World*, Herman bought whiskey in the drugstore, off the lobby.

Prohibition drinking was a game. But there was a booby prize. "Twelve Killed by Wood Alcohol in Two Days" was a *World* headline. And with typical twenties extravagance the subhead elaborated: "Victim Points at Woman Who Sold Poison Rum as He Goes Blind and Dies of Its Effect."

Almost every night somebody was giving a party somewhere, and anybody who knew about it was welcomed. Herman regularly invited his friends to other people's parties. One of the rowdiest party places was the West Forty-eight Street publishing house of Boni and Liveright, which in the twenties published more authors of enduring reputation than all other New York houses put together: Eugene O'Neill, Theodore Dreiser, Ezra Pound, Sigmund Freud, e. e. cummings, T. S. Eliot, Ernest Hemingway, William Faulkner, among others.

Herman relished the late-afternoon groups that drifted together in Horace Liveright's sitting-room office to laugh over such weighty matters as a proposed undress production of *Hamlet*, a successor to Liveright's production of *Hamlet* in modern dress. They cast Bernarr Macfadden as Hamlet and Texas Guinan as Queen Gertrude. Herman suggested "costumes by Elizabeth Arden" and, as he left, announced, "A private undress rehearsal will be held February twenty-ninth."

Herman's four years in the New York of the 1920's were his heyday. In the words of F. Scott Fitzgerald in *The Great Gatsby*, "everything afterward savored of anti-climax." In the Broadway world he had dreamed about in Wilkes-Barre, Herman was a man of consequence. His job commanded respect. He was a prized companion. He knew everybody. Helen Hayes remembers: "The New York group was so grateful for the freshness of Mank's wit and approach. It was as if God had sent the sunshine after all the flowers."

For Herman, the New York years were a crucial episode. His dream was to be a writer. He knew he had talent and proved it daily to himself and his friends with the sparkle of his conversation. The challenge for Herman was to bridge that gulf between speech and the blank sheet of paper. That required a combination of schooled inspiration and craft. The question for Herman was whether he would take on the struggle to develop it, or skate brilliantly on the surface of his life.

Two of the strongest influences on Herman in New York were Ben Hecht and Charles MacArthur, fresh from their newspaper days in Chicago. Among the celebrated Hecht-MacArthur collaborations were the play *Front Page* and the later movie *Wuthering Heights*. Both were extraordinarily gifted, especially Hecht, an opulently fluent sentimentalist and cynic. But they both were adventurers, and like Herman, their semi-legendary status had less to do with what they created than with the way they lived. Their clutch on youth very likely set a limit to their creativity. "I never achieved a real goal in my life," Ben Hecht wrote in his last years. "My chief goal was to remain 18, never to grow up or old. I missed that goal." Helen Hayes once remarked that her husband, Charlie MacArthur, was *youth*. And when he entered middle age, she said, it was as if he had come into a foreign, unknown land. Without being aware of it, he was not at home there.

So Herman in his Broadway days and nights with Hecht and MacArthur was literally one of the boys. They were particularly dangerous models. Jingling their talents like coins in their pockets, they had the kind of flair that turned irresponsibility into romance. Herman understood this and longed for the same quality in himself.

He once described the night he and MacArthur shared a box seat at the opening of an Earl Carroll *Vanities*. "We had been drinking—drink for drink, nobody loafing. The chorus girls suddenly appeared on the stage dressed as musketeers, nude to the crotch, and bearing weapons. Carried away by the glamour and gallantry of the spectacle, MacArthur leaned out of our box and applauded like an idiot. He kept applauding till he fell out of the box and landed on the stage, where he bowed several times, with ass to the audience, and tottered into the wings. If such a thing had happened to me, all you would have heard the next day was, 'Mank was drunk as a beast last night and fell out of a theater box—and he is ruining his life.' Well, about MacArthur, they said, 'Did you hear about Charlie playing D'Artagnan last night?' "

Drinking, according to Sara, was still not a large problem in New York. Sometimes Herman was able to cajole a reluctant Sara to join him at parties and speakeasies. But there were also those nights when Herman was out alone, and as the hour grew late, Sara would wait at home in a panic of worry. In extremis, she would telephone Professor Mankiewicz, who lived miles away in Brooklyn, and he would dutifully get on a subway and journey to her side. A few times he sat through the entire night looking out the window for his son. During those vigils perhaps guilts surfaced inside him. As a great teacher the professor knew about problem children. How many times must he have said to worried parents, "Perhaps if you tried to understand your son a little bit."

Arriving home, Herman sometimes paused in the shadows of the central courtyard of their apartment house and was loudly ill. Then upstairs he was met by the reception committee. The professor would simply say, "Herman! Go to bed! We'll talk about this later." "Pop was the wrong guy," says Joe Mankiewicz, who at age fifteen was sometimes dispatched to find Herman. "The last thing Herman needed was to be seen in a state of disgrace again in front of Pop."

Herman never attacked his father in talking to Sara. She had few inklings of their true Wilkes-Barre relationship. She knew only the benevolent professor, whom she called Father and everybody else, even students, called Pop. She blamed most of Herman's boyhood damage on his mother. Nevertheless, reflecting some knowledge, she says, "What was wrong with me? Getting Father there! Sometimes I wondered, 'Am I blaming Father?' You know—'Let *him* suffer too. I'm not going to take this alone!' "

The next morning Herman usually would attempt to charm Sara and to explain away the night before. While he dressed, he would plead with her, "Sit down. Stay here. Let me talk to you."

"I had children and a household," Sara says, "but in no time I would be lulled into sitting there, and then I began looking around. I'd see discrepancies—lipstick on the handkerchief, matchboxes that said the Hotsy Totsy Club. I always caught him at everything. And I didn't mean to either. I didn't want to have trouble. I would have preferred to feel at ease about him. It was almost as though he wanted to be discovered, do penance, flagellate himself. He'd say how unworthy he was. Remembering that makes me cry because he was *not* unworthy."

Herman did try to atone to Sara. His abject apologies were sincere. One reason he kept his life in compartments was to protect her. As a form of repayment, he gave her a degree of luxury. Sara had a full-time servant. Even with two babies she had enough leisure time to take courses at Columbia, where she got an A in English. She was able to summer on Long Island, and Herman came out on weekends. He himself had little money in his pocket. When somebody asked him for change for a $5 or $10 bill, he would say, "No, but thanks for the compliment."

Herman was spending about $200 a week—$80 from the *Times* and roughly $120 from all manner of moonlighting jobs. In the summer of 1923 he took a leave of absence to become a press agent for the American production of Max Reinhardt's *The Miracle*, conveniently forgetting all his Berlin scorn of the Master.

Herman decided to emulate the Broadway producers whose profiles he was writing for the *Times*. While working for Kaufman, he staged a play called *Love 'Em and Leave 'Em*, written by John V. A. Weaver, a Round Table member and Brooklyn *Eagle* book editor. Weaver was described by his own father-in-law as "a used piece of soap." The play was a quick failure—though in 1926 it was revived and rewritten under the aegis of Producer George Abbott.

Herman's second venture was almost foredoomed. In 1924 he was invited into a partnership by the debonair, back-slapping S. Jay Kaufman, who wrote a gossip column for the *Telegraph* called "Round the Town." They were a curious collaboration, since S. Jay was scorned as a pretentious pest by the Algonquin group. George Kaufman derided him as "the *nice* Kaufman." Herman dubbed him "the diarist for the illiterati" and composed the couplet "I count each day lost on land or sea/ That S. Jay Kaufman does not call on me." The Round Table at its birth had only one bylaw: that S. Jay Kaufman be forever banned from the table.

Yet, with Herman as president and S. Jay as treasurer, Jayman Productions was formed to put on a revue called *Round the Town*, exploiting the S. Jay Kaufman column. Both men were billed as the show's director. "I was absolutely opposed to it," says Sara. "I knew he wasn't cut out for that. He had to select the sixteen most beautiful girls for the chorus line. Well, that was the sorriest line you ever saw—too heavy, not really professional. Every one of them had either given him a sob story, or they were down and out friends of friends. I'd say, 'Herman, that one is just awful.' He'd say, 'Sick mother.' "

It was a measure of the affection the Round Table had for Herman that they rallied to help him. Dorothy Parker, Robert Sherwood, Marc Connelly, and George Kaufman contributed skits and songs. Victor Herbert composed some of the music. Heywood Broun and Robert Benchley agreed to give monologues and wanted to be billed as "B & B." Herman collaborated on a skit with Kaufman and wrote a satire on etiquette and an "allegorical ballet" called *War and Peace*, whose satiric summary in the program ended, "Eventually the dragon dies in a pool of blood and the faint dawn of Liberty is visible in the West."

Before the New York opening Herman's college drinking pal Lorenz Hart, later of Rodgers and Hart, wired him: "May tonight make you a greater and more cerebral Ziegfeld. All the luck in the world." But not even that much luck was enough. During an intermission the *Women's Wear Daily* critic Kelcey Allen met John Emerson, president of Actors Equity. "Do you want to be a public benefactor, John?" Allen asked.

"Yes," Emerson replied.

"Then," said Allen, "call a strike before the second act begins."

Benchley, who had sensed disaster and dropped out of the show, wrote in the original *Life*: "The net effect of *Round the Town* was that of having been sold a book on 'How to do Card Tricks.' " A Chicago critic wired his paper: "The play ran late, the audience early."

Jayman Productions had issued $25,000 worth of stock in $100 certificates, which were not exactly snapped up. Costs exceeded the budget. Herman was bailed out by a loan from his acquaintance Otto Kahn, who had financed *The Miracle* on Broadway and was a member of the regally rich Jewish aristocracy. And Herman paid him back.

Producing, however, was a tangent. Herman's real goal was to be a playwright. He had been writing skits for *Ziegfeld Follies* and *George White Scandals* and the *Little Shows*. And in that time of witless comedies and puerile romances, everybody felt ready to write a play for Broadway. As the producer Arthur Hopkins said, "You could ask your postman, 'How's your second act?' and he'd tell you." Herman's pals were doing it successfully. There were Hecht and MacArthur. Edwin Justus "Eddie" Mayer went to Italy and in a few weeks wrote a play called *The Firebrand*. It was a big hit, with Herman's friend Liveright the producer. Another friend, Maxwell Anderson, sat in the *World* coffee shop listening to the war stories of still another friend, Laurence Stallings, whose leg had been shot off in the war. Anderson made them into a play, working nights in the reading room of the New York Public Library at Forty-second Street. Then Stallings rewrote Anderson. Their play, *What Price Glory?*, was a World War I classic. Stallings, said Herman, had "the only lost leg with a listing in *Who's Who in America.*"

Kaufman stimulated Herman's vision of himself as a playwright. Herman wanted to *be* George Kaufman. The ambition to be a comedy playwright lasted much of Herman's creative life, a byway leading him away from his strength, the serious political erudition which created *Citizen Kane*.

Following their collaboration on the skit in *Round the Town*, Kaufman quietly invited Herman to help him with his play *The Butter-and-Egg Man*. It was the one play that Kaufman, who always worked with a collaborator, was supposed to have written by himself. But according to loyal Sara, Herman took a complete script and virtually rewrote it. According to Arthur Sheekman, who wrote for Groucho Marx in Hollywood, "Kaufman got Mank to add a few jokes."

Somewhere between these two opinions was Herman's contribution, which was never acknowledged by Kaufman. "Herman expected to get some cocredit on it," says Sara. "And it wasn't like George not to acknowledge Herman's work."

However, Herman's blood was up. He constantly tried out plot ideas on his theater friends. Walking down Fifth Avenue with actress Peggy Wood, he described in detail a play he wanted to write. As he ended, saying, "And I think I've got a big hit!" Peggy Wood said, "But, Mank, that's already been written, and I've read it."

Herman, nonplussed, was silent for a moment. "Well," he said, "at least I've got a coincidence."

He allocated his August vacation to work on a political satire, *We the People*, but chose to do it at a house that Hecht and MacArthur had borrowed in Woodstock, New York. He arrived with his notes inside a suitcase gurgling with bootleg scotch. Remarking that if you'd seen one tree, you'd seen them all, Herman settled semipermanently in the corner of an old couch, attacked his scotch, and joined in long nights of lurid reminiscences of the war and newspapering. The notes stayed packed. Sara arrived, and MacArthur departed, waving from the rear of the train the $20 bill Hecht was sending to the indigent poet Maxwell Bodenheim. Herman, says Sara, commented to nobody in particular, "I have a feeling one rabbit has just been given a piece of lettuce to take to another rabbit."

On their return to New York, Herman who was accident-prone slipped in a bathtub, sprained his back, and was encased in adhesive tape like a medieval knight. Leaving Herman free to work on his play, Sara departed for Long Branch, New Jersey, to spend two weeks with the Aaronson family. Before leaving, while Herman was at his *Times* office, she moved his bed into the relatively airy living room.

But that evening at Tony's speakeasy Herman encountered Hecht, MacArthur, and Sam Hoffenstein. The four adjourned to the Plaza Hotel suite of Prince Bibesco, the Rumanian consul who had left on a trip and lent his key to MacArthur. Toward morning Herman passed out. Hecht and MacArthur rolled him onto his stomach and across the white expanse of adhesive tape penned racy declarations of eternal love. They signed them "Gladys" and chuckled at the vision of Herman undressing in front of Sara.

Meanwhile, all that night, Sara had been fruitlessly phoning Herman from New Jersey. Frantic and furious, she got him at the *Times* the next day. He explained that he had been very tired and slept through the phone call.

"Herman," said Sara, "your bed was made up in the living room right next to the phone!"

"Oh, shit," Herman said.

Herman confessed all to Sara. "For the next weeks," she says, "Herman was apologizing and perspiring over it, no matter how often I said, 'It's finished, Herman. You should forget it now.' But no, he kept calling me long distance in Long Branch saying, 'Do you really, truly forgive me?' "

Herman's play *We the People* did finally get finished and with Kaufman's help was accepted by a producer, though no production date was set and no money paid. He worked, too, on an uncompleted play about Hearst.

Herman, however, decided that the best way to become another Kaufman was to collaborate with Kaufman, and with *his* collaborator, Marc Connelly. At that time the two were the most successful writing team on Broadway. They must have respected Herman's potential because they agreed. According to Connelly, "Mank was bright, enthusiastic, and had a lot of general gusto. We liked him and wanted to help him."

With Connelly, Herman started *The Wild Man of Borneo*, a play about a medicine show faker pretending to be a great actor. But Connelly was almost as dilatory as Herman, and the project dragged on endlessly. "Connelly was too busy meeting boats," Herman said. So in 1925 Herman and Kaufman began *The Good Fellow*. It was Herman's idea, the machinations of a backslapping blowhard to get the Ancient Order of Corsicans to hold their convention in his hometown, Wilkes-Barre, Pennsylvania.

One morning the rigidly scheduled Kaufman came into his study ready for work. Herman kept on reading the morning paper. "You'll never get any work done that way," Kaufman said impatiently.

"Who's working!" Herman replied cheerfully.

Two of Herman's weaknesses were Kaufman's greatest strengths. Kaufman was a silent man who saved his humor. And he was a hyperstructured worker who never paused, not even to savor success. During his thirty-seven-year career, he had forty-five plays produced, twenty-seven of them hits.

Herman once described the difference between himself and Kaufman. He told his friend Marion Spitzer that if Kaufman were walking down Broadway and saw a panhandler a few paces away, George would stride by without a qualm or a look. But he, Herman, seeing the beggar, would cross the street to avoid him.

"That was a good summing up of both characters," says Marion Spitzer. "George was truly, basically a hard man. He had no problems saying no. If he was vulnerable, it was deep within him. He instinctively took care of himself. Protect George. Herman never wanted to face anything unpleasant."

By late 1924, Herman, age twenty-eight, seemed to be a minor prodigy. Despite the ill-advised play production attempts, he was respected in elite company as a theater critic and reporter. Two of the town's best playwrights were working with him. He was a master of double caustics at the Round Table. The boyish, self-doubting side of Herman was now hidden from all eyes but Sara's.

Herman's prestige on Broadway was validated when Harold Ross, a Round Table member, invited him to help launch his fledgling humor magazine *The New Yorker*. For many months Ross, then editor of *Judge*, had been carrying a dog-eared mock-up in his pocket, whipping it out at the faintest sign of interest. "I'm afraid," Kaufman recalled, "that he was rather a bore about it."

A spin-off from the Round Table, the magazine was even named at one of the lunches by John Peter Toohey, but only, joked Herman, "after 154,628 suggestions, 217,614 of them received at lunch by the editor." Ross had offered a reward of one share of stock for the name he picked. In the first issue there was a tongue-in-cheek announcement of the results of "our $25,000.00 prize Name Contest." Written by Herman, it was an example of a special brand of "crazy humor" developed by the Algonquin group:

> The *New Yorker,* thus, will be The *New Yorker.* The First Prize—of three thousand dollars in escrow—has been won by Charles Dana Gibson of No. 115-A Railroad Street who submitted The *Country Gentleman.* Mr. Gibson will receive one-third of the sum, which was divided into three parts, since two other people failed to submit a similar title. For a time it seemed that the *Saturday Evening Post* might be the name selected. This was abandoned, however, when it was learned that the New York *Evening Post* uses a similar name for its Saturday edition. The *New Yorker* thanks the participants for their generous economy of time and patience.

The beginnings of the *The New Yorker* were in many ways an attempt to translate Round Table humor onto paper, and Ross expected his famous friends to help. They did not. With a few exceptions they waited until the magazine was firmly established. But as Herman consolingly pointed out to Ross, "The half-time help of wits is no better than the full-time help of half-wits."

Herman, a utility writer and *The New Yorker's* first drama critic, took the job less for the cash than for the cachet. His salary was $50 a week, and Ross, short of funds, tried to pay him in stock. Herman, fuming and goddamning the certificates as worthless paper, insisted on half stock, half money and talked himself out of what would have become a substantial fortune.

But at *The New Yorker* there was a potential for Herman far more important than money. Ross was a meticulous, directive editor capable of forcing Herman to explore and master writing technique, and thereby carry his work far beyond his first spontaneous rush of words. Indeed, under Ross Herman produced the finest, most disciplined prose of his life. Beside the mannered quippery which nearly killed the magazine, Herman's writing leaped to the eye. "We were always eager to read what he had to say," says Brooks Atkinson. "He was a very good reviewer, a very able guy, and he was saturated with the theatre."

"*The Green Hat* to be sure, is unreal," wrote Herman about Michael Arlen's hit play. "It is as unreal, say, as the Kaiser's Christmas dinner in Paris; as the success of Pickett's charge; as the possibility that the young woman who sang 'They Always, Always Pick on Me' with slides, in the Wilkes-Barre, Pa., Bijou Dream, in August, 1911, is still radiant, dewy-eyed, rose lipped, personable, eighteen. . . . *The Green Hat*, then, is not for those who lisp in skyscrapers, who merge railroads and do their 18 holes in seventy and who get out of every day in every way the utmost in sense, health, and achievement."

The fact that *The New Yorker* was not a memorable magazine during its first year meant that Herman was later ignored or forgotten as an important member of its founding staff.

5

□ □ □

For the first of the Algonquins, who will
someday laugh at his sophomore contemporaries and that day will achieve all.

—DAVID O. SELZNICK,
An inscription to Mankiewicz

IN NEW YORK HERMAN AVERAGED AT LEAST ONE LUNCH A
week at the Algonquin Round Table. Set in the center of the
Algonquin Hotel's Rose Room, the table was reserved for the
celebrated clique which included Alexander Woollcott, Robert
Benchley, Dorothy Parker, Franklin P. Adams, Harold Ross,
George Kaufman, Marc Connelly, Robert Sherwood, and
Heywood Broun. The Round Table had convinced itself—and
much of America—that it represented the acme of 1920's
sophistication. To be sophisticated in that decade was to be
unshockable, up-to-date, expert at sleeplessness, gossip, and
clever insults, to be smart, to be like Dorothy Parker, who in
a review "thwowed up" at *The House at Pooh Corner*. There
was even a magazine, edited by the revered H. L. Mencken,
frankly called *The Smart Set*.

Admirers like John Mason Brown, then a hopeful young
writer, came to the Rose Room and goggled at the Round
Table from afar. He later wrote:

> We could not at our side tables hear what was being said
> by those men and women whose plays and performances we
> were seeing, whose books, columns, and reviews we devoured,
> and who seemed to us the embodiment of Times Square sophisti-
> cation, gaiety, and success. We could only gape at them, and

hear their distant laughter, and be hopefully certain that what they laughed at was the ultimate in wit and drollery. Countless older New Yorkers felt as we did—and solid out-of-towners beyond numbering flocked to the Algonquin as part of their Broadway pilgrimage.

Herman had managed the acquaintance of many members, but it was George Kaufman who brought him to his first Round Table lunch. Soon, elated, he was given to understand that he would be welcomed on his own. Membership in the Round Table was rigidly limited. Partly this was done to preserve its exclusivity, partly because the table seated only a dozen people comfortably.

The maître d' of the Rose Room, George, cut off most interlopers with his velvet rope. Intruders who got to the table were so bloodied they never returned. One elaborated at length on her ancestry until Kaufman said, "Yes, I also had an ancestor in the Crusades. As a spy, of course." Herman told a gushy actress, "A voice that sweet should be saved for convicts on the morning of their walk to the electric chair."

It was Alexander Woollcott, according to member Murdock Pemberton, who "appointed himself the majordomo, the czar of the thing. If you brought a guest Woollcott didn't approve of, he'd wave his crossed finger at you, which meant 'See you later.' And on the way out he'd grab you and say, 'Not that guy again.' "

Woollcott was a peremptory mix of tour director and wit snob, described by James Thurber as "a pompous Grand Marshal of his own parade." He once rented a house in Salem, New York, for the winter and simply announced to Beatrice Kaufman and Alice Duer Miller (novelist and author of *The White Cliffs of Dover*) that they were to share it. In the same letter he enclosed the address, phone number, key, and each one's portion of the bill. It was Woollcott who was determined that only women with jobs would be acceptable at the Round Table. It was Woollcott who never hesitated at sledgehammer rudeness and once announced to a guest, "Your brains are popcorn soaked in urine." It was also Woollcott who repeatedly said, "Mankiewicz is the funniest man in New York."

Other members regarded Herman as "impressive" and "the brightest of the lot." Murdock Pemberton considered him "the one real wit," and Robert Sherwood called Herman "the truest wit of all."

However, despite the sweet warmth in Herman, there was also a lurking violence which set him apart from the undiluted gaiety and *joie de vivre* the other members tried to maintain. Ring Lardner described an example in a 1925 letter to F. Scott Fitzgerald:

> One night Herman Mankiewicz called up from Petrova's and said he would come and see us if we'd come after him. We did and I took them, Mank and Dorothy [Parker], to Durand's. The place was full of Durand's big, husky Irish clients. After a few drinks, Mank remembered that he had been in the Marines and ought to prove it by licking all the inmates of the joint. I, as usual, acted as pacifist and felt next day as if I'd been in a football game against Notre Dame.

If Herman was not part of that small, inner core that sought each other out noon and night and weekends, he was an unquestioned member who came and went in the group as they partied at speakeasies and at each other's apartments, played poker in their Thanatopsis and Inside Straight Club, and turned their luncheon institution into an attitude toward life. In fact, next to his father, the Algonquin group was the most powerful and formative force in Herman's life.

Sara could always tell when Herman had eaten at the Round Table. "You're talking like Woollcott," she would tell Herman, "and you're wearing your hat like him." Woollcott began affecting a cane for the opening nights, and Herman bought one, too. George Kaufman's little two-fingered salute became Herman's lifelong gesture of farewell, or hello, or "I'm sorry." And throughout his life Herman continued the Round Table quirk of saying "ain't." "He thrived under their approval, and he took on their coloring," Sara says. "But it was subliminal. Something he could not resist."

Herman not only was trying on the mannerisms and attitudes of the various Round Table members, but was trying out their various careers—playwright, producer, critic, essayist, reporter—each of which required different talents. The part of Herman shaped by his tyrannized boyhood hungered not for perfection of a particular art, but for *success*. Dorothy Kahn, his Columbia friend who later became a Hearst writer under the name of Waring, was by coincidence George Kaufman's distant cousin. Dorothy recalls: "George lived in a limestone town house, and you entered below ground level. There was thick carpeting on the stairs—you sank into it—and Beatrice had wonderful furnishings and objets d'art. Beatrice was very fond of Mank, and he used to go up there. Now I presume that every time Mank went into this house . . . well, I can just hear Mank saying to himself, 'One of these days I'll have all this. One of these days I'll show the world.' "

As a Round Table member Herman was indeed *somebody*. In a way he had achieved success. But that world prized the talents which came easiest to Herman. It could not push him into maturity. While the Algonquin environment satisfied his temporary cravings, it was in the long run exactly what Herman Mankiewicz did not need if he was to become a writer, an artist, profound within himself and comfortable with solitude.

Mildred Knopf, a friend of Sara's, says, "Anybody who had any contact with the Round Table and any sort of natural wit never really got over a hunger for center stage." Ben Hecht said, "For a young novelist or playwright with his roots not yet down, to sit in such a clique of know-it-alls was to get the art frightened out of him. Any writer who makes critics his cronies is almost certain to quit writing."

With the possible exception of Dorothy Parker, the *raison d'être* of the men and women around that table in the twenties was the enjoyment and gift of light entertainment. Cleverness was deified. Though the cleverness was sometimes as rare as wisdom, most of the group had middleweight minds buttressed by heavyweight personalities. And though the group produced a considerable body of writing, little of it has endured. Alexander Woollcott, who considered himself "potentially the best writer in America," confessed toward the end of his life, "I never had anything to say." They were verbal alchemists who turned triviality to gold. That could be overwhelming, particularly to a Herman Mankiewicz. Even Thornton Wilder said, "I know I'm better than that whole Algonquin crowd, but I can't act it when I'm with them." Other contemporary Americans who never sat at the Round Table were Eugene O'Neill, William Faulkner, Henry Mencken, Theodore Dreiser, Edmund Wilson, Malcolm Cowley, Christopher Morley, Thomas Wolfe, and Ernest Hemingway.

The Algonquin group was living in a decade with grave problems. Police kept the lid on labor unrest, while "Cautious Cal" Coolidge, full of "strive and succeed" copybook maxims, kept the status quo. There was a depression on farms and in southern textile regions and New England shoe factory towns. There was a serious overproduction of goods as business became superheated by the invention of easy-payment buying and high-pressure advertising. As part of the worship of big business, Americans bought stocks on margin as though purchasing tickets to Utopia. And in 1929 the dues had to be paid.

The Round Table's attention was elsewhere, mostly on itself. As Heywood Broun later wrote, "Humor is the grit in the evolutionary process. The underlying mood of humor is 'Does it matter?' And of course it does matter." The members affected cynical disillusionment or resolute lightheartedness. Robert Sherwood, theater critic for *Vanity Fair*, mentioned a movie advertisement that trumpeted, "As Big as the Heart of Humanity"—and Herman shot back, "Must be a one-reeler." Robert Benchley said, "I'd *like* to worry. I *try* to worry. But I just *can't*."

The weight the group gave to public affairs was summed up by an entry in F. P. A.'s once-a-week column, "The Diary of

Our Own Dr. Pepys," written in mock "olde" English: "News cometh that Lloyd George hath resigned, and I am sorry about it, albeit any feeling I have about anything political is only tepid. Had luncheon with Nellie Leavitt who tells me about two suitors her daughter had, and one had gone to China and one to California, whereupon the child quoth, Love me and see the world."

Herman, who continued to read most of the city's papers and violently argue with his father, was the one member with strong political opinions. He despised Coolidge and Harding, was pro-union and an early supporter of the American Civil Liberties Union. He regularly sent money to the imprisoned Tom Mooney because the anarchist had an ulcer and needed a special diet including ice cream. Herman had a fully developed social consciousness, and spun off aphorisms: "The poor are always suspicious of innovations. They feel instinctively—and almost always rightly—that the new is merely an improved way of exploitation."

When Herman and Sara were invited to dinner parties by Herbert Bayard Swope, young Herman would authoritatively contradict the *World* editor's politics. A bristling Herbert Bayard Swope would rise up in rage, saying, "You whippersnapper, what do you know!" Herman adopted as his own an expression he often heard from Swope: "Where is it written that it has to be like that?"

"Mank," says Marc Connelly disapprovingly, "could be a little bit insistent—more forceful than we. He was a man whose convictions came out as obsessions." In that world sincerity and concern about tomorrow were generally considered out of step, and Herman kept as quiet as he could. Finally, in 1927, the trial of Sacco and Vanzetti did activate Broun, Parker, and Benchley politically. Thereafter Broun became a Socialist and in his column a political crusader.

Curiously for a clique of writers, there was a strain of anti-intellectualism. Dostoevsky was an author to be read for use in charades, but not for a continuing study of the human condition. Real understanding and seriousness were for the grinds so disdained at college.

Woollcott once said, "Reading Proust is like lying in somebody else's dirty bath water." Beatrice Kaufman, on her way to Carnegie Hall to hear Stokowski conduct Bach's B Minor Mass, said, "In heaven's name let's hurry, or we'll miss the intermission." F. P. A. finished Virginia Woolf's *Mrs. Dalloway* and wrote: "Save for what she had to say concerning doctors and their insensitiveness, I found the book uninteresting."

Reviewing Shaw's *Caesar and Cleopatra,* starring Helen Hayes, even Herman wrote: "It is not unreasonable to demand that a play be intrinsically interesting and have merits other than demonstrating that ancient Romans weren't always writing commentaries and Cleopatra wasn't always playing with asps."

As for their own writing, the group took pains not to appear serious. Many worked hard, but they did so almost in secret, pretending never to write. "My typewriter is covered with brambles," said Dorothy Parker. They all played a great deal. Procrastination was made somehow charming and part of the mystique by such rueful wit as Herman's remark "A final draft is what you put in the typewriter the night before it's due." Benchley once handed in a magazine article two weeks late. Entitled "I Like to Loaf," it was accompanied by a note saying, "I was loafing."

The major exception was the obsessive Kaufman, who once asked Marc Connelly about the play he was supposed to be writing. "It's all done," Connelly said.

"Wonderful," Kaufman replied. "When can I read it?"

"Oh, it isn't on paper yet."

"Not on paper!" Kaufman exploded. "What is it on? Birch bark? Yak skin? Unborn elephant hide?"

The Round Table obviously could be fun. But that was one of the lesser reasons for its existence and its endurance for a decade.

On a psychological level, those celebrated men and women, in 1922 only in their late twenties and early thirties, may well have needed the Round Table for emotional support and reassurance. With some exceptions, they were a bizarre collection of oddballs. Like Herman, their personalities were Maginot lines defending childhood damage which might have crippled lesser people. Also, they grew up "different" in the American provinces and may well have been insecure about their success, so much greater than their original hometown hopes. The Round Table was certainly a safe harbor where their shaky authenticity could be confirmed by peers and where their oddities were simply amusing quirks that enhanced the legend. Kaufman once said, "I never want to go any place where I can't get back to Broadway and Forty-fourth by midnight."

Alexander Woollcott grew up in Red Bank, New Jersey. Kaufman came from Pittsburgh, the son of an erratic businessman. Connelly was the child of a McKeesport, Pennsylvania, hotel owner and ex-actor. Ross's father mined silver in Aspen, Colorado, silver mines. Benchley grew up in Worcester, Massachusetts, where his father was a city official.

Heywood Broun was indigenous to New York almost. The son of an ultra-British Scot in Brooklyn, he was fat as a boy. "I was a child prodigy myself," Broun said. "At the age of five I already required twelve-year-old pants."

Dorothy Parker was reared in New York; her mother died when she was a baby, her father when she was nineteen. She was educated in a convent, until she was expelled for insisting the Immaculate Conception was spontaneous combustion. "Dorothy was wedded to despair," says her close friend Donald Ogden Stewart. At least three times she attempted suicide, but she always managed to be saved at the last moment. After one of her attempts George Oppenheimer, later a screenwriter and Hollywood friend of Herman's, went to see Parker in the hospital. "She was crying," Oppenheimer remembers. "I put my arms around her, and she said, 'I want to tell you the whole thing,' and she was still crying. Then I saw her ring the bell

Herman's father, Franz Mankiewicz, was an imposing Prussian presence when at age 33 he settled in Wilkes-Barre, Pa., to edit a German-language newspaper.

Born in New York where he lived for his first seven years, Herman stands in the snow on the stoop of the Mankiewicz apartment house. His father, a frustrated teacher, was even then severely pressuring him to achieve at school.

Encased in the bombazine and leg-o'-mutton sleeves of the era —and at 26 a lighthearted, tiny woman of 98 pounds—Johanna Blumenau was a successful dress maker when she married Franz Mankiewicz in 1896.

In the trappings of new manhood, Herman spent his fourteenth year in the coal mines. A prodigy who passed the Columbia College exams at age 13, he was too young to enter. On the picture, Herman penciled, "Alias 'Mike' Mankiewicz."

As a Columbia freshman, Herman posed in his Sunday best. Constantly impecunious, Herman was usually sloppily dressed. Says a classmate, "I don't know how he subsisted other than by sponging." But the great professor/author John Erskine considered him a brilliant mind and made Mank a protégé.

A Marine private in World War I, Herman mocked his post-Armistice military career in a portrait he sent Sara Aaronson in Washington, D.C. He married her a year and a half later. He wrote on the picture, "Winding up the watch on the Rhine."

Herman came directly from the War to Sara Aaronson's arms. He proposed, she accepted. And they solemnized their engagement with a public embrace. Herman always hung this photograph in his many offices in his many studios.

Working as a press officer for the Red Cross, Herman with the rank of Captain served in Paris for six months in 1920. Back in Washington, D.C., Sara received this picture, featuring what a friend called "The celebrated Mankiewicz leer."

From Paris, Herman wrote Sara, "My wonderful darling, when I think that I've been lucky enough to win your love, I begin to believe that I could dig a tunnel single-handed or swim across the Atlantic. For neither of these things is any more incredible than that you should love me." They were married on July 1, 1920.

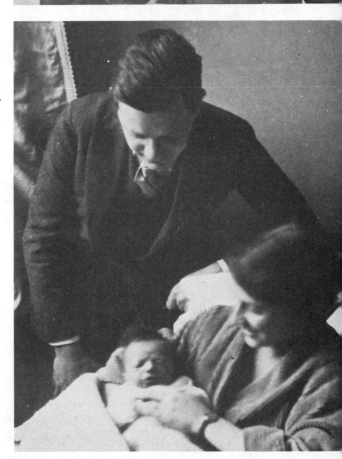

S. S. Kroonland
Coming Over – 1920 – a

The excited newly-
weds sailed for post-
World War I Berlin,
and spent their first
two years of mar-
riage in the most ex-
citing city in Europe.

In Berlin in 1922
Don Mankiewicz
was born to a sub-
limely happy Sara—
unaware that Her-
man had to borrow
the money for the
hospital room.

Herman had the use of the Chicago *Tribune*'s Berlin office. While Herman wrote for the *Tribune*, *Women's Wear Daily*, and *New York Times*, Sara (left, in hat) often waited before an evening at the theater.

Congenitally fascinated by politics, Herman relished watching from the inside the peregrinations of the Weimar Republic. Here at a Chancellor's garden party, he sits at the left hand of the Chancellor himself, Josef Wirth.

To earn American dollars in inflation-torn Germany, Herman did press-agent jobs. One client was boxer Jack Dempsey, the heavyweight champion. In suits given him by a smaller man, Herman guided Dempsey and his manager, Jack Kearns (left), around Berlin.

In 1922 Isadora Duncan, 48 and pudgy, came out of Russia to Berlin, newly married to the 33-year-old alcoholic poet, Sergei Essenin. Hired to handle her publicity during a tour, Herman complained of a "fleshiness and lack of fire" in Isadora's dancing.

Late in 1922 Herman and Sara returned to prohibition era New York and that swirl of journalists, playwrights, and wits. Here Herman and Sara are with **Ben and Rose Hecht** in a **Coney Island** photo parlor.

The epicenter of Herman's world was the Algonquin Round Table. A friend—and the kindest in that clique—was Robert Benchley, who also felt he threw away his talent in Hollywood making movies.

Already launched as a great comedy playwright, George Kaufman was the drama editor of the *Times* and hired Herman as his assistant.

Harold Ross—shown here with his wife, Jane Grant, about the time he started *The New Yorker*—made Herman the magazine's first theater critic.

A second son, Frank, was born in 1924 in New York, and Sara with her two sons was like a Jewish Madonna. Don grew up to be a novelist and a screen and TV writer. Frank achieved celebrity as Robert Kennedy's press secretary and George McGovern's national political director during the 1972 presidential election.

for the night nurse, and I asked her what she was doing. She said, 'That will insure us three-quarters of an hour of complete privacy.' " When Woollcott visited her the next day, she used the same joke all over again.

George Kaufman's imperious, overprotective mother made her son into a hypochondriac, terrified of germs and imminent disease. For years he would open public doors only with his hand inside his jacket pocket, gripping the doorknob through the cloth. Kaufman was a virgin until age twenty-nine and then became a compulsive Don Juan. Jed Harris, producer of many Kaufman plays, remembers him as a severely inhibited man. They once went on a Florida vacation together, and Kaufman always undressed alone at night, reappearing in a nightgown down to his ankles. He went on the beach just once, walking to the water with his long robe tight around him. He lifted one foot out of his bathing shoe, put his toe in the water, withdrew it, put his foot back in the shoe, walked back to the hotel.

There was another occasion, however, when Harris, in his New York hotel room, perhaps with malice aforethought, sat totally nude through an entire business conference with Kaufman. Finally, Kaufman, opening the door to leave, turned and said, "Jed, your fly is open."

An agonizedly insecure man, Kaufman had little faith in his gifts as a playwright. He fearfully remained at the *Times* for thirteen years, long after he was one of Broadway's most successful authors. He always considered himself a lucky newspaperman who might be exposed at any moment.

Alexander Woollcott was a last, unwanted child reared by women descended from the leaders of a Fourierist communal society called The Phalanx. At Hamilton College he was a skinny, mollycoddled, priggish misfit nicknamed Put, short for Putrid. He grew into a short, 230-pound eccentric, once described as a hoot owl perched on a bag of potatoes. He told his longtime friend Mrs. Hawley Truax, "I don't think any woman whom I could respect would every marry me." When a lecture chairman mentioned his boyhood success in female stage roles, Woollcott howled in a raging scream, "Look at me, boys and girls: half god, half woman."

At *The New York Times* he was the youngest drama critic in New York. Shortly after going to work there, he contracted mumps, which left him a desexed semieunuch. This was not widely known, and his lack of sex life was considered a fit subject for humor. Once, after arriving from Paris, he went immediately backstage at *Animal Crackers* to visit the Marx Brothers. The four men lifted him up, then plunked him bodily into a chair, where Groucho put his face close to Woollcott's and demanded, "Did you get laid in Paris, Alec? Did you get laid?"

Woollcott, with Olympian dignity, replied, "Infinitesimally."

Robert Benchley was another product of strong women. His mother's favorite child was her older son, Edmund. When Robert was ten, Edmund joined the Army and went to Cuba with Teddy Roosevelt. On the Fourth of July, 1898, a reporter from the Worcester *Spy* came up the walk, bringing the news that Edmund had been killed. In her anguish, and fully within Robert's hearing, his mother cried out, "Oh, why couldn't it have been Robert?"

Edmund's beautiful, dominating fiancée took over the administration of Robert's life, charting his education and paying his way through Harvard. She made it clear that though it might take a decade, she was grooming him to be her husband, a substitute for his dead brother. Instead, Robert married his grammar school sweetheart, but lived apart from her much of his life.

Benchley grew up in an intensely religious household of aggressive teetotalers, particularly his father. Benchley had to spend long Sunday afternoons in a Christian Endeavor Church, where he heard Carry Nation rant about alcohol. When he first arrived in New York, he was a puritan suburbanite in galoshes. He soon became an alcoholic. Years later he confessed to a young lady friend that when he took his first drink each day, he felt stentorian breathing behind him. And he never dared turn around, certain he would find his father there, glowering.

Herman must have found some comfort in these histories. Childhood damage need not be fatal. And comparatively, Herman was normal. His drinking and gambling, socially *de rigueur* in New York, were still propensities, not habits. Herman was the only one intensely involved in family, a novel posture the others found amusing and engaging. "I have a new baby boy, born today, his name is Frank," Herman announced proudly at a Round Table lunch.

Marc Connelly glanced up from his soup and said, "Does Sara know?"

When members came to dinner at the Mankiewicz apartment, Dorothy Parker would envelop Sara with gushy questions about "the little ones." "I even showed her my baby pictures," Sara says, "and she'd say, 'Ahhh, the baby.' I soon realized it was all venom to turn me into a simpering mother. I could just hear her afterward saying, 'Sara gave me all that crap about babies. Jesus Christ, don't ever let me talk to that woman again about her children.' "

Sara would get her private revenge later by imitating Parker to Herman. "She did a great deal of dropping her eyes," Sara says, "and butter wouldn't melt in her mouth, and she was such a lady and sweetness itself. Actually she was a real two-fisted drinker and a foulmouthed, funny, terribly witty, brilliant woman. She was a man, really, except that she was feminine with it all."

Herman also had the only enduring marriage. Heywood Broun was divorced by the feminist Ruth Hale. Robert Sherwood divorced actress Mary Brandon to marry the wife of Marc Connelly, his best friend. Dorothy Parker divorced her second husband, Alan Campbell, and then later remarried him. F. P. A. married twice and Harold Ross had three wives.

Publicity was an important value of the Round Table in the lives of its members. Its photosynthesis depended not on sun, but limelight. The very existence of the group was a publicity gimmick devised by Frank Case, the shrewd, celebrity-loving manager of the Algonquin Hotel. When an early nucleus began gathering there informally in 1920, Case decided to institutionalize the aura they projected. The round table he reserved for them limited the size and guaranteed snobbish exclusivity, created a locus, a cachet, and, most important, a memorable name. Naturally the members were delighted to exhibit their cleverness and eliteness center stage in one of New York's most popular literary and theatrical gathering places.

The publicity value of Round Table membership was hugely multiplied by the members themselves. With constant, clubby little mentions of each other's names and doings and works, these widely read columnists and magazine writers built their mutual fame. "So to the playhouse," wrote F. P. A. in his Dr. Pepys column, "and there saw *The Good Fellow* by G. Kaufman and Herman Mankiewicz, and I enjoyed it greatly." Herman once started a review literally arm in arm with Woollcott: "A critic who shall be nameless—Alexander Woollcott—has called for public dancing in the streets to honor the production of *In a Garden*, Philip Barry's new play at the Plymouth. With our left arm tenderly around the Woollcott waist, and our right hand trustingly in his giant paw, we are prepared to dance till exhaustion."

The early issues of *The New Yorker* were filled with limp intramural jokes: "Deems Taylor, walking along Park Row, was hailed by Robert C. Benchley. 'Hello, George,' said Benchley. He thought it was Murdock Pemberton."

The magazine was so parochial that Herman could entertain himself with mentions of his friends and relatives: "Miss Estherlea Aaronson is a New York visitor of her sister, Mrs. Herman J. Mankiewicz, by marriage."

F. P. A. with his two columns in the *World* was a sort of Ben Jonson to the Algonquin group, propagating the impression of a superfraternity of wits living from one sophisticated, merry encounter to another. And in the twenties there was an avid audience for such dazzle, a naive public described by Ben Hecht as "nine million human wallflowers." They thrilled to newspaper peeks at romanticized queens and chorus girls, theater stars and literary lights. Adams's "Conning Tower," a compendium of light verse, witty aphorisms, and sage comments, was the common man's whiff of culture and was studied by everybody with literary pretensions. The first to print Kaufman and Parker, Adams repeatedly used Algonquin contributions and thereby became a power in the group. The jokes he made and heard during their mutual diversions were the guts of his Saturday "The Diary of Our Own Samuel Pepys," the egotistical, name-dropping trivia of his week. For example:

Saturday, July 10
Lay long at Orchard Farm and waited for H. Ross to awake, which he did by ten o'clock, and we lay there talking over many scandalous things, bandying this name and that one about to our great glee. Thence in my petrol wagon to O. Paine's and on the way discussing whether Rye was the place where faces were made, and we asked a man on the road whether he knew where the Rye Face Factory was, and he said, No, he was a stranger there himself.

Monday, June 18
Waked weary, having slept ill, because of the coffee I had yesterday noon, and served me right, too, as my age is now great enough to teach me some wisdom. So to the office early and my scrivening. Dorothy Parker come to see me, and she in fine fettle and very gay. She told me about her peregrinations abroad, and I asked her about Ernest Hemingway, and how old he was. And she said, "Well, I don't know. But all writers are either twenty-nine or Thomas Hardy." So home to dinner, and then as luck would have it, seven lads came in. What to do now? quoth I. How about a game of poker? quoth M. Connelly. Agreed, cried all, and naught short of an inspiration, though I doubt that there was $20 included in the entire crowd of us. Had a highly adventurous game till late, and so to bed.

Wednesday, August 12

To the office early, and essayed to write a ballade with the refrain "The primrose path is a oneway street," but it would not come out to be aught but silly. To lunch with Herman Mankiewicz as my host. He tells me how difficult it is to hear what a bearded man is saying. Lord, quoth he, he cannot speak above a whisker.

In my petrol wagon up the Drive and met A. Woollcott and Miss E. Ferber walking. A. Woollcott, home from his holiday, hath now a goatee which I think detracts from his beauty, if I may coin a phrase. Thence I drove them up the Drive, being so pretty a day, and E. said, I could almost write a poem about the Hudson, I am so glad to be alive. Almost? I echoed, and forthwith fashioned this couplet:

> It fills me full of joie de viver
> To look across the Hudson River,

which I deemed as fine a poem as ever I wrote, but which occasioned no comment soever from the prosaic pair in the back seat.

Another purpose of the Round Table was sex. Enjoying the 1920's liberation from Victorian taboos, the Round Table became a clearinghouse for both gossip and affairs. A 1961 reunion of only ten Round Table alumni included three once-upon-a-time alliances. Herman always delighted in shocking Sara with the day's stories of the Algonquinites' peccadilloes. Once, after hearing the latest Broun gossip, Sara said to Herman, "Don't you think it would be a good idea if Heywood Broun just never zipped his pants?" The next day Herman hurried to the Algonquin to repeat the crack.

Robert Benchley, the father of two boys, always deprecated himself as a lover. "I tried it twice," he would say, "and it worked both times." Dorothy Parker, lonely and dependent despite her acrid tongue, was an easy mark for the men in the Algonquin circle. She had affairs with Deems Taylor, Ring Lardner, and Charles MacArthur. Once during an evening of drinking at the apartment of Mr. and Mrs. Vincent Sheean, she made love to screenwriter Ross Evans on the couch, while the astonished Sheeans studied the New York skyline. "We must have been awfully picturesque," she said afterward by way of apology.

The group tolerated a young socialite and press agent named David Wallace because he could provide an introduction to almost any actress in town. The members rewarded him with their companionship and with the role of butt for a long playing joke. Wallace was not a wit. But when he attempted a joke, the circle would collapse with fake laughter, calling to each other across the table, "Did you hear what Dave said?," repeating his line to more raucous laughter.

One specialty of the Algonquin group was cruelty. A parlor game they played involved rating each other's qualities on a scale of one to ten: intelligence, sex appeal, honesty, and so on.

When the group was not elevating the lowly pun—"Paroxysmarvelous city"; "Atwater Kent be the Atlantic"; "I wonder where Herman Mankiewicz"—their humor was often cruel. It was a textbook example of Freud's analysis of wit as a socially acceptable way to discharge generalized hostility.

Helen Hayes, married to Charles MacArthur, wrote about the Round Table: "It could be so corrupting and so destructive. The smallest infraction could result in lacerating ridicule." When Herman once unguardedly revealed earnest, private emotions to Woollcott, he was immediately answered with a joke. They were in the card catalogue room of the New York Public Library, and Herman went through the "MA" drawer checking the Mankiewicz cards. "You may not think so," said Herman, his heart momentarily on his sleeve, "but someday my name's going to be here."

Woollcott later told everybody his put-down retort, which was built around an author named Pearson, famous for books on criminals. "I'm sure it will," replied Woollcott. "I can see the title now: Herman J. Mankiewicz by Edmund Lester Pearson."

There was an elaborate joke played on the table's token bore, John Peter Toohey. A press agent whose favorite expletive was "Jesus, Mary, and Joseph," the kindly Toohey was genuinely liked as a willing audience, victim, and straight man. Toohey had a deep, booming voice and a habit of making every sentence seem like an oration. He also talked constantly about what things cost, what his wife paid for various items. One of his favorite complaints was the cost of the Round Table lunches, which were usually under $2. Murdock Pemberton, Marc Connelly, and Herman Mankiewicz concocted a special luncheon menu with all prices tripled. The Algonquin's Frank Case printed up several copies and put them on the table the next day. On cue, Toohey exploded with anger the moment he saw them. The rest of the table vociferously joined in his outrage, and a plan was devised to bring Case to heel. The whole group would abandon the Algonquin, and each person was assigned several different restaurants to try out for a new meeting place. And while Toohey, still steaming at Case, went down his list day after day, the others came to the Round Table and roared with laughter.

Nobody was exempt from the cutting edge of the Round Table humor, from such wisecracks as Herman's "She could give you an eyewitness account of the Crucifixion and put you to sleep."

The *World* theater reporter, Laurence Stallings, sometimes talked about his wooden leg, thereby creating sympathy, embarrassment, and a silence in which he could take over the conversation. Once when he did so, Herman leaned forward and loudly said, "I am going to lay upon you a terrible curse. MAY YOUR LEG GROW BACK!"

Sara went to lunch at the Round Table once. "You could hear them all as you walked in," she remembers. "Herman wanted to show me off so badly, wanted me to be funny. I wasn't. I didn't make any outrageous remarks. But I think I handled myself pretty well. I remember standing up and saying, 'Gentlemen, I'm deeply honored,' and a roar of applause went up. But I never wanted to go again. There was too much brilliance. They had such reputations by then, and everybody was quoting everybody."

But beneath the fun and sparkle, like the hostility, was the competition of egos. Herman saw this clearly. When Marc Connelly's play *The Green Pastures* was a major hit, Herman said to Kaufman, "If I told you a month ago that Marc Connelly was going to write a play all by himself about a bunch of Negroes, that it was going to take place in heaven, that the main theme was going to be a fish fry, and that Marc Connelly was going to direct the play all by himself—would you have seen any reason why you and I should worry?"

Donald Ogden Stewart, one of the Algonquin group, is perhaps more accurate and honest about the Round Table than the usual romanticizers. "I don't think," he says, "that the lunches were as witty as legend would have them because they were such a strain. It wasn't just a gay, whimsical, upper-class group of people enjoying themselves. There was always somebody to stick the dagger in. You had to have your guard up all the time. It wasn't what you might call the ladies friendly association."

Stewart adds, "You had to have three or four jokes before you went, and it got to be a kind of rehearsal for a musical comedy. It got too artificial. You went to get a laugh and also to be talked about until the next luncheon: 'Did you hear what Herman said?' The way people did with Dotty. They were the best ones. And I can remember one talk that Bobby Benchley and Dotty and I had when we decided not to go to the Round Table much anymore. Dotty was a terribly shy person. Her nature was to hide in a corner and shoot in her cracks unobserved. And she didn't like them to be publicized in the columns the next day. When it all got to be a kind of publicity thing . . . well, if you know one of your cracks may be in the newspapers the next day, you begin to think about what kind of cracks you can make. And Dotty hated the reputation of being funny. She was always afraid that somebody would think that she was working at being funny. Often at the Round Table she'd whisper, 'Let's get the hell out of here.' And then the next thing she said was so tremendous they wouldn't let her go."

When Harold Ross's third wife sued him for divorce, she delivered from the witness stand a cold-eyed summary of the Algonquin group and the influences that were so potent on Herman. "The defendant," she stated, "is a habitué of that circle of literati, actors, musicians, playwrights, authors in which the unconventional at all times dominates. Ordinary pleasantries and common amenities are tabu as banal. Courtesy is a cliché and only the barb or mot and the adroit witticism are tolerated. Ethics, decency, real values as understood by the man in the street are socially archaic. In this arena of pseudo brillance, consideration is the mark of the tenderfoot and survival depends on the ability to compound a bright remark."

CHAPTER

6

☐ ☐ ☐

Hollywood money is something you throw
off the ends of trains.

—CHARLES MACARTHUR

"HERMAN COULD MAKE A FORTUNE IN HOLLYWOOD." THOSE
words, uttered in 1925 by an MGM press agent friend, rang
like bells in the heads of Herman and Sara. For a while Herman professed indifference. He continued to dream of the day
when Americans would be asking, "Have you seen the new
Herman Mankiewicz play?" And at the Algonquin there was
a class distinction between playwrights and screenwriters.
Movies were a minor art form. In the theater Brooks Atkinson
or George Kaufman, not some nonentity, reviewed you. Nunnally Johnson once asked Harold Ross for the job of movie
critic on *The New Yorker*. "You don't want that," said Ross.
"That's for women and fairies."

The press agent Miller persisted, urging Herman to develop
a silent movie idea on the Marines. Herman eventually did.
At the Round Table he made much of the fact that the idea
for the movie came to him while he was sitting on the toilet.
Metro-Goldwyn-Mayer offered him $500 a week to come to
Hollywood and write a scenario. That sum was more than
twice what he made in New York. "We nearly lost our minds
with joy," Sara remembers.

Herman accepted but considered the trip only a lark during
which he would make a little quick money to support his New
York writing career. He always maintained everybody initially
came to Hollywood "in pursuit of a lump sum." In his case,

he said, it was $2,200 to pay a debt. And since he was passing through Chicago, he agreed to stop over and address the prestigious Book and Pencil Club on the subject of the New York theater. The speech he carried with him was written by Sara because she was sure he would never get around to writing it himself.

In Chicago the *Daily News* offered Herman a job as drama critic. He wrote Sara: "It's probably childish of me, but I do enjoy being a fake literary lion. Next time I come, I hope it will be real."

When he boarded the train for California, he had lost his cash and the lecture fee in a poker game at the home of his Chicago hostess. And in Hollywood, MGM had lost interest in his Marine story. Herman was asked to help find a vehicle for Lon Chaney, the master of disguises. So he wrote his first movie for Chaney, a silent melodrama called *The Road to Mandalay*, billed as "A Thrilling, Throbbing Romance of Singapore."

Herman was captivated by the life in what was recognizably the newspaperman's land of milk and honey. He wrote Sara: "Los Angeles is delightful beyond belief with its tropical vegetation and its mad, colored, pretty bungalows."

To Herman's consternation and astonishment, he received a telegram from Harold Ross firing him from the staff of *The New Yorker*. The cause was an attitude of Herman's that made him a lifelong thorn in other people's sides. He regarded most men and women, no matter how celebrated, his inferiors in scholarship and intellect. He would give vent to his frustrated feelings of superiority before people like Ross. Herman respected him but became impatient with that yokel quality which stuck out like straw from a scarecrow.

As the organizer and chief visionary of a monument to big-city sophistication, Harold Ross appeared as an incongruous figure. Born in Aspen, Colorado, Ross looked like a western hayseed. Equipped with only an incomplete high school education, he had become a tramp reporter, and had roamed from paper to paper. Herman said he looked like a dishonest Lincoln, then quipped, "At the theater, Ross is afraid to sit in a box seat." Herman would say to him, "Don't behave as though you just arrived from Colorado. You know better than that." Newspaper publisher Ralph Ingersoll, then a young "Talk of the Town" reporter, remembers that Herman "terrified and enraged Ross," adding, "Mankiewicz considered his opinions worth more than those of a naive Ross."

Herman took the same attitude with most of *The New Yorker* staff. Katharine White—Mrs. E. B. White—at that time a lowly first reader, later a key editor of the magazine, remembered that "On Mondays in a frenzy of typing he rewrote copy for the then brief 'Talk of the Town.' I was scared of him and stayed out of his way. He talked very loudly and acted as if he owned the place. I assume he was an experienced journalist, but to me he seemed merely lofty and very, very sure of himself."

Returning from Hollywood in February of 1926, his pride badly hurt, Herman proclaimed his outrage. He vowed to administer retribution to Ross with the heavy end of his cane. The Round Table group gleefully described to Ross the justice that awaited him. At *The New Yorker* one day word was flashed to Ross that Herman was in the elevator on his way up. Ross hid in a coat closet. Herman whacked Ross's desk with his cane and departed.

The collision did come soon afterward. "The editorial office at Twenty-five West Forty-fifth Street," Ralph Ingersoll remembers, "was a miniature city room with a seven- or eight-foot high wall partitioning off one end. For some reason, Ross and Mank's confrontation took place behind it, and the whole staff—there couldn't have been more than four or five of us—stood there listening. Ross had an office of his own, but maybe he felt safer from Mank's rage closer to possible help. After Mank's 'But you *can't* fire me' reaction, and as they got madder and madder, roaring at each other, first ties, then coats—and could be a shirt—came flying over the partition, stripping out of sheer excitement, much to our great delight. And in the end the red-with-rage Mank came flying out in tatters. Shortly thereafter I inherited the unhappy job of being Ross's conveyor of bad news. Firings were too much for Harold after Mank's."

Herman never told Sara that he had been dismissed by Ross.

Herman's departure from *The New Yorker* was the coup de grâce to his formative years as a prose writer. Ross's influence had been too brief, and Herman never explored and developed his own writing as a serious craft. Even so, Herman could have been superb at the quick, spontaneous effect, a talent which would have been memorable over the short distance of a political column. If he had chosen to harness his most intense interest, he could have been an angry Buckley, a witty Lerner, always with a strong point of view, often outrageous, never dull. But he did not pursue that possibility, perhaps because he doubted his ability to move his opinions from the parlor to a public forum. Perhaps it was because nobody ever offered him the chance, or perhaps the reason was stated by Herman in a 1925 review of Phil Baker, the comedian. "He is so good," Herman wrote, "that we again devote a moment to our favorite speculation as to why he is not better. The best guess is probably that rousing audiences to mirth comes too easily to him and so he consequently does little about it."

Or perhaps Herman ultimately wanted a success grander than that of a newspaper columnist, for which he would have had to develop laboriously a $100-a-week skill into a $300-a-week profession.

Herman decided to go west again. His collaboration with Marc Connelly on *The Wild Man of Borneo* was dragging out interminably. When the *Times* theater critic Stark Young was fired in 1925, the paper hired Brooks Atkinson instead of promoting Herman. A production date for *We the People* was being postponed out of existence. He still had great hopes for *The Good Fellow*, which was due to be produced that fall. But all those doors of opportunity that had been so wide open now seemed barely ajar. It was time for new fields to conquer, the money-green pastures of Hollywood.

Herman turned down an MGM contract, and his producer friend Walter Wanger arranged a one-year deal with Famous Players-Lasky Corporation, which soon became Paramount Pictures. His income was quadrupled. Overnight his salary increased to $400 a week, plus $5,000 for each original story filmed. The studio guaranteed to buy at least four of Herman's scenarios. But Herman took the precaution of stopping by to see Brooks Atkinson. Would the *Times* take him back in his old $80-a-week job if he failed in Hollywood? Atkinson promised yes.

In July, Herman reported for work in Hollywood, while Sara joined her family on the New Jersey shore for a last summer together. Herman now plunged into good times even more extravagantly collegiate than in New York and with even more glamorous companions. Herman was an usher at Donald Ogden Stewart's wedding and attended the bachelor dinner with America's romantic idol John Gilbert, novelist Joseph Hergesheimer, and Charlie Chaplin. Robert Benchley was there, his leg in a cast as a result of a fall. A girl danced on the table. The men drank champagne toasts and smashed their glasses against the wall. They broke Benchley's crutches into kindling and lit a fire under his chair. Then the party adjourned to Gilbert's hilltop house for more drinking and more girls, while Stewart discreetly departed. Herman wrote Sara: "You'd be surprised how much fun you can get out of breaking a cripple's crutches into thousands of pieces, while the cripple glares at you in impotent rage. But the dinner was only mildly alcoholic and everybody behaved beautifully."

Sara, proud of Herman and happy to be leaving their New York life, wrote to Herman from New Jersey: "My darling— this morning (it was 7:15 and I had been awake for half an hour, lying in bed thinking of you) we had such a nice phone talk. And you said so sweetly, 'I love you, schnucks,' so all day I've been sort of happy with moist eyes, if you can understand that kind of happiness. Good night, my darling—I kiss you right on the mouth."

Herman returned to New York in September to bring his little family west—part of the general migration in 1926. Greta Garbo journeyed from Sweden to appear in *The Torrent*. From Broadway came W. C. Fields. The dead body of Rudolph Valentino returned from New York in a black-draped funeral train. A new name appeared in Hollywood when a midwestern housewife won the *Movie Weekly* contest by rechristening Lucille Le Sueur, an ex-sales clerk, Joan Crawford. A device named Vitaphone came west, offering the possibility that sound might someday be synchronized with film.

Herman and Sara traveled in a private drawing room on the posh Super Chief, as befitted a Hollywood writer. Their two children and a nurse were ensconced in another car. Hovering black servants served meals on white tablecloths in their private compartments. As they approached Hollywood, elated by their entrance into paradise, Sara and Herman watched the rows of orange trees mile upon mile that bordered the track from San Bernardino to the end of the line at Pasadena, where a studio limousine waited for them.

Although the population of Los Angeles had doubled in every decade since 1850, the Hollywood which greeted them was still a peaceful, pastoral town, surrounded by bean fields and orange and lemon groves. On the flat-roofed, false-fronted stores there were only a few signs: "The Auto House—Auburn and Cord Cars—Front Drive." Palms and pines, pepper and eucalyptus trees provided shade for squat one-story bungalows with steeply pitched roofs and the two-story Victorian homes with scrollwork eaves and front porches bordered by thick-ankled columns. The corner of Hollywood and Vine—ten years later Hollywood's busiest intersection—was bounded by two churches and orange trees. "You can see Catalina Island every day," wrote Herman to his father, "but this is not obligatory."

Sara rented a house on upper Vine Street. High above them,

on the empty hillside, were huge wooden letters spelling "Hollywoodland." Herman moved about his new home, singing, "We're in the money; we're in the money." Herman bought a closetful of expensive clothes—white flannels and black and white wing tip shoes. He bought golf clubs, and joined a country club. He acquired a soft-top convertible Cadillac from the director Ernst Lubitsch. It had huge spoked wheels and wide running boards, and inside, above the back seat, was a little wall vase in which a delighted Sara kept flowers. Herman also bought a gray plush lap robe monogrammed H. J. M. He hired a tall black chauffeur named Stafford. Across the middle of the car was a window that could be folded shut to seal off the driver. But Herman considered this egregiously undemocratic and decreed that the window never be closed. Sometimes, however, a tight-lipped Sara, poised for argument, did push it shut, saying, "Do you mind?"

Herman also purchased a two-seater Buick, which lasted only until Christmas Eve. Herman's pal Eddie Mayer had arrived, also hired by Paramount, and settled a few streets away. On his way to a party at Eddie's house Herman drove down the steep slope of upper Vine Street. As he passed a policeman, he looked him in the eyes, lifted both hands from the steering wheel, and called out, "Look! No hands!" Unfortunately the Buick swerved and was demolished against a telephone pole.

Herman was soon talking about buying a house. Sara, driving her own small Chrysler, searched in Hollywood and then drove through the farmland to a new luxury suburb called Beverly Hills, where movie people were building huge homes: French châteaux, twenty-five-room cottages with fake thatched roofs, Spanish haciendas, English manors. Inside were "antiqued" rafters, "aged" fireplaces, wormholed picture frames, Sheraton furniture, coats of arms.

Through Beverly Hills and vegetable farms and open country ran the five-cent Red Car Line, whose trolleys carried farmers and Los Angeles city dwellers to Santa Monica and the ocean for all-day excursions. At noon the streetcars stopped for a half hour while the conductors and motormen sat in the sun and ate their sandwiches.

Sara did find an English house and garden for $90,000. But without cash of their own, the monthly payments were too terrifying, and they settled for a series of rentals, the last of which, a Spanish-style house on Tower Road, they eventually bought.

Herman, one of the first New York theater writers to come to Hollywood, was immediately an impressive success. Symbolic of his importance at Paramount, Herman was not housed in the shedlike building where most of the writers labored in tiny cubicles. Production chief B. P. "Ben" Schulberg wanted Herman close to him in the long Spanish stucco administration building. Outside Herman's lavish office, a secretary, Rachel Linden, awaited his summons. Beyond his window lay a grassy quadrangle where Jack Oakie tossed a football around with friends. Beyond loomed the silent film shooting stages, vast frosted glass barns like gargantuan greenhouses.

Herman flourished in a joyous tumult that perfectly suited him. Ben Hecht, in his autobiography, has described it:

> The loneliness of literary creation was seldom part of movie work. Movies were rarely written. They were yelled into existence at conferences that kept going in saloons, brothels, and all-night poker games. You worked with the phone ringing like a firehouse bell, with the boss charging in and out of your atelier, with the director grimacing and grunting in an adjoining armchair. Conferences interrupted you, agents with dream jobs flirted with you, and friends with unsolved plots came in hourly.

Herman, nervous, fretful, happy, head down, and half looking out the corner of his eye, ready to pounce, presided over a constant influx of friends like an antic, defrocked bishop. "A compliment from Mayer," he would say with a Mephistophelian grin, "is like having Nathan Leopold tell you that you're lovable."

Hearst columnist Louella Parsons was soon berating the studios for giving carte blanche to "eastern scribblers such as Herman Mankiewicz . . . who have never proved they know anything about the tricky essentials." The *Hollywood Reporter* wrote about "The famous 'bachelor's table' in the Montmartre restaurant—Herman Mankiewicz, high priest. Here writers pledge themselves to a 'few more years of tripe and then something worthwhile.' "

In silent films the only words that existed flashed on the screen as titles, a sentence or two that explained the plot or helped a characterization. Herman was a virtuoso at titles— one of the writers described in *Liberty* magazine as "The Titular Bishops of Hollywood—The nine editorial prima donnas of the motion picture industry who roll around in high priced limousines." Producers wanted titles that "hit the back wall," that got big laughs and could turn a clinker into a hit. "Derely Devore, the star, rose from the chorus because she was cool in an emergency—and warm in a taxi," Herman wrote for *Take Me Home*. For *Three Week Ends* he wrote: "I've got as much chance to wash in private as a six months old baby." In another of his titles, these words flashed on screen: "Paris, where half the women are working women." Then an instant later: "And half the women are working men."

The prima donna director Josef von Sternberg worked only with the men he considered the best at Paramount, and for him Herman titled *Drag Net*, *Thunderbolt*, and the famous *The Last Command*. In a cutting room, silent film footage could be arranged into three or four entirely different movies. Working with the director, Herman could deliver a critic's insight on the concept or story line and make the difference between a film's failure or success.

When a movie was previewed in an outlying town, Ben Schulberg would take Herman and Sara along in his Lincoln limousine, embellished with real gold trim, petit point cushions, wall vases whose flowers were coordinated with the chauffeur's puttees. After the screening was over and the audience had gone home, Herman would stand on the sidewalk with Schulberg and say, "Well, that whole scene comes out," and would shush Schulberg's wife, "For Christ's sake, this is not a philosophical treatise we're making." Sometimes on the drive home Schulberg would say, "Now you all be quiet and let's hear what Sara thinks."

"Those were the biggest moments in my life," Sara recalls. For Herman and Sara—not yet thirty—it was a halcyon time of high hopes. Together they partook of the pleasures of California: luxury weekends in Palm Springs, driving down in the evening through air fragrant with orange blossoms, trips to the pine forests of Lake Arrowhead, summer days on the beach at Malibu, ebullient San Francisco weekends for football games, cruises to Catalina Island. "Herman was dear and adorable," says Sara. "Young love."

In the fall of 1926 Herman's ambitions as a Broadway play-wright—and his belief that he could leave Hollywood any day he wished—received a setback. His collaboration with Kaufman, *The Good Fellow*, went into production. Howard Lindsay was the director and Kaufman himself codirector. At the out-of-town tryouts in Long Branch, New Jersey, audiences sat in painful silence. One evening Kaufman encountered the actress Ruth Gordon, who was in nearby Atlantic City struggling through the tryouts of a tragic drama. Despondently she complained that her audiences just sat and laughed. "I've got a great idea," said Kaufman. "It'll save both shows. Let's switch audiences." Opening in late 1926, *The Good Fellow* ran for just six performances on Broadway. It was the worst failure of Kaufman's career.

In the winter of 1927 *The Wild Man of Borneo*, Herman's collaboration with Marc Connelly, was also a quick failure.

Herman in New York had not faced the fact that universal drama, including comedy, requires painfully explored emotions and sensitivities. He still had not yet assembled himself and written out of his whole being. He may have been having too much fun. He may have enjoyed too many other kinds of distinction. Or he was afraid to risk his shaky self-esteem on what he could do at a typewriter. Maybe the necessity of self-scrutiny, plumbing the sources of his self-doubts and violence, was impossible. He transmuted his deep feelings into jokes, which helped him insulate himself from introspection and pretend his problems did not matter. So Herman tried to take his wit and make it do the work of everything inside him. But the wit alone was not enough. Perhaps Herman knew all that, choosing as he did to move away from the theater into a silent medium.

But if the failure of his plays caused a hitch in Herman's Hollywood stride, he did not show it. He turned his disappointment into rueful laughs. He framed the two telegrams that told of the devastating reviews and titled them "The Regrettable State of the American Theater." Fortunately, he was flourishing. "Mank was a man who liked to manipulate people and the job," said screenwriter and director Nunnally Johnson. "And when he came out here, I think Mank figured, 'These are my kind of people and I can handle them.' He was so damned smart he charmed everybody from stuffed shirts like Walter Wanger all the way down to almost idiots and hustlers. Bringing Mank to Hollywood then was like throwing the rabbit into the briar patch."

It was natural for Herman to invite a pal to join him on easy street. In late 1926 Herman invaded Schulberg's office, carrying in his hand his one-year contract. Herman insisted that Schulberg hire Ben Hecht. If he failed to write a successful movie, Schulberg could tear up Herman's contract and fire them both. Schulberg, a betting man, agreed. The telegram Herman sent to Hecht summed up his attitude toward his new world: "Will you accept three hundred per week to work for Paramount Pictures? All expenses paid. The three hundred is peanuts. Millions are to be grabbed out here and your only competition is idiots. Don't let this get around."

In Hollywood, Ben Hecht received Herman's cynical short

course in silent-movie writing: "I want to point out to you that in a novel a hero can lay ten girls and marry a virgin for a finish. In a movie this is not allowed. The hero, as well as the heroine, has to be a virgin. The villain can lay anybody he wants, have as much fun as he wants cheating and stealing, getting rich and whipping the servants. But you have to shoot him in the end. When he falls with a bullet in his forehead, it is advisable that he clutch at the Gobelin tapestry on the library wall and bring it down over his head like a symbolic shroud. Also, covered by such a tapestry, the actor does not have to hold his breath while he is being photographed as a dead man."

In one week Hecht wrote the first gangster movie, *Underworld*. Schulberg gave him a bonus check of $10,000, which Herman calmly snatched out of Hecht's hand. "I just want it for a few days to get me out of a little hole," Herman said.

The gambling he had found in Hollywood in the last years of the 1920's made the Thanatopsis games in New York seem like tea party whist. As in all boomtowns, "real men" gambled. At dinner parties out came the poker chips. Studio employees doubled as bookies. In odd corners and offices knots of men pitched pennies and rolled dice. On weekends half the studio traveled down to Mexico to gambling casinos and racetracks at Tijuana and Agua Caliente. The *Hollywood Reporter* and *Daily Variety* printed racing charts and bulletins in their pages, and during the season studio telephone bills skyrocketed. Off Sunset Boulevard there were illegal casinos called the Colony Club and the Clover Club. Says Ben Schulberg's son Stuart: "It was a status symbol to come to the Colony and show off how much money you could afford to lose and not go under."

In 1929 Samuel Goldwyn won $155,000 in a poker game, and two weeks later he lost $169,000—the kind of gambling that continued while the rest of the nation was devastated by the Depression. It was guilt, in part, that fueled the extravagance of Hollywood gambling. According to Donald Ogden Stewart, for a time the highest-paid screenwriter in Hollywood, "Telling the truth was what originally made you try to be a writer. But you were getting an incredible salary for creating dreamland and fairy tales while there were breadlines and your friends had jumped out of windows on Wall Street. The gambling was wanting to get rid of all that money which was on your conscience." Herman's friend David Selznick, married to the daughter of MGM chief, L. B. Mayer, once considered his poker hand for a long minute. Finally, he threw chips into the pot, saying, "The overpaid son-in-law raises a thousand dollars."

Dr. Fred Hacker, a psychiatrist friend, believes Herman subconsciously gambled to lose, "and partly it was to show he was a good loser, and partly it was self-punishment." Making the big bet, the bad bet, the bet he could not afford, had become the most highly charged act in Herman's life. "Pawn all your furniture," said Herman, "and give the money to Max to bet on the first race at Bowie. That will give you such a rapid pulse that three nurses will have to hold your hand while it is being counted."

During his career, at least $1 million passed through Herman's hands and left no residue. Crosby Gaige, a friend and producer of *The Good Fellow*, began trying to collect a $3,000 debt in late 1926. After a year of stalling, Herman wrote Gaige's lawyer: "The situation frankly and honestly is that I have absolutely no funds and nothing of any value to be converted into funds." Then Herman, angry at Gaige for harassing him over a mere $3,000, enjoyed a subtle dig at what he considered his tormentor's low-brow taste and meanness. "I am trying hard to finish a play of my own," added Herman in a letter of apology to Gaige himself. "It's about Hollywood and its title, which I hope you like, is 'Nigger Rich'—which I'll send along to you as soon as it's finished."

Herman once gave Sara a worthless household allowance

check on a Friday afternoon, after the banks were closed. Nunnally Johnson asked him, "Why the hell did you do that, Mank?"

"Well," Herman said, "I didn't want to spoil her weekend."

Not long after their arrival in Hollywood, a friend met Herman on the street. "How's Sara?" asked the friend.

A look of mystification came to Herman's face. "Who?" he asked.

"Sara. Your wife, Sara."

"Oh," said Herman, comprehension dawning. "You mean Poor Sara." Henceforth that was her name around town— Poor Sara—like Mary Lou or Joe Anne.

An October 1926 *Variety* carried the item "On football wagers everybody phones, rushes and probes to find out who Mankiewicz likes—to bet the other way. His rep is becoming national. Columbia teams—he dropped in there—have kept him in the red so long he's a beacon. Agents clamor to handle him, charging you 10% of your winnings."

Herman liked to bet on long shots. "You either win or lose," he irrationally insisted, "so it's always even money." Just once this bizarre philosophy paid off spectacularly. The Columbia College football team, known as the Lions, arrived in Los Angeles to play in the 1934 Rose Bowl against mighty Stanford. Columbia was given no chance, but Herman bet heavily on them. In a pouring rain, Herman and his boys were the sole welcoming committee at the train station for the team— "a group of short, bespectacled men who wore suits and ties and read from calculus texts," remembers Don Mankiewicz. Herman, who brought a fetid, toothless old·lion for window dressing, fled, leaving the astonished coach, Lou Little, holding the lion's leash. Columbia spent the entire game setting up a special play. It worked and the sophomore halfback, Al Barabas, scored around end. Columbia won, and Herman finally had his big killing.

At cards Herman was, by his own admission, "a well-known pigeon." George Kaufman, visiting Hollywood, drew Herman as a bridge partner. Finally, Kaufman said, "Herman, I know you just learned to play bridge today. But what *time* today?"

Herman sat at poker tables gambling $100 chips against the industry's chieftains and its most feared players: Joe Schenk, Eddy Mannix, Irving Berlin, Zeppo Marx, Sam Goldwyn, Syd Grauman, Ben Bernie—taciturn circles of watchful men, no jokes, no amenities. Thousands of dollars routinely changed hands in the Malibu mansions. Herman lost sincerely from genuine incompetence. These men liked to win from Herman. There was small sport in taking money from producers who deliberately lost to ingratiate themselves. But only in prodigal and imperial Hollywood could Herman's debts have been a Byzantine kind of benefit. "Don't worry," he told Sara. "They can't fire me. I owe them too much money."

Herman usually paid his debts one way or another. Once, for $10,000, Herman sold Schulberg a plot idea for a prize-fight film concocted at lunch with Laurence Stallings. Herman took the film rights, Stallings the theater. The amount Herman owed Schulberg just happened to be $10,000. The movie was never made.

Herman had a son-and-father relationship with Ben Schulberg, another literate, rebellious ex-newspaperman. At night they played pinochle together in Schulberg's den, thick cigar smoke, drinks, outrageous sarcastic anecdotes, guffaws of laughter, and, at dawn, Herman invariably writing a check. "My father and Herman," says Stuart Schulberg, "believed that the courage you showed through gambling was a badge of honor, of manhood."

When Ben Hecht tired of waiting for his $10,000, which Herman had soon lost, Hecht took him to see Schulberg. They negotiated a $500-a-week raise for Herman, which Schulberg would pass directly to Hecht. Thus, Herman became the high- est-paid writer at Paramount.

In 1929 sound came as a catastrophe to a considerable segment of the movie industry. International gods and goddesses, beautiful faces earning $12,000 a week, reported like schoolchildren to take voice tests, then to be told by a young technician from Western Electric whether their careers were dead. Heavily accented foreign stars could be heard practicing their English enunciation: "Sweet Sister Celia seated ceremoniously 'neath the sun kissed spruce." Zasu Pitts told friends, "I can't go out tonight. I have to go home and learn my titles." When Clara Bow heard there was a fire at Paramount, she rushed from her dressing room, shouting, "I hope to Christ it's the sound stage."

For Herman Mankiewicz, the gravy train accelerated with the arrival of sound. As a Broadway critic and ex-playwright he was one of the few men in Hollywood experienced with dramatic dialogue. Schulberg put him in charge of a crash program to create a staff of dialogue writers. Herman went back to New York to recruit friends for "The Herman J. Mankiewicz Fresh Air Fund for Writers." The newspapers announced his triumphal arrival. One headline said simply, "Herman is Here on Trail of Genius." Naturally he stayed at the Algonquin, where, said Herman, "writers are so thick they get in your hair."

On those trips Herman would see his revered father, and the professor's superiority would again be underlined. One night Herman took him to the comedy team of Clayton, Jackson, and Durante and afterward to a speakeasy, the Puncheon Club, later "21." But the man at the peephole, Charlie Berns, refused Herman entry. Herman, embarrassed in front of his father, protested violently.

Charlie said, "Sorry, we don't know you."

"God damn it, I came here last night with Robert Benchley, and I was told I could come back any time."

"Sorry, our rules are very strict."

"Look, my name is Herman J. Mankiewicz and I . . . ."

"Mankiewicz! Are you any relation to Pop Mankiewicz at Harlem Evening High?"

Herman's father stepped forward, saying, "Oh, hello. Hello, my boy."

"Professor Mankiewicz! Come right in. Come right in." And Charlie Berns rushed off to get the professor's other ex-student, Jack Berns.

On another occasion Sam Jaffe, Schulberg's brother-in-law and the Paramount production manager, was also in New York. Jaffe was in Herman's hotel room, and they were arguing politics. And Herman was yelling, "What the hell would a goddamn idiot like you know?" The telephone rang. It was Professor Mankiewicz, who was in the lobby and on his way up. After the professor arrived, the argument continued. "Herman's father took over the whole discussion," Jaffe remembers. "Herman started to challenge him, and Professor Mankiewicz interrupted: 'I don't have to listen to you. I know what you're going to say.' It was exactly the way Herman had been with me, except that Professor Mankiewicz was on top and Herman was down."

The screenwriting recruits Herman found on his several trips east—one was Nunnally Johnson—helped change the course of Hollywood movies, according to *New Yorker* critic Pauline Kael. The movement of New York writers west was inevitable, but Herman was a prime and initiating catalyst. He picked newspapermen in his own image, and these sophisticated, iconoclastic veterans of big-city newsrooms ridiculed the romantic sentimentality then in vogue in Hollywood. They introduced to motion pictures a smart-talking worldliness which audiences loved. In particular, the ex-newspapermen created the tough, sardonic reporter as a stock movie character. Newspaper movies were popular: *Front Page, Five Star Final,* the *Torchy Blaine* series, *Blessed Event, Advice to the Lovelorn.* And *Citizen Kane* in 1941, of course, was the newspaper movie at apogee.

Herman himself wrote the story or titles for about thirty silent movies at Paramount and the script or dialogue for fourteen talkies, some with collaborators. His pictures had major stars: William Powell, Kay Francis, Carole Lombard, Jack Oakie, Nancy Carroll, Zasu Pitts, Dennis King, Jeanette MacDonald, Miriam Hopkins, Jean Arthur, Ruth Chatterton, Richard Arlen, Adolphe Menjou, Fay Wray, Mary Astor, Fredric March, Clara Bow, Ina Claire. Two sound movies were hits: *The Vagabond King* and *The Royal Family of Broadway*, an adaptation of the George Kaufman-Edna Ferber play. When David Selznick, at age twenty-nine, became production chief at RKO, he borrowed Herman to write *Girl Crazy*. And Herman was the producer for a celebrated comedy called *Laughter*. In most there is Herman's quick, ironic touch. Noted Louella Parsons in her column: "Mr. Mankiewicz, while independent as he can be, is still one of the favorite children."

"He was the kind of guy who could pull a picture through to completion," says James M. Cain, a fellow writer with Herman at Paramount. "If some actor couldn't play a part, he knew somebody else who could. When everything was all jammed up and they were stuck, he could take a walk down around over to the commissary and come back and have the answer. Nothing could blow him down or faze him or get his nerves." And Herman feared nobody. In *Million Dollar Legs* there was a moment when Jack Oakie is fingering what is apparently parchment. "My grandfather," says Oakie. An assistant producer came to Herman's office bringing word that Schulberg wanted the line removed. "No," said Herman brusquely. "I like it. It's in."

The turn of the twenties into the thirties was one of the times when Herman could have returned east with enough momentum to launch a second try in New York. However, as he wrote his father, "Things are going quite nicely for me and I think I will probably be here for another year or more."

Gambling had prevented Herman from harvesting that cache of gold he came to find. He was happy with the indigenous disorder of studio life. But also, at last, he had his tangible success and power. Herman delighted in pointing out that when talkies arrived, actors and directors dropped by the wayside like fall leaves, but not one producer was considered unequipped for the new medium. Herman was surrounded by executives who had risen to power when the industry had nothing at all to do with the spoken word—and very little with the written word. Herman, eloquent, erudite, outlining an idea, delivering a judgment, was Dizzy Dean blowing his fastball past high school batters. His incisive, peremptory, overpowering manner, his facade of confidence and independence reassured his bosses. They treated him as an oracle.

Part of Herman's power came from the potent fact that all sorts of people prized him. Though he could be bellicose, he worked to make them laugh. He lost money to them. In a place not noted for those qualities, he was known to be honest and a soft touch who identified with every unlucky underdog. On a rainy day he would buy out the entire stock of papers from the crippled newsboy outside the Brown Derby. When occasional panics swept Hollywood and the studios economized by cutting secretaries' salaries, Herman himself would pay his secretary the money she lost.

One New Year's Eve he discovered that David Selznick's secretary, Marcella Rabwin, had no party invitation. Though Hollywood social life ran according to a rigid caste system, Herman invited Marcella to his party, along with such names as the Ronald Colmans. Marcella recalls: "Herman and Sara treated me as though I was their favorite guest in a roomful of people who were darling to me at the studio, but if they saw me at Chasen's, they didn't know who the hell I was."

"He was a tragic guy," says James M. Cain. "Inside was something terribly decent. A very kindly guy. And at least out of his mouth, very gifted. Worth knowing, worth hearing."

Much of Herman's clout at Paramount came from his

friendship with Schulberg. In a nice way Herman enjoyed flexing his power by obtaining jobs for friends. One young writer named Dore Schary was fired twice—and twice almost gave up and left Hollywood. Both times Herman arranged new jobs. Ultimately Schary became head of MGM. In 1929 Herman obtained writing jobs for his brother, Joe, and sister, Erna. "My mother writes, too," he told Schulberg, and took an ad in *Variety*:

MANKIEWICZ IN HOLLYWOOD
ERNA, JOE AND HERMAN
WATCH US GROW
AVAILABLE FOR CONTRACT OR BY THE HOUR
DONALD (Aged nearly 9) *
Frank II (Aged nearly 7) *

* Santa Fe and New York Central Railroads:
This is just a joke. They're really under 5.

Erna had previously been a public school teacher in New York with no professional writing experience. She had Herman's aggressiveness of mind, but not his geniality and wit. She infuriated Herman by finishing his sentences for him and explaining his jokes. When someone called the Mankiewicz home asking for Erna, Herman would say, "Don't be silly. If Erna were here, wouldn't she have answered the phone?" Erna was eventually fired from Paramount. She worked for a time at Columbia Pictures, her salary, unbeknownst to her, paid by Herman. Finally she went back to teaching.

Joe had already followed in Herman's footsteps by working for the Chicago *Tribune* in Berlin. Even before he reached Hollywood, Herman was building up his brother to his friends. As proof of Joe's credentials as a Mankiewicz, Herman proudly circulated his brother's wire from Albuquerque announcing his arrival: "Two hours late. Horses eaten by wolves. Gold safe however."

Joe came to California full of adoration for Herman. "When I was a boy," says Joe, "I used to bare my heart in the most childish way . . . actually open . . . no defenses

to Herman. I think the only person I confided to on paper
was Herman. He was the father figure I wanted. Three
thousand miles away in New York I would fight my way into
the Paramount Theater to be the first one to see *The Last
Command*."

Marion Spitzer, Herman's friend, remembers that in Hollywood, "Joe seemed like a nice, bright, modest, sweet, more
respectable version of his brother." Herman put his considerable influence behind Joe, who showed immediate talent.
Soon Paramount gave him a one-year contract at $60 a
week. Late in 1929 Herman got David Selznick to use Joe
for "additional dialogue" on a sound movie, *Fast Company*,
which made Jack Oakie a star and launched Joe. *Cinematters*
magazine that year picked him as one of the ten best dialogue
writers. *Skippy*, in 1931, earned Joe an Academy Award
nomination and the offer of a raise from $60 to $75 a week,
plus a five-year contract that would culminate at only $500
a week. Herman thought the contract outrageously cheap
and had a violent fight with Schulberg. Herman quit in protest. To his surprise, Schulberg accepted the resignation.

What followed was the quintessence of Hollywood, the
never-never land. Herman telephoned his agent, David Selznick's brother Myron, who was elated at the news. "I've
always said you were a twenty-five-hundred-dollar-a-week-
writer, and that's what you're going to get. Call you back in
an hour." No call came. Days went by. A week. Two weeks.
Any period at all in the Mankiewicz house without income
was a disaster. Herman called Myron and told him that Paramount would take him back at his old salary, $1,500, and he
wanted to go. Myron was furious. "Look," he said, "I told
you that you were going to get twenty-five hundred dollars
a week. That's what you're going to get, even if you don't
work for a year."

Herman soon arranged for his return to Paramount, and
as long as he remained "a favorite child," Joe's rapid rise
was an occasion for family pride. But Joe's worship of Her-

man was rapidly corroding. When Joe's salary reached $125 a week, Herman dictatorially made Joe put $25 of it away in a savings account. Six months later, to pay a debt, Herman borrowed all the money in the account.

Joe, furious and terrified, some years later refused to borrow on his life insurance for his brother. Herman told Joe to come to the office of their mutual friend Charlie Lederer, a writer and Marion Davies's nephew. When he arrived, Herman, to the astonishment of all present, announced, "This is a trial." And turning to writer James McGuinness, Herman said, "Now will you kindly tell this little SOB what a brother is—that everything he has is mine."

Herman expected others to be as extravagantly generous as he himself. "He really was a sweet sucker," says Dr. Fred Hacker. Any hard-luck story could extract help and money from Herman. Sam Jaffe, going into Herman's office, met a Catholic priest coming out. The priest, Jaffe learned, had got a pledge from Herman for $1,000. "Where are you going to get a thousand dollars?" Jaffe asked.

"Borrow it, of course," Herman said casually.

Even if he had to go out and get the money, Herman tried to follow his personal code when he lent to friends. He gave twice the amount asked. People, he said, borrow the bare minimum to solve the immediate problem and then have no money to get going again.

By the early 1930's the profligacy of studio life was beginning to suit Herman too much. If anything, the boomtown feeling of Eldorado seemed even greater. In the depths of the Depression, Hollywood was the fifth largest industry in the world. Seeking eighty minutes of escape—or in the popular triple bills, 240 minutes—80 million Americans a week went to 17,000 movie theaters. At twenty-five cents for an adult, ten cents for a child, movies were the one entertainment they could afford. As the twenties merged into the thirties, movies like *Min and Bill*, with Wallace Beery and Marie Dressler, told Americans that poverty was not so bad.

Busby Berkeley musicals and singers like Grace Moore in *New Moon* stroked American fantasies. And crime movies like *Little Caesar* administered a shot of sensationalism. Social realism, like King Vidor's Depression movie *Our Daily Bread*, dialogue by Joe Mankiewicz, turned into box-office poison.

Herman knew how to exploit all that money and the inevitable slippage and waste. "Everything came so easily for Mank," Nunnally Johnson recalled. "He was handling it all like a pro player who had just found himself in the middle of a bunch of children. He couldn't help but take advantage of it. He got careless."

There was Herman's episode with the four Marx Brothers. As a member of the Algonquin group, he had known the anarchic comics in New York, and Ben Schulberg assigned Herman, in 1931, to be the producer—called supervisor—of their first movie made in Hollywood, *Monkey Business*. The two neophyte writers on the project were S. J. Perelman and Will Johnson. Perelman remembers Herman as "a sort of Johnsonian figure in the industry." Perelman has written, "Luckily his duties as our overseer lay lightly on him. He stressed the fact that we were to proceed as fancy dictated, cynically adding that, in any case, the Marxes would keelhaul us."

Describing the Marx Brothers to Johnson and Perelman, Herman said, "They're mercurial, devious, and ungrateful. I hate to depress you, but you'll rue the day you ever took the assignment. This is an ordeal by fire. Make sure you wear asbestos pants."

Herman did not reappear for six weeks. At that point Groucho voiced the general opinion of the script. "It stinks," he said. Everybody went to work—or the Marxes' version of work. The brothers appropriated Herman's office and secretary. When Sara came there, she says, "My life was in jeopardy." She would be goosed from behind, or Harpo, with his stage leer, would grab Sara and toss her through the air to

Chico, who flung her on to Groucho. Herman presided, if that is the word, over five months of group writing sessions, bedlams of shouted ideas, insults, trade-offs, and general dementia.

Monkey Business, of course, was an instant hit. With typical Hollywood logic, Herman was assigned to produce another movie, a bizarrely unsuitable project called *School for Sweethearts*. He treated it with offhand contempt, and when it was ultimately abandoned, Herman resigned his producership. "I can't afford any new enemies," he explained. In the latter part of 1931 he wrote *Dancers in the Dark*, with Jack Oakie and Miriam Hopkins, and the Wheeler and Woolsey musical comedy *Girl Crazy*.

Then, in January 1932, he was assigned to produce the Marx Brothers' next movie, *Horse Feathers*. This time the lunatic script meetings included the songwriting team of Bert Kalmar and Harry Ruby. A writer named Henry Myers, hired by Herman to think up jokes, remembers one of the sessions. Herman opened it, saying, "Let's do this sensibly. Let's analyze." Myers had some notes, and he started reading them. One of the Marx Brothers got a Dixie Cup and put it in the middle of the floor. Each brother put a dollar bet on the floor and took his turn trying to spit into the cup.

Policing the Marxes was hopeless, a good pretext for Herman to indulge his own whims. "Mankiewicz wasn't much good because he was either boozing or playing cards with Schulberg," said Groucho Marx. "But he was a funny man. He was an interesting character—and a provoking one." Needless to say, Groucho considered himself the prime shaper of the Marx Brothers films.

After six years at Paramount Herman was getting fed up, and so was Paramount. By the early thirties Herman was trapped in a vicious circle of contempt. Regarding movie writing as child's play and beneath his talents, he condemned himself for doing it. And the longer he did it, the more he scorned himself and the work, so the more ready he was to neglect the work.

It was hard for Herman to treat anything in Hollywood with committed respect. And that included the Marx Brothers. He appreciated their unique comedy but regarded it essentially as a sort of *Hellzapoppin* shenanigans. He fought any attempt to put systematic plot in their pictures, saying, "If Groucho and Chico stand against a wall for an hour and forty minutes and crack jokes, that's enough for me." He was delighted to have them as friends. Harpo, wearing a green baise roulette layout as a yarmulke, used to lead the little Mankiewicz boys in Indian war dances through the middle of family Passover Seder ceremonies.

But Herman had the same superior attitude that had undone him with Ross and *The New Yorker*. Herman regarded the Marx Brothers' humor as inferior to his own. In writing conferences, he could be disdainful, particularly of Groucho's favorite writer, Arthur Sheekman. Herman would reject Sheekman's jokes with "For Christ's Sake! Gene Bendini's *Chuckles*. 1928." Or, "Eddie Cantor in *Whoopee*, the first version which was rewritten." To S. J. Perelman, Herman would say such things as, "For God's sake, Perelman, go back to your hutch and bring out. . . ."

Though he regarded Groucho's entire personality as the creation of a few scriptwriters, particularly George Kaufman, Herman did value Groucho's comic mind and intelligence. But during the filming of *Horse Feathers* Herman realized that Groucho was using jokes from the script to amuse his friends at the comedians' table at the Hillcrest Country Club. The jokes lost their freshness, and soon Groucho was demanding new dialogue. So Herman began saving the best jokes until the very last minute.

In Herman's opinion, Chico Marx's talents were limited entirely to an Italian accent. On the set one day, using a dollar-bill serial number, Chico did a parlor trick which ap-

parently required a photographic memory. Harry Ruby turned
to Herman and said, "This is amazing!"

"Yeah?" said Herman disgustedly. "But in a few minutes
they'll start shooting and he won't remember his lines."

As soon as the scene started, Chico was yelling, "Hey,
bring that script over here."

Herman, like everybody else, loved Harpo, who originated
all his own antics. But Harpo began to take himself seriously.
In New York Alexander Woollcott had been trumpeting him
as the new Chaplin and the greatest pantomimist in the world.
Harpo asked Herman for the script of *Monkey Business* because "I want to find out what my character is."

Herman looked at him sourly and said, "You're a middle-
aged Jew who picks up spit because he thinks it's a quarter."
That, Harpo told friends, punctured his pretensions forever.

Despite his disdain and misbehavior, Herman always remained a man people valued, even the Marx Brothers. After
Horse Feathers, Herman wrote to Sara from New York: "The
Marxes were extremely glad to see me. They insist I'm crazy
and that they wouldn't think of doing a picture without me."
One of the writers on *Horse Feathers*, Nat Perrin, has a more
objective memory than Groucho. Says Perrin: "Mankiewicz
was kind of lax, but I never knew him as a drunk. I think
the boys had a respect for him as a man of the theater and
as a writer—and he influenced the script. You know, just a
few words here and there can keep a story in line. And Mankiewicz had taste. He always made sense, even if he seemed
to be taking things lightly. I think he may have been able to
accomplish more despite his indifference than a lot of guys
who attack things with their bodies and souls."

In 1933 Herman was assigned to the Marx Brothers' new
Paramount movie *Duck Soup*. The studio was in financial
trouble, and there were threats of pay cuts. In answer to a
worried letter from Herman, Professor Mankiewicz consoled

his son with a typical homily: "If less money helps you to experience the difference between life's pleasure and life's happiness, I'd call it a blessing."

Herman's protector, Ben Schulberg, had been fired by the board chairman, Adolph Zukor. Passed over for choice assignments, Herman placed an ironic joke ad in *Variety*:

HERMAN J. MANKIEWICZ

WROTE	DIRECTED	PRODUCED
"THE TEN COMMANDMENTS"	"THE KING OF KINGS"	"SEVENTH HEAVEN"
"THE BIRTH OF A NATION"	"THE BIG PARADE"	"WAY DOWN EAST"
"TOL'ABLE DAVID"	"SKIPPY"	"THE COVERED WAGON"
"THE HUNCHBACK OF NOTRE DAME"	"ALL QUIET ON THE WESTERN FRONT"	"THE GREAT TRAIN ROBBERY"
"BEN HUR"	"THE LOVE PARADE"	"BEAU GESTE"

ALL I ASK IS A CHANCE

Despite his shaky status, Herman spent the early weeks of *Duck Soup* throwing darts for money with the movie's director, Leo McCarey. To palliate his generalized contempt and anxiety, Herman was nipping scotch more and more. And as a joke, Herman spread the word that it was Ruby, a near teetotaler, who was enticing him to drink. A Paramount executive summoned Ruby and ordered him to stop feeding Herman liquor. Apoplectic, Ruby stalked into Herman's office and said, "Open that drawer!" Herman complied. Ruby said, "What's that?"

Herman said, "That's scotch; that's rye. What do you mean, 'What's that?'"

"Herman, you have a job here!" expostulated Ruby.

"This is a free country," Herman said.

Ruby's lyricist partner, Bert Kalmar, once quipped about Herman, "To know him was to like him. Not to know him was to love him."

Herman was removed from *Duck Soup*. The Marxes could have kept him. But as usual, Herman's verbal victories, like his crack to Harpo, ultimately served to defeat him. He was assigned to write a political musical called *The Phantom President*, starring George M. Cohan and with Jimmy Durante and Claudette Colbert. Soon he was battling the producer over political naivetés in the script. In March 1933 Herman left Paramount by mutual consent.

7

Out of the thousand writers huffing and puff-
ing through movieland there are scarcely
fifty men and women of wit or talent. Yet,
in a curious way, there's not much difference
between the product of a good writer and a
bad one. They both have to toe the same
mark.

—BEN HECHT

ONE WEEK AFTER HIS INGLORIOUS DEPARTURE FROM
Paramount, Herman was hired by Hollywood's richest, most
prestigious studio, MGM. Holding sway in an office next to his
new patron, David Selznick, Herman's salary was reduced only
briefly from $1,250 to $1,000 a week. "Thus do the wicked
prosper while the righteous moan and beat their breasts," he
gloated by letter to his father. "I propose to write for Don and
Frank a new version of the saga of the ant and the grasshopper,
with particular emphasis upon the sachel [good sense] of the
grasshopper and the all-around idiocy of the ant."

For a time in a burst of optimism and resolve, Herman enjoyed an era of importance and productivity at MGM. Selznick, valuing his skeptical irreverence, put him on projects and
sought his advice. Herman wrote a series of successful adapta-
tions, beginning with a collaboration on a Helen Hayes vehicle,
Another Language. He worked on Selznick's *Dinner at Eight,*
the 1933 movie version of the George Kaufman-Edna Ferber

play and one of the most popular motion pictures ever made. In 1934 MGM lent Robert Young to Fox in exchange for Spencer Tracy, needed for Herman's script of *The Show-Off.* Herman's 1934 spy drama *Stamboul Quest* starred Myrna Loy. Herman did another Myrna Loy script, *Escapade,* but she decamped to England after a salary argument. So Herman rewrote the script for Luise Rainer, and in 1935 the movie made Rainer a major star. That year Herman did a newspaper screenplay, *After Office Hours,* and according to an MGM film history, "the biting wit of the Herman Mankiewicz dialogue got the rosiest bouquets tossed by the critics."

Success eased the pressure on Herman. MGM was known as "the country club." It was hard to get fired and, says Joe Mankiewicz, "easy to hide." Herman moved under the kindly wing of an important but ingenuous executive named Bernie Hyman, who adored him. More and more Herman began to enjoy himself.

His day began at MGM around 10 A.M., when he entered the studio through the ersatz grandeur of the main gate with its ten wooden Corinthian columns. In his office he immediately placed a dry spoonful of bicarbonate of soda on his tongue, quickly drank a glass of water, and burped loudly. Then he telephoned Sara. "What's new?"

"Honey, you just left," Sara would say.

"Who called?"

"Nobody."

"Give me one thing and I'll hang up. Something must have happened."

Herman getting to work was like Robert Benchley trying to leave a party. "It isn't that I can't toddle," said Benchley. "It's that I can't *guess* I'll toddle." Herman, in the throes of procrastination, once wrote Harold Ross:

> I am replying to your letter promptly, chiefly because I have promised M.G.M. to deliver a finished script by Monday, faith-

fully and without fail. Answering your note to me, however, and, if necessary, dictating a comic letter to the Editor of the Yellow Book, asking why my December, 1898, copy hasn't arrived, will have to take so much time that I won't be able to let them have the script as promised. God damn them!

Before he could begin writing, Herman, by telephone, had to place bets, set up lunch at Romanoff's, rehash last night's party, try to get jobs for friends. When Horace Liveright went broke, Herman found him employment in Hollywood. One day the MGM story editor, Sam Marx, received a call from Herman. "Listen, for God's sake, F. P. A. is starving to death. He's lost his column. Can't you get him *something*?" Marx managed to finagle a writing job at $500 a week. Frank Adams, in a fury, rejected the offer. "How come Sidney Howard gets three thousand dollars a week?" demanded the former lord of the Round Table.

On the telephone Herman aided charities, corralling a collection of friends to make monthly contributions for Jewish German refugee children. He listened to horse races by phone, solved other writers' script problems, gave advice to young writers. He told one writer to complain *immediately* about his office, get some painting done, have his desk moved, let them know he was in the building. He should demand a couch: "It's a matter of prestige." He instructed another neophyte, "Never explain in this town. Deny."

Between calls there was *Variety* and other required reading. Studying the Daily Racing Form, Herman said, "I've always felt that when a man stops reading, he stops learning."

There was usually a joke to be put in motion. He tried to rent a blimp to float across a University of Southern California football game towing a sign, saying, "Send Your Boy to an Eastern College." Goodyear turned him down. The *Hollywood Reporter*, however, was happy to take Herman's ad announcing a facetious chain letter.

POOR SARA!

SPORTSMAN $100,000 GROUP
PROSPERITY CLUB
(In God We Trust)

Herman J. Mankiewicz, 1105 Tower Rd., Beverly Hills,Calif.
Sara Mankiewicz, 1105 Tower Rd., Beverly Hills, Calif.
Donald Mankiewicz, 1105 Tower Rd., Beverly Hills, Calif.
Frank Mankiewicz, II, 1105 Tower Rd., Beverly Hills, Calif.
Herman J. Mankiewicz, 1105 Tower Rd., Beverly Hills,Calif.

FAITH — HOPE — LUCK

This chain was started in the hope of bringing prosperity to YOU. Within three days, make five copies of this letter, omitting the top name and address, and adding your name and address at the bottom of the list. Deliver a copy to five of your friends to whom you wish prosperity to come.

In omitting the top name, send that person one hundred thousand dollars ($100,000.00) as a charity donation. In turn, as your name leaves the top, you should receive 15,625 letters with donations amounting to $1,562,000.000.

IS THIS WORTH A HUNDRED THOUSAND DOLLARS TO YOU?

John Houseman, a friend of Herman's, diagnosed his procrastination not as laziness but as "neurotic inertia." Among the Mankiewiczes, *Schreibfaulheit* (writing laziness) was regarded as a family trait. Though Joe Mankiewicz was more disciplined than his brother, Professor Mankiewicz sent him a carefully lettered sign for his office wall. It said: "EHEU! Fugaces Labuntur Anni!" "Alas! the Fleeting Years Slip By!" Herman was more colloquial and fatalistic about the problem. "A loafer is a loafer is a loafer," he said, evoking Gertrude Stein. "Not, mind you, that one—even a loafer—doesn't intend wholeheartedly to write. But hour follows hour, day follows day, week follows week—and that's how it is."

To help a friend in trouble over a deadline, Herman would cheerfully go right to work. When his friend Jim McGuinness, a top writer and heavy drinker, was incapacitated, Herman would half kill himself night after night to write McGuinness's pages. Sometimes McGuinness did the same for Herman. On one occasion, after Herman had sobered up, McGuinness handed him pages to turn in. Herman glanced through them. "These stink!" he said. "They're not my style."

When the pressure of Herman's own deadlines became finally irresistible, Herman would tell his secretary to come after dinner to Tower Road. An exceptionally fast writer, he would dictate dialogue late into the night. Dictating had become his solution to transferring verbal gifts to paper. He reworked the typed-up pages with a pencil—and the secretary retyped. Dictating provided the stimulation of an audience, and solved the writer's burden of loneliness, particularly onerous for Herman. But the technique could also be a tempting way to get maximum output with minimum effort, a short cut around the painful, laborious composition of the first draft.

Those home sessions would escalate into frantic days and nights, with secretaries in relays—what he called "doing twelve hours in eight hours." When finally under way on a script, Herman had a certain industry which carried him through. He never failed to finish an assignment. He rationalized his work habits with the idea: "My half effort is worth everybody else's full effort."

Though extreme, Herman's *Schreibfaulheit* was not exceptional in Hollywood. Harry Cohn, head of Columbia Pictures, is supposed to have stood outside the apparently empty writers' building and screamed, "I'm paying you bastards. Get to work!" Immediately the air was full of the rat-tat-tat of typewriters. "Liars!" bellowed Cohn.

While some writers skylarked, there were authentic literary names, helpless in the unfamiliar medium, who withered in idleness simply to ornament the studio roster. "The boss," said Ben Hecht, "who hired Dostoyevski to write like Horatio Alger somehow became Feodor's superior." However, those names were in Hollywood for the same reason that Herman came—and stayed. They wanted the money. Not even William Faulkner could earn enough writing books.

Herman received an invitation to a dinner "to acquaint Liam O'Flaherty with the secrets of keeping from being found out in Hollywood and to welcome him to our graft (typographical error)." Thomas Mann was there, considered rather boring and a difficult person to place at a dinner table.

William Faulkner was hired by Howard Hawks to work for Nunnally Johnson, who was producing a picture called *Road to Glory*. Faulkner arrived in Johnson's office, carrying a brown paper bag. During their desultory talk about the film, Faulkner asked for a glass and pulled a pint of whiskey from the bag. He opened the bottle and cut himself. Johnson was eager to call a doctor. But Faulkner dragged the wastepaper basket to his chair. And while Faulkner's hand dripped blood steadily into the basket, the two men got drunk.

F. Scott Fitzgerald was in Hollywood, now largely forgotten by the reading public, sad and shrunken, the flamboyance gone. He was desperately hoping for a new career at MGM but could not write movie dialogue and was being rewritten by Joe Mankiewicz, who had moved to Metro. Perhaps because misery loves company, Fitzgerald enjoyed being with Herman, who was described by his friend Marion Spitzer as "a kind of German Jewish Scott Fitzgerald." And Donald Ogden Stewart says, "Scott had a bit of the death instinct. I think Mank and he were closer to each other than any of that generation."

Fitzgerald, to whom Herman lent money, sometimes came to dinner at the Mankiewicz house. After one party he wrote Sara a thank-you note: "I've never had a better time in these my latter days, with the leaves dropping hour by hour. I spend my time composing dithyrambs to guide my first-born through college, but they are going to forget their rubbers anyhow and no harm done."

There were, of course, what Herman called, "discourteous demands on my time by my employer." Rewrites would be required "because the leading male part has sixteen one-syllable words and seven polysyllable words less than the female part."

Herman was sometimes called to a shooting stage to redo lines which did not play. Says director George Cukor: "He used to exasperate me. I remember Ina Claire complaining about a certain scene, and Herman said, 'It will work. Just hear it.' And he had the gall to read it to her, this most expert actress."

Days were spent sitting outside producers' offices and then inside in the conferences called "to lick the story." When George Seaton, director of *Airport*, came to Hollywood as a $35-a-week junior writer, he was ushered into David Selznick's office for a conference on *Meet the Baron*, the saga of Baron Munchausen. Says Seaton, "In that office, which was a little larger than Mussolini's was Herman Mankiewicz, Norman Krasna, Alan Rifkin, P. J. Wolfson, Arthur Kober, about five gag writers, the director, Walter Lang, Jack Pearl, and the comic Ted Healy—and they were sitting as if they had been there for weeks, which they had been. There was still no beginning for the script. They couldn't motivate Munchausen. I went back to my little hotel room, worked all night, and when I came in the next morning, everybody was sitting in exactly the same position as the day before. I had two ideas, and I gave the first one. Herman said, 'That's it. That does it.' And everybody agreed. So I was assigned to work with Norman Krasna to put it in screenplay form.

"I went to Herman later and thanked him very much for liking my idea. And he said, 'It's not that I liked it. I just wanted to get out of Selznick's office.' "

It was in just such conferences that Herman earned his salary. Fast of mind and tasteful, Herman could articulate problems and produce ideas and blast open a stalled screenplay. And he pronounced his judgments with the authority of a witty Zeus. In a meeting to consider the purchase of a script called *The Marriage Mask*, Herman said, "I don't understand what the story is about. It reminds me of the fear I get now and then of having to drink a glass of water without the glass. I think this script was sent in the way somebody would send in a collection of useless toys he found in the attic to an island where he heard the two-headed Ubangis were paying fabulous prices for any goddamned thing at all."

Herman was also expert at "punching up" another writer's dialogue, adding wit and sparkle. "Give it to Mank for a couple of weeks," producers would say. In his career he worked on perhaps a hundred or more scripts without credit. The MGM story editor, Sam Marx, rated Herman at the top of writers of sophisticated, witty dialogue. He says, "Even though at times my faith may have faltered, I pushed Mank a lot and was usually pleased that I had."

Herman, of course, was writing full screenplays and was better equipped for doing that than many of his cohorts. In terms of craft, if not art, he was a professional, and he survived when other cutups were fired. Producer after producer continued to set about "straightening Mank out." They were certain that if the wellsprings of Herman's oral wit could be tapped, a great script would emerge.

However, Herman could be easygoing about story construction, the building of plot turn upon plot turn. Often, like George Kaufman, he needed a coauthor, and, said Herman, "Nothing puts me to sleep faster than the sound of my collaborator's typewriter." In Orson Welles's opinion, "Mank was a collaborative artist and was most innovative within that framework. But that doesn't cut half the melon away. It's just another way of doing it. Herman wrote marvelous single lines and speeches. I conceive of his talent as narrow, but very tall."

In addition to the writer's endemic dread of the typewriter, Herman's dilatory ways were part of his anguish at being trapped in a creative process he considered insane. It produced the superbly commercial, homogenized mass product now revered by movie buffs. But at MGM in the 1930's Herman was a cog in a movie factory seemingly designed to debase writers into hacks, drying up their aspirations, satisfactions, and self-confidence.

Perhaps *the* gratification for a writer is the communication of closely held ideas and insights, the sovereign control over plots and characters and phrases. But Herman, like all studio writers, was simply an employee obliged to devote himself to whatever he was handed, no matter how trashy. "You were a lucky writer if something crossed your path that you really liked," says writer-producer Bert Granet. "Most of the time you were like the guy with a call girl who you'd invested fifty dollars in—and you'd better like her."

When Herman began a script, he knew it might never be filmed. And just as he himself worked on other men's scripts, Herman knew that his own would almost surely be processed in the studio mixmaster. Each studio carried 75 to 100 screen-writers, and a script was rarely the work of one author. Irene Selznick, David's ex-wife and the daughter of L. B. Mayer, says, "Sometimes writers worked in succession. Sometimes they worked in teams—or several writers worked separately on the same script, and each one thought he was alone on it. Sometimes one writer did the outline, someone else did the synopsis, someone did the dialogue, someone did the revision, someone did a complete rewrite. Who the hell knows who wrote anything?"

Periodically Herman came home early in the day, discouraged and miserable, carrying a load of studio pencils and paper. "To hell with that," he would say. And Sara knew immediately that somebody else had been put on his script. Says John Houseman: "When that happens to you three or four times after you've really busted your neck, you say, 'Screw it!' "

It was particularly devastating when the replacement writer became the one listed in the screen credits, the only testimony to a writer's output. In those days credits were assigned capriciously by the producer. "You waited until your agent knew the shooting date," Donald Ogden Stewart recalls, "and then he would suggest to the producer that you might be able to help out. And then you'd remove as much of the other person's dialogue as you could and get the screen credit. It really was a bitches' game. But the stakes were so bloody high."

Herman wrote *Comrade X*, designed for Clark Gable, cast as an American reporter in Russia. To be sure of defeating two competing Gable scripts, the producer then gave Herman's screenplay to Ben Hecht, Herman's most admired and trusted friend. Hecht got the screen credit by rewriting the movie in twelve days with the aid of Charlie Lederer, Marion Davies's nephew. Hecht helped sell the script by reading it aloud to the studio executives.

"They all aspired to be Ben," says Irene Selznick. "The resourcefulness of his mind, his vitality were so enormous. His knowledge. His talent and ambition. He could tear through things, and he tore through life. They'd see this prodigious output of Ben's, and they'd think, 'Oh, hell, I'm a bum.' I think it must have been devastating. Ben did it to MacArthur, who died in time to save his reputation. And I'd hate to have been Herman, caught between Kaufman and Hecht. And then to have had Joe come along in addition. That's very rough, particularly when you've got no self-discipline and you're frittering your talents."

The studio assembly line was run by a proliferating army of producers. In 1927, 24 producers made 743 pictures. Ten years later 220 producers made 484 pictures. Only half the producers had better than a high school education. Nobody read books. Some, of course, were skillful, intelligent men. More often they were muddleheaded, interfering egotists with no loyalty to the intellect, crude men controlling culture. "Harry Rapf," said Herman, talking about one of L. B. Mayer's assistants, "has bought a lovely piece of English suiting which will be made into a jacket especially waterproofed for eating chicken soup at the MGM commissary."

And yet these men unhesitatingly criticized, revised, and OK'd scripts. Herman sourly described story conferences as the time "when the producer says to you, 'Now in reel three the fellow shouldn't kiss the girl, he should kiss the cow.' And then the whole picture unravels, and you can't stand it." In the early thirties producers were called supervisors. Herman called them "pissants," "ragpickers," "blintze brains," and "Jew tailors." He called Mervyn LeRoy "the San Francisco newsboy."

Herman's self-expression, his self-respect as a writer were under the thumb of powerful executives like Harry Rapf, who once advised Herman on a script, "It should have a big exciting finish—like an earthquake. A catechism of nature!" Another producer commissioned Herman to adapt *The Man with Red Hair*, a horror story by Hugh Walpole. "It's about a crazy old guy who likes to kill people," said the producer. "He ties them up, sticks pins in them, and stuff. You can do anything you like with it, but I'm asking one thing: Take the morbid element out of it."

At one of the annual MGM Christmas parties a friend found Herman sitting at his desk drinking scotch while tears streamed down his face. "I am sick and tired of pretending that I know less than Bernie Hyman."

These producers were hired by the hard, enterprising, often ruthless men who were equipped to win and to create an entire industry. Hollywood was founded by a glove salesman, the sons of a butcher, a bouncer at an amusement park, two furriers, an upholsterer, two clothing merchants, a jeweler, and two drugstore owners. Louis B. Mayer had been a junk dealer, and his grandson, Daniel Selznick, remembers that notes accompanying Christmas presents were ungrammatical and misspelled and that the beginnings of sentences were not capitalized.

Such men, of course, built the industry as a business, not as an art form to satisfy the creative urges of writers and directors. Nevertheless, those executives did have a kind of vision. They wanted to make, by their taste, good movies, and they spent enormous sums on an extraordinary pool of creative people. Marvelous motion pictures were made—but mixed in with a river of mediocrity. All movies were guaranteed exhibition because the moguls controlled both the factories in Hollywood and chains of movie theaters around the country.

The writers who had imagined a higher destiny for themselves were miserable. Says Helen Hayes: "Through all the laughter and jackanapes and desperate merriment, they were fiercely unhappy people out there." In the second half of the 1930's Herman was the prototype of the screenwriter besieged by disgust—furious and guilty over his own betrayal of his intelligence—and incapacitated for giving his best. He called his screenplays "slop," "shit," and "vomit" and with acid derision would say, *"Weit gebracht in Amerika"* ("I've gone very far in America"), an expression used by disillusioned immigrants.

When movie attendance briefly plunged in the thirties, Herman attended anxious gatherings of exhibitors, directors, writers, executives. "I'll tell you what to do," he told one meeting. "Show the movies in the streets, and drive the people back into the theaters."

Increasingly the crest of Herman's day, the hours when he recharged his ego, was lunchtime. Sometimes he ate in the studio commissary at the prestigious directors' table. He arrived as to a performance—up—often kindled by a shot of whiskey. And he reigned over a regular band of senior writers, directors, and such stars as Clark Gable and Spencer Tracy. They were the beneficiaries of the energy and invention most writers husbanded for the blank page. And much of it was directed at Herman's oppressors.

There was discussion of Maurice Revnes, a failed literary agent whose job at MGM had recently been arranged by Myrna Loy. Somebody asked what Revnes did. "Well," said Herman, "it's his job to sit on the third floor and look west down Washington Boulevard. And if an iceberg comes down Washington Boulevard, it's his job to run in and tell Louis B. Mayer. Also there was another man looking south." In truth Revnes had been put in charge of the studio's junior writer program. "Ach," said Herman, "the guy with the worst clap is running the clinic."

Any name that came up brought a joke. The group was discussing a mediocre out-of-work director. "Don't waste your sympathy," said Herman. "His real job is looking for a job. If he were to find a job, he'd be out of work." Assigned to collaborate with a Hungarian screenwriter, Herman complained, "His characters always start their sentences, 'When a woman . . .' or 'If a street car . . .' " Joe Louis, predicted Herman, would knock out Jack Roper "in round zero." "If people don't sit at Chaplin's feet, he goes and stands where they're sitting," Herman said.

One day Herman began ragging his friend George Oppenheimer, a bachelor. "George, why don't you marry my sister?" Herman proposed. "There she is. I'm supporting her. You wouldn't have to sleep with her. And look what you'd gain in income tax. You'd get community property." Enthusiastic now, Herman began to create, perquisite by perquisite, a fantastic, teetering tax scheme that would render Oppenheimer a rich man. When Herman finished, another writer quietly left the table, went directly to Universal Studios, and sold the idea under the title *Income Tax Wife*. Herman once confessed, "I talk too much, and so my ideas appear in print or on the stage before I get around to writing them—and sometimes to uttering them."

Often Herman left the studio for lunch at a restaurant. Sometimes it was to meet a bright, pretty woman, one of a platonic retinue which, at one time or another, included actresses Margaret Sullavan, Nancy Carroll, Miriam Hopkins. Sullavan wrote him: "I'm the girl who thinks you're much more of a genius than Ben Hecht." He called her "Missy" and "you goddamn southern belle" and told her to "knock off that husky voice with me. Save it for the directors." She gave Herman a picture endorsed "From lover number two."

Herman was gallant, opening doors, passing compliments. He made women feel amusing, and they remember him with such words as "flirtatious," "appreciative," "flattering," "cuddly," "enchanting," "sweet," "very warm." One, a young writer named Decla Dunning, recalls: "Mank needed somebody he could pick up the phone and call and make jokes with and talk to. Sara knew all the answers. He needed somebody to take his advice. Sometimes, when he was drunk, he would say, 'Do you love me?' and I'd say, 'No, Herman, I like you,' and make some corny remark like half a loaf is better than none. He needed love."

Though they were only his Beau Brummell fantasy, he did not discourage gossip that he was having affairs with these women. Sara doubted the stories that came to her, but she did have fears. Herman's secretary phoned Sara from a studio Christmas party to say that Herman had bought her a diamond bracelet and after many drinks had casually dropped it in his pocket and departed, probably for Miriam Hopkins's house. Sara hurried in pursuit. "My heart pounded," Sara says. "Jealousy did it to me more than anything else. I got an actual ache." Herman's car was parked at Miriam Hopkins's beach house. Sara had to force herself out of her own automobile. Filled with dread, she rang the bell. Miriam Hopkins opened the door. "Sara," she said, "I'm glad to see you. Come in here and get this man of yours and take him home." Inside, Herman was sitting calmly by the fire, smoking, a drink in his hand.

"I was smart about those things," Sara says. "I immediately made those women my friends. It was the best thing I could have done."

The women were evidence to Herman that he was valuable. He often took them to lunch at a restaurant that offered the same reassurance—Romanoff's in Beverly Hills. It was the realm of the ex-confidence man who called himself His Imperial Highness Prince Michael Alexandrovitch Dmitry Romanoff. His fakery so fascinated Hollywood that Herman threatened to ruin him by claiming Romanoff was in actual fact a true prince, passing himself off as an impostor.

Romanoff's was a walk-in litmus test for Hollywood status, and Herman was ushered to a prestige booth across from the

long bar. Again he was the center of attention—an event—
and a flow of friends joined the group to delight in what Herman had to say about the topic of the day. In the forties
Herman explained why a jury acquitted Errol Flynn of statu-
tory rape. "That's easy," he said. "There were several middle-
aged married women on that jury. And the girl testified that
Flynn laid her on the boat Friday night and laid her on Saturday and again on Sunday afternoon. Now the husbands of
these middle-aged women had assured them that it is physically impossible for a man to copulate more than once a week.
So the girl had to be a liar!"

Sometimes the laughs came from the same cutting wisecracks which used to rock the Round Table. Orson Welles
says, "Mank's humor certainly didn't come from the fact that
he found the world irresistibly entertaining and funny. He
simply could express his hatred best and most elegantly in
terms of humor." Because the hostility came forth as humor,
not only was it socially acceptable, but all those who laughed
became his allies. Herman himself saw his sarcasms as playful
verbal gymnastics and was vaguely disappointed when his targets were upset.

A fellow screenwriter never forgave Herman for remarking,
"It should be against the law for that fellow to be alone with
a typewriter." Herman skewered a producer's wife, saying,
"She's one of the nicest women I'm sorry I ever met." Not even
Ben Hecht was exempt. Herman was asked in the 1940s why
Hecht had become such a radical Zionist advocating violence.
"It's very simple," said Herman. "You see, six years ago Ben
found out that he was a Jew, and now he behaves like a six-
year-old Jew."

A highly paid writer of jokes for other writers' dialogue once
rhapsodized about New York, saying he would work there for
$25 a week. "Doing what?" said Herman. Herman was so cut-
ting to one man the victim left the table. Decla Dunning remonstrated, asking what the fellow had done to him. "He
talked," Herman said. "There are some people who should

talk and others who should keep quiet. He is the one who should keep quiet." At another lunch, however, Herman was gracious to a man he particularly disliked. Again Decla Dunning asked why. "I found out he likes me," Herman said. "There is nothing so irresistible as being loved."

Herman never attacked Sara. "We always knew he cared tremendously," says writer John Lee Mahin. And the one-time college cadger now made a fetish of always picking up the check.

There were times at Romanoff's when Herman was, as he put it, "in a cup or two." Invited to a preview of *The Lost Weekend*, he declined: "Would you invite Admiral Halsey to play with the boats in your baby's bathtub?" When a lunch companion suggested that he go home sober for a change, Herman protested, "What! And have Sara throw me out as an impostor?"

At four o'clock in an otherwise-empty restaurant he would still be at the center of an audience, a glass of scotch on the table between his hands, a light grin on his face. By then, back home at Tower Road, Sara was impatiently waiting for his after-lunch call, when he again phoned for news and delivered the gossip he had gleaned.

If the call had not come by three o'clock, she began to worry. She telephoned his secretary at the studio. If he was not there, she called Romanoff's, or the Brown Derby, or Mike Lyman's, or Lucy's, and the headwaiters disclaimed any knowledge of Herman. "Everybody protected him," Sara says.

Then, in her car, she made what she called her "survey," cruising by the parking lots of his favorite places. When she found his car, she marched into the restaurant. "Wherever he was there would be a circle around him, aiding and abetting," Sara recalls. "I couldn't count on anybody to be my ally."

Standing by the table, while Herman was sheepish or expansively cordial, Sara would say, "Let's go, Herman."

"It was like the truant officer is here," says Sara. "I didn't care for that role. But that didn't stop me."

He always came obediently, even gratefully. He worried about getting home alone. He was safe with Sara. If Don and Frank were at Tower Road, she took him to her sister Mattie's house, where he was put to bed like a little boy. "Don't be mad on me," he would say to Mattie. When he woke up, he would talk to Mattie's two children because "they are still too young to know that their uncle spiritually lives in Berchtesgaden and was a member of the Dillinger gang until expelled for depravity."

Often, of course, there were days when Herman made a conventional return to his office. And there were times when Herman announced resolutions and routines of work. He would swear off alcohol, lay out schedules, promise early bed-times. "My industry has definitely returned, or perhaps it were better to say, made its first appearance," Herman wrote to his father. "But I need not stress that there is little danger of Sara dying of lethargy and anemia due to a personal life barren of the worry that is so good for the soul."

The professor answered, "Your letter was unmistakable proof of a new era, and we would all love to have more proof of a victory over the procrastination which robs us of the joy of creative work."

Sooner or later another crisis would explode. Sometimes it was a producer needled once too often. During a story conference the cry of "fire" sounded in the hallway. "Do you smell smoke?" Herman asked Harry Rapf, who was famous for his enormous nose.

"No," Rapf said.

"Then there's no fire," Herman replied.

Sometimes the blowup came because Herman still cared about what he wrote, despite his contempt and the corruption by the studio system. He exploded at producers in a fury of frustration. "You goddamn idiot," he would yell. "You're ruining the picture." He told one producer, "Given a more favorable personality than you have, you could make a fairly good living as the proprietor of a small candy store. In good times, that is."

Often the crisis was a missed deadline. Despite the continued recklessness, there were still friends willing to expend their power to save him. Says Orson Welles: "One of the things that bound his friends to him was his extraordinary vulnerability. His condition was a constant topic for conversation. He liked the attention he got as a great, monumental self-destructing machine. That was his role, and he played it to the hilt. He was a performer, as I think all very successful personalities are. He couldn't be affectionate or loving outside his family. You never felt you were basking in the warmth of his friendship. So it was his vulnerability that brought the warmth out from the friends. And people loved him. *Loved* him. That terrible vulnerability. That terrible wreck."

At MGM Herman would go to Selznick, saying, "Jesus Christ, you've got to help me. If Sara finds out. . . ." Selznick would talk to Herman's producer to soothe damaged feelings or would arrange a rescheduling or the addition of another writer.

Everybody loved and felt sorry for Sara. "She adored him so," says Irene Selznick, "and she was so pure, such a marvelous wife and mother, a good housekeeper, and so worried and concerned. It was all so alien, these wild goings-on." And for her sake, Herman could usually get forgiveness or a reprieve.

The process began when Herman returned home drunk and uncontrollable. "OK, Herman, what is it?" Sara would wearily say. "Is it money? A script? Who have you insulted? Have you been fired?" And he would confess. The next day Sara would go to the studio. At Paramount she would see Schulberg; at MGM, Selznick or Bernie Hyman. To Hyman she would say, "Please have a little patience. That deadline is making it impossible for him to write. Let him do it in his time, and I guarantee that he'll have it in."

When debts were the emergency, Sara appealed to Louis B. Mayer, the most powerful man in Hollywood and the highest-salaried man in America. Though employed by Loew's Inc., Mayer regarded MGM as his extended family, whose members he nurtured and groomed upward through the ranks. He took for granted their total loyalty and for two decades considered himself MGM incarnate. Once, walking the streets of the studio lot with thirteen-year-old Danny Selznick, Mayer put his arm across his grandson's shoulders and said, "Someday, my boy, all this will be yours."

He was capable of rages so brutal that one of them sent Dore Schary running from the room to vomit. But Mayer, the paterfamilias, could be sentimental, benign, almost indulgent. This was the side which Sara and Herman evoked. When she phoned, Mayer would say, "Come right over." At one end of his vast office Mayer sat inside a circular white desk like a pilot operating a giant airship. "I always felt as though I were explaining a naughty child's acts to a father," Sara recalls. "Mayer liked that role. He made it easy for me." After extracting his pound of humiliation from Sara, and then Herman, Mayer had the debts paid and the sums deducted from Herman's salary.

Herman managed a grudging, backhanded respect for Mayer and his skill at manipulating situations and even the biggest of stars. Herman began taking flying lessons with Margaret Sullavan and her husband, Leland Hayward. Anybody whom Herman had driven in a car knew this was paying for a course in suicide. Sara asked Mayer for help. He called Herman in, but no argument had any effect. Finally, Mayer sagged, the picture of defeat. "Herman," he said, "you're a stubborn man. I give up."

Herman, triumphant, started for the door. Instantly Mayer roared, "Herman, have you ever heard of a Jewish flier? Who? Who? Name one!" Herman's mind went blank. "Are you going to give me your promise?" Mayer demanded. Herman nodded. He was defeated. "All right, my boy, go back to work," Mayer said. It was the only time Herman was ever stopped.

"Louis B. Mayer may be a shit," said Herman, "but not every shit is Louis B. Mayer."

In the mid-1930's the movie industry—and Herman—were confronted by the formation of the Screen Writers Guild. Herman had always been antiboss and procollective bargaining. He considered United Mine Workers leader John L. Lewis a great man and was a champion of the less fortunate. He described going Hollywood as "being able to sleep at night as long as *your* belly is full and *your* car's in the garage full of gas and *your* butcher's coming in the morning with roast beef for dinner. Going Hollywood has nothing to do with Hollywood. You can go Wilkes-Barre, Pa. You can go Norfolk, Va."

But he regarded the founders of the guild as fools, not unfortunates. He fumed at those village idiots who did not even know the name needed an apostrophe. He believed, too, that the guild was founded by Communists as part of their infiltration of Hollywood, and therefore, they had no real concern for wages, hours, and working conditions. He was triply outraged by the hypocrisy of movie writers spouting Communist working-class cant while living high on their plutocratic salaries. "Look at that son of a bitch Communist," Herman would say. "Look at him driving his Jaguar!"

He did not want this group to have practical control over his work and future. He argued that unionization would debase the writing profession to the craft level of carpenters and electricians. The cynical side of Herman also considered it risky to unionize what was actually a ridiculously overpaid racket. "Stop yelling for your rights," he warned. "Somebody's likely to give them to you, and we'll all be working for seventy-five dollars a week.

"Look," he remonstrated, "we flush our toilets with hundred-dollar bills," and he took an ad in *Variety* proclaiming, "Writers of the World Unite! You have nothing to lose but your brains." A guild member argued back, saying, "Herman, we're *not* doing this for the twenty-five-hundred-dollar-a-week writer; we're doing this for the two-hundred-fifty-dollar-a-week writer."

"All the two-hundred-fifty-dollar writers I know," Herman said, "are getting twenty-five hundred dollars."

A strike was threatened. Herman launched into an orgy of ridicule. "I think it's a great idea," he said. "Chasen's can dispense the vichyssoise on the pickct line. I want to see the accounting of the first guy who applies to the union good and welfare fund—two hundred dollars a week for school tuition, a hundred twenty dollars for the psychiatrist, three hundred dollars for the cook, two hundred dollars for . . . You'll all go out on the streets carrying big signs saying, 'Help! Help! We're only being paid seven and a half a week.' And everybody will say, 'How about those poor guys? Seven dollars and fifty cents a week.' And then somebody else says, 'No, seven *hundred* and fifty *dollars* a week.' And then duck because you'll all be stoned to death."

Herman was throwing in with his natural enemies, the producers and company bosses, perhaps as the better part of valor. He joined the studios' counterunion, the Screen Playwrights, which was reviled as reactionary right-wing. Feelings ran deep. Preposterous rumors circulated: that Herman had crawled into an air-conditioning duct to spy on a guild meeting. Says Sara, who was in favor of the guild, "A lot of people never forgave Herman."

In 1936 Herman pulled himself together and made a brave effort to leave Hollywood. He had been there a decade, unreconciled and still considering himself a transient held over in a hick town. Later, when Sam Jaffe went off to war, Herman accused him of "yellowness" for leaving "this Pneu-

monia Paradise where it's not actually cold and not actually
warm; where the sun shines, to be sure, and yet you can't always be sure it is shining; where, when it isn't raining, it isn't
raining and I don't know which is worse. There isn't even
spring, as spring is understood in civilized places."

He still believed that the only form that could honestly be
called writing was New York writing. Herman remained un-
shaken in his determination to achieve a successful Broadway play, both his dream and his deus ex machina escape
from screenwriting. Even after the nonsuccesses of *The Good
Fellow* in 1926 and *The Wild Man of Borneo* in 1927, Herman continued to try. He filled notebooks with play ideas,
sitting in his bedroom chair or his chilly office over the garage
at Tower Road.

In the mid-1930's he wrote the first act of a never-pro-
duced play called *The Tree Will Grow,* a drama about Dillinger. Interestingly, it was the precursor of *Citizen Kane.*
The plot begins with the news of Dillinger's death under the
guns of the FBI, and it is designed as a complex portrait of
the gangster, assembled from the conflicting memories of
men and women who knew him.

Herman completed *The Meal Ticket* in the fall of 1937.
It is a satiric comedy about an itinerant vaudeville family
whose eighteen-year-old girl is on the brink of big success in
Hollywood. She falls in love with a young doctor, and instead of accepting the studio contract, she runs away with
him. Herman found a man to finance the production, his acquaintance John Hay Whitney, a close friend of Robert
Benchley's and a frequent visitor to Hollywood. The director
was a man by the name of Harry Wagstaff Gribble.

Both Herman's freedom and his confidence in his creativity
were riding on *The Meal Ticket.* In January 1937 he sneaked
away to help at the rehearsals for the Philadelphia tryout,
though a script was due at MGM. There was serious trouble
when the studio discovered his absence. With his usual pen-

chant for self-damage, Herman had bought his New York friends their theater tickets through MGM.

From Philadelphia Herman wrote Sara forlornly:

> I had forgotten how hopeless, purposeless and generally disorganized a troupe of actors can look at this stage of rehearsals, fumbling for lines, trying to work out business, getting mixed up on cues, tired—and they're so tired—and in general indicating that they're in a state of inextricable confusion. I can't help getting very depressed regularly. The jokes, charm and humanity will just have to stand up!

Nothing stood up. Herman received lacerating reviews. The Philadelphia *Record* critic thought: "A cheaper, more poorly constructed play has seldom been seen on any stage. It's characters are funny only when they are disgusting. It lacks tone, timing, scenario, good lines, acting ability and competent direction."

And so in Herman's fortieth year the bloody demise of *The Meal Ticket* shriveled his Broadway ambitions to mere talk. Almost from habit, especially at home with Sara, he carried on his role of frustrated author. But he spoke less about escaping from "The Devil's Island of the U.S.A.," about getting even at the bank and saving a little money ahead for a move to Wilkes-Barre or New York, some place where he could concentrate and write.

That dream never did have Sara's all-important support. She would have followed him to New York, but whenever he talked about "getting out of the goddamn sunshine," she could never see how ice and snow—and the old temptations of the city—could bring new inspiration. "Absolute nonsense," says Sara. "There's no such thing as a mental block. That's just humoring nonsense. If you have something to write, you write." And she would say to Herman, "Now you tell me what you could do in New York that is so literary and creative that you can't do here."

For Herman, the practical considerations were on Sara's side. Says John Houseman: "When you can earn twenty-five hundred dollars a week making jokes, and working two or three hours a day in the studio, and having long lunches, and getting drunk and making more jokes, why would you go to an attic and beat your brains out doing something you're afraid you might not be able to do? You can make a fortune as a dramatist. But you can't make a living as a dramatist."

However, Herman's screenwriting career was also on the wane. He had no credits at all in 1936, though in 1937 three movies with his credit were released. His old friend and boss Ben Schulberg, now flunking as an independent producer at Paramount, borrowed Herman to write *John Meade's Woman*, which failed at the box office. Like *Kane*, it dealt with a tycoon, a lumber baron played by Edward Arnold. At MGM a lavish spy story for Luise Rainer, *The Emperor's Candlesticks*, proved a disaster. His one success, however, was special. A comedy farce called *My Dear Miss Aldrich*, a seminewspaper movie and Walter Pidgeon's first MGM starring performance, was Herman's own original story and script. Thereafter at MGM the screenplays on which Herman worked were either shelved or he was replaced and received no credit.

One of these was *The Wizard of Oz*. He knew the whole panorama of *Oz* books well; his sons read every one and discussed them. Herman was convinced *The Wizard of Oz* could not be translated into a movie, and wrote a long memo to that effect. Then he set about getting off this disaster as quickly as possible. In three days he turned in a seventeen-page treatment notable for the folksy, Orphan Annie sweetness of Dorothy and Toto—and for a lost, chauffeur-driven limousine containing a rich woman and daughter, equally unpleasant, plus a Pekingese, Adolphus Ajax Rittenstaufen III, who is "too valuable to play." Five pages of satiric dialogue compare Adolphus with Toto, who "can count up to eight." After Herman turned in a fifty-six-page script five days later, unknown to him two more writers were assigned to *The Wizard*. Within two weeks Herman was off the film.

Herman was now beginning to compete with a new generation of screenwriters, young, Hollywood-grown writers who gave their work their full respect, intensity, and ambition. They were pushing the frustrated playwrights and novelists trapped in Hollywood by big money, and as Orson Welles put it, "deprived of the freedom of a decent living."

Ironically, one of those hustling young writers was Herman's much younger brother, Joe Mankiewicz. The ex-whiz kid at Paramount was in 1937 a twenty-eight-year-old wonder boy at MGM, earning $3,000 a week. Already a successful writer at MGM, with ambitions to direct his own scripts, Joe had been forced to become a producer by L. B. Mayer. Mayer was grooming Joe as a possible successor to the recently dead Irving Thalberg, the former vice-president in charge of production. Clearly, Joe had passed Herman.

There was a primal bond between the two brothers, the Mankiewicz family stamp—the bulldog look, the sense of superiority, the speed of tongue. Joe and Herman ignited each other in evenings of hysterical laughter. They felt that others in the room were mere straight men, privileged to hear the brothers Mankiewicz build their brilliant oral edifices. Theirs was the intoxication of shared snobbery as two fast-draw gunslingers might have felt in a saloon full of cowboys. "We used to take people on together and tear them apart," Joe remembers. "We had wonderful times."

But they were also yoked together by rankling disparities and jealousies. "There was a close hatred, within which they were inseparable," says actor James Mason's ex-wife, Pamela, a close friend of both the Mankiewicz brothers. A disciplined worker, a moderate drinker, a gambler who was able to quit gambling, Joe served as an implicit rebuke to Herman, who must have believed his brother's public success could have been his. Herman once said, "I've been an influence on Joe's life, but it's been mostly negative. Like Shaw said, 'Parents should be a warning to their children, not an example.' Nobody can deny I've been a good bad example."

In Herman's mind the successful Joe had become self-important, ruthless, and somehow fraudulent. Herman could not subdue his feelings. He would publicly refer to Joe as "Joe the genius." When Joe arrived late at a party, Herman said to a distant cousin of Sara's, Robert Pirosch, "Here's the little son of a bitch now." When screenwriter Frank Davis was about to collaborate with Joe at MGM, Herman took him aside and told him, "I think you ought to know that my brother is a shit." When Joe seemed poised to marry an English socialite, Herman scornfully explained to Nunnally Johnson, "He wants to be able to name his son Napier." He told another friend that Joe had picked her because she was no competition. "Joe can be a star on all levels," said Herman. "Even looks."

At Tower Road the attitude hovered that Joe did not deserve his eminence, that he was not all *that* good a writer. Herman let it be known to his family that he, not Joe, had actually written the hit *Million Dollar Legs* but had given the credit to Joe to boost his little brother. This was almost certainly not true, though Herman may well have worked on the script. A number of people had. In a contemporary review, the *Film Daily* listed Joe as "author" and named two "adapters," Henry Myers and Nick Barrows. Myers says the final script came out of *his* typewriter. Joe furiously insists that he himself wrote the movie.

But Herman took satisfaction in the fact that unlike his own credits, virtually all of Joe's successes, including Academy Award winners *All About Eve* and *A Letter to Three Wives*, were based on other writers' ideas. *The Barefoot Contessa* was Joe's only major original. *The New Yorker* once pointed out that somebody had plagiarized Joe. Said Herman to Joe: "I thought it was going to be the other way around."

The steadfast Sara echoed whatever feelings Herman had. When, in 1935, Herman was hired to write a film in England,

Sara wrote from Washington: "Did you show that big producer Joe and his wife your English contract, and was he properly impressed and depressed? Please be very superior and important with him."

Joe Mankiewicz had his own freight of bitterness. First the professor betrayed Joe by ignoring him as a boy. Then Herman, the admired father image, let him down. "When Herman kept demanding money, my rage and fear were so intermingled that I thought it would go on for the rest of my life and there was no way I could stop it. I was terrified of Herman. I never felt I could call on him for help. Everybody else in the world could. But if I did, somehow he'd bawl me out for what was happening to me."

Moreover, Joe considered Herman's fabled generosity an illusion done with other people's money for the sake of a *grande geste*, though Herman did pay most of his debts. It must have galled Joe that he himself had no reputation for openheartedness, while he was forever being asked to lend money to the "generous" brother and act as cosigner or comaker on Herman's loans from the Morris Plan. And he was the son with the money, who funneled it to their parents, who paid for their round-the-world trip.

It must have galled Joe that no matter how hard he worked on his homework, no matter how glittering his success, his brother maintained a kind of supremacy. Herman was the one who was the legend, the one famous for brilliance, the one everybody loved, the one who eventually achieved the greater masterpiece, *Citizen Kane.*

In contrast with Herman, Joe was liked but not adored. He had little talent for friendship. He had charm and impressive wit in his own right. But, says their mutual friend Dr. Fred Hacker, "Joe was essentially a solitary man." In Joe's boyhood the professor saved money by moving yearly from one tiny apartment to another, and Joe once said, "I became skillful at taking on the color of my environment without absorbing it, at participating in almost everything without becoming a part of anything." His onetime bachelor roommate, producer Bill Wright, says, "Joe's a fickle fellow. He extends himself chiefly to new enthusiasts." "Sometime," said Herman sardonically, "I'd like to meet somebody at Joe's birthday party I'd seen the year before."

Analyzing her two brothers, Erna Mankiewicz said, "Joe is a man of high principles, a fighter for causes. But you could sit for an entire evening and be practically in tears, and he wouldn't notice. If there was something bothering you, and you walked into a room where Herman was sitting, reading, after three or four minutes he would look up and say, 'What's the matter, kid?'"

Women did love Joe. "He was seeking love," says Pamela Mason, "and he was awfully lovable. He made you feel that he was desperately in love like a boy, taking your handkerchief home and sleeping with it under his pillow. He had a sweet quality, and you felt he was very open, probably because he was a very good talker." Joe talked to Pamela about his Hollywood conquests, which included Judy Garland, Linda Darnell, and Joan Crawford. "They were all famous," Pamela says. "It had to be a brand name. I realized he was operating from ego and competition. I think he spent his life competing with his father and then Herman, and presumably Herman was doing the same thing."

The studio day ended at five or six o'clock, though emergencies sometimes kept Herman later. If the day had been wasted, he was assailed with guilt and apprehension. "You make enough mistakes," said Herman, "and you lose your job, unless you're a nephew. You don't make too many mistakes, you keep your job, unless a nephew wants it."

Though Herman was an optimist, he must have felt his self-doubts were being confirmed. His Broadway hopes seemed finished. The studio system was riddling his confidence. He was protecting his pride by scorning his work and his bosses. He was nourishing his ego by entertaining himself and his world. He was retreating into the little boy part of himself, the delinquent child who actually thrived on failure and fed on the love that was proved when people rescued him. His primary protector was Sara, who constantly bandaged his life, perhaps saving him from an abyss, perhaps keeping the child from growing up, perhaps both.

Herman regarded himself and the world through the eyes of a superbly educated cynic. It was a devastating combination. As he once said about himself, "I read too much. I set myself too high a standard. My critical faculty has prospered at the expense of creative talent." The more Herman the intellectual knew that everything had been written already, the harder it was to see why anything was worth writing, and the easier it was to be overwhelmed by obstacles. "Where is that masterpiece that nobody has thought of?" Herman may have wondered. Oddly, it lay only a few years in his future.

In 1937, however, Herman told a friend, "I was to have been a distinguished American literatus along about this time. Various matters have interfered." That year Herman wrote a short satire titled "On Approaching Forty." Harold Ross rejected it, and Herman finally had to settle for the *Hollywood Reporter*.

The article began:

> Right before me, as I write, is a folder in which my wife keeps the blotters from Mr. Eschner, the insurance man, Don's first report card, the letter from the income tax people about the gambling loss at Tijuana, the press photograph of me greeting Helen Kane (in behalf of the studio) at the Pasadena Station, and my literary output. There are four separate pieces of this output and they are all excellent. I hope some friend will gather them into a little book after my death. There is plenty of ninety point Marathon in the world, and wide margins can't be hard to find.

Each tiny, unfinished fragment was presented in its entirety. The article ended:

> The fourth note looks rather naked now, all by itself on the

desk. It says, simply: "Write piece for *New Yorker* on reaching thirty-fifth birthday. No central idea. Just flit from paragraph to paragraph." People who complain that my work is slipshod would be a little surprised to find that I just am *not* always satisfied with the first thing I put down. I'm changing that thirty-fifth to fortieth right now.

There is, from a city editor's point of view, no news to report. Your Ma has not spent a weekend adrift in a leaky yacht, sails, engines, rudder disabled, in Santa Catalina Channel; your brother has not been found by a frantic searching posse after being separated from his fellow Boy Scouts on a hiking trip up Mount Wilson; your sister has not disappeared, to be discovered thirty-five hours later under a neighboring porch tearstained but otherwise unharmed—your sister, of course, not the porch—and I have not held the winning ticket on a sweepstake, Irish or otherwise.

—HERMAN MANKIEWICZ,
A letter to his son Don

THE INSOUCIANT YOUNG NEWLYWED PHOTOGRAPHED ON THE steamship sailing to Germany in 1920 posed seventeen years later for another eloquent picture. This time Herman Mankiewicz, forty years old, is standing on the lawn in front of his Beverly Hills home, a long two-story Spanish house with a tile roof extending over a wood balcony. Sara is not standing next to Herman in the picture. Instead, one sees his thirteen-year-old son, Frank, lean, handsome, vigorous in sharply creased white duck pants, necktie and sports coat.

In contrast with Frank, and himself in the 1920 photo, Herman's stocky body is plump. His pinstriped suit is double-breasted, a tailoring style useful for concealing bulk. The

Slavic face is now rounder and soft with flesh. Receding hair has extended the great sweep of brow. But the mischievous smile still slightly curves his lips.

This house at 1105 Tower Road, later purchased after years of rental, had become Herman's permanent home. Living next door, at one time or another, were Oscar and Dorothy Hammerstein and Alice Faye and Tony Martin. Mary Astor lived on the corner near Arthur Rubinstein. Maria Montez moved in later, across the street. And almost every day, taking her morning constitutional, Paulette Goddard walked by Herman's home, her brown hair tied by a white bow.

Inside, instead of Hollywood luxury, there was New York solidity: plumped chairs and sofas, print patterns, ruffles at the bottoms, all meticulously placed; Sara's grand piano; the Capehart, and books lining the walls. Nevertheless, Hollywood was present. Over the years various couples came to cook, serve, and chauffeur. Upstairs lived a white-uniformed governess. In a rear cell a laundress labored. A Japanese gardener came once a week—plus a man who cleaned the frog-shaped swimming pool. Herman would impulsively raise salaries, saying, "I will not allow anybody to work for me who doesn't make a living wage." Sara was not allowed to fire servants without getting them a new job. Herman insisted: "Nobody is going to leave my house not knowing where they're going to sleep or get a meal."

Upstairs, by mutual agreement, Herman and Sara had separate bedrooms. And for herself Sara had created a self-portrait of the Hollywood Sara, a decade older than the young girl in Washington. Her wallpaper consisted of butterflies on a white background. The oversized bed was pale oyster. The figured coverlet was edged in lace. The telephone was white, with buttons for ringing the servants. The satin-covered chaise longue was cream-colored; the chairs were elegantly curved copies of French antiques. Her bureau drawers held perfumed sachets, silk stockings rolled like pastry, rows and rows of leather gloves—light brown, medium brown, dark brown, gray, black, russet, green—pristine, as if never violated by hands. In a mirror-paneled dressing room, ranks of perfume bottles stood on a glass table.

Sara believed separate bedrooms "made it all the more romantic." But Herman knew that if he was going to join her in bed, he had to bring his own pillow because, says Sara, "I couldn't stand the thought of that greasy head on that beautiful. . . ."

Herman's room made a dramatic contrast: a massive bed, huge bureau bearing the silver-handled carafe swiped from Twentieth Century-Fox and a big bottle of Emperin codeine for recurrent headaches, vials of sleeping pills. Books and newspapers lay everywhere. For Herman, the geographic center of the house was the huge, overstuffed easy chair. Here Herman peacefully read his books, smoking, wearing pajamas under his worn bathrobe, bare shanks, and feet in carpet slippers on the footstool.

Herman's evening routine at Tower Road began when he yelled from the foyer, "Schnucks! Where are you?" "That," says Sara, "was the wonderful moment in my whole day. Then I knew he was sober and he was fine, and it was my husband coming home from a day's work like all good husbands should."

Joseph P. Kennedy, for a time the owner of RKO Pictures, once remarked that the only men in Hollywood with a true family life were Sam Goldwyn and Herman Mankiewicz. While Sara lay on his bed, Herman from his chair would quiz her about servant problems, her shopping trips, her soirees in her bedroom at which the butler passed coffee and little cakes on a silver tray. All minutiae of the children had to be reported and commented on. Frank, at ten, was reading Sandburg's biography of Lincoln. "I haven't the heart to tell him the book has an unhappy ending," Herman said. Don was picked as running guard on his class football team. "I have a feeling he'd be more comfortable as sitting guard," Herman commented. The boys' school had had basketball games. "They lost a closely contested game in the last second of play by the score of fifty-five to four," Herman declared.

From boyhood Frank was an extroverted athlete with a talent for turning on charm. In his school memento book he wrote "Frank" opposite the categories "Richest" and "Likely to Be Most Successful." Frank was later a good student and eventually valedictorian of his class at UCLA. Following his father's political interests, he went on to be a lawyer, the director of the Peace Corps in Latin America under President Johnson, press secretary for Robert Kennedy for two years prior to Kennedy's assassination, national political director for Senator McGovern's campaign for the presidency. "I always figured that if people got scores on tests, you should get the highest scores," Frank says. "And if there was a game, you should win it."

Together Herman and Frank went to midget auto races and high school basketball games, and at home played a football board game involving strategy and plays. Writing to Don away at school, Herman said, "Frank is a bit on the subdued side on a account of a bad thrashing—33 to 0—I gave him via the Layden football game. I'm really worried about him because this sudden enforced realization of his physical inadequacy has come at the same time as the news that Margaret Sullavan, who unsuspected by us has been a special dream princess, is now in her third marriage—a deplorable fact that is causing great disturbances and readjustments in his outlook on life. I suggest that you make no preparations to leave at a moment's notice, because if you *should* have to come, everything humanly possible will have been done before your arrival anyway."

Where Frank was bright and competitive, Don was brilliant. Herman called him "the intellectual." Don completed high school in two and a half years and entered Columbia at age sixteen. Ultimately he patterned himself after the writer side of his father, giving up his law studies to become, for a time, the successful fiction writer his father wanted to be. Don wrote three novels, including the Harper Prize novel *Trial,* and then settled into movie and television writing. He did the pilot TV scripts for *Marcus Welby, M.D.* and *Ironsides.*

But Don, as a boy, was a worry to Herman and Sara. He was overweight, deeply introverted, sloppy, given to bouts of nonachievement, and his marks plunged. Herman would lecture him sternly, but more often nudged with affectionate irony. Once he parodied his reproofs, wiring Don, "Want it distinctly understood we are not sending you to school to crack ribs Stop Do not see why you don't feel you can crack ribs on your own time in Tower Road during vacation Stop Under no circumstances are you to crack any more ribs without first checking with us Love Pop."

On nights that he and Sara were going out, Herman would circle the boys' dinner table, talking and picking up lamb chops off plates and taking bites, allegedly to test if the food was good. Then he would criticize what they were eating, telling them, for example, that salads are bad for you. They should not be eaten. He would say, "Do you know that in England a man was once tried for murder, and it was proved that he had threatened his wife and that he had gone to the pharmacist and bought the rat poison, and traces of this poison were found on her plate and in her body, and the jury refused to convict simply because it was shown that an hour and a half before her death she had eaten a salad?" The boys and their friends would nod their heads and for years believed what they had heard.

When the boys were older, dinners at Tower Road were often shouted political debates, as in Herman's youth. "Apparently in your day patriotism has become an elective," Herman yelled. "In my day it was a required course." The movie business was regarded as unfit for conversation. "If I hadn't known what he did," Frank says, "I wouldn't have known what he did." And Herman did not do *all* the talking. It was only an illusion that meals were one-man forums on the history of Tammany Hall, on the ignorance and idiocy of Eleanor Roosevelt, or on the role of the Winchester rifle in the settling of the West. "It was just that other people spoke in a normal tone of voice," notes Frank, who considers his hours with his father among the most interesting and instructive in his life.

Sometimes Herman and his sons competed with elaborate puns. Herman concocted a long story placing Leo Durocher, the Chicago Cubs star Phil Cavarretta, and Congressman Emanuel Celler all on the same train. A traveler, walking down the aisle, said, "There's Manny asleep twixt the Cub and the Lip." It was Herman who invented the famous pun on the search for Syngman Rhee's missing son, a reporter for *Life* magazine. The policeman who found him says, "Ah, sweet Mister Rhee of *Life*, at last I have found you."

Frank, the achiever, was closer to Sara, and Don favored his father, perhaps because the two shared a guilty and unspoken bond. Don was also a gambler. As a boy he would bet on which friend playing catch would first drop the ball. At Columbia University he was so deeply into horse racing that he published a profitable campus tip sheet. Repeating his father's habit, Don probably shared the same psychological causes. Psychiatrist Dr. Robert Custer, a specialist in compulsive gambling, believes its roots are in "psychic pain." This pain comes from a corrosive situation the gambler cannot solve: a domineering wife or husband, an unpleasant job, feelings of inadequacy begun early in life, often triggered by an overly demanding father. "Whether gamblers win or lose," says Dr. Custer, "just being in action relieves the pain."

Later, in the 1940's, when Don was courting his first wife, Ilene Korsen, they would go to Pacific coast baseball games. There would be Herman wearing a long-sleeved, blue gabardine shirt tucked into tight gray flannel pants. It was a virtual uniform among the gamblers bunched near third base, betting on the runs per inning, on whether the batter would get on base, on whether he would strike out. Seeing Don, Herman made his little salute, no words, just that signal which meant Sara should never be told.

Frank married Holly Jolly from San Bernardino, California, in 1952. Where Ilene Korsen was Jewish and therefore acceptable to Sara, Holly Jolly was not only a divorcée but a fallen-away Mormon. Sara would say, "Now, look, James and Pamela Mason are coming to dinner, and I'd like you to look nice. Wear that nice black Kimberly knit I gave you."

Sara once asked Holly if there were any professionals in her family. "What do you mean, professionals?" answered Holly. "My father installs refrigeration equipment."

"Are there any doctors and lawyers?" Sara asked.

"No," Holly replied.

"Dentists?"

"No."

"Writers or painters?"

"No." (Holly says, "I could have given her Uncle Wayne, who painted the WPA mural on the wall of the post office, but since he did it by the hour, I didn't think she would care!")

Whenever Herman encountered Holly churning with angry dismay, he would comfort her with teasing. His eyes would twinkle and he would say, for example, "Mormon, huh?"

"Not anymore, Herman. I left the church."

"Don't give me that. You left. How did you do that?"

"I wrote a letter."

"Give me that address. Where can *I* write?" And then Herman would add, "Let's get some things clear. I don't mind that you're not Jewish. But there are two things that bother me. One, if you're going to be a gentile, you cannot look so Jewish. Some blond dye would be a big improvement. We cannot bring in this dark-haired girl with a big nose. Secondly, is there anybody in your family who has any money?"

"Nobody, Herman."

"Well, think about it. Maybe there's some relative that you

don't know very well with things to inherit and you'll get it when he dies?"

"Nobody. I can't think of a soul."

"OK, I'm not talking about big money now. I'm reduced to asking if there's anybody with ready cash."

"Nobody."

And then Herman, who had always told Frank that it was just as easy to fall in love with a rich girl as a poor one, would look up at the ceiling, shrug, and say, "A lifetime of instruction gone."

Failing to cajole Holly out of her misery, he would address the problem directly. "You know, you've got a lot to learn," he once said. "Sara's a funny combination of sophistication and sheer provincialism, and you gotta learn to ride with it a little bit. Don't be too harsh in your judgment of her. She's capable of great tenderness. She's a fine woman."

"Of course, I love Sara very much now," Holly says. "She fascinates me. I think Sara may be the only person I've ever known who has no self-doubts."

By the late 1930's Sara had established herself as a personage in Hollywood. And Herman joked about abandoning all resistance to her queenly authority. "I have left my seat in Her Majesty's Opposition," he said. "A blinding flash of insight showed me that not only was I the leader of this group, I was its sole membership."

Most Hollywood wives spent their time cultivating the wives of important executives, discussing how much they paid their butlers, how to take a $500 I. Magnin dress out for approval and then get it copied, and which girls might be their husbands' latest mistress. Says Lillie Messenger, who did verbal book precis for L. B. Mayer, "In a community in which everybody looked up to people because they were famous, she was Sara Mankiewicz and she stood *for* something."

Sara had matured into a classic Old Testament Jewish

beauty: large brown eyes in a small, oval, sweet face, delicate skin, black hair. She had intrinsic dignity. She radiated concern and was the first person on the phone to friends in trouble. Their friend Eddie Knopf remembers: "We used to say that Sara was a bad-weather friend." She had a knack for creating intimacy, for being adored. In her way she was a seducer. Sara was so liked and respected that mere acquaintances feared banishment from her affections. She was very strong. "In a situation like hers," says Marion Spitzer, "you either develop a steel core or you die. And she wasn't going to die." When angry at Sara, Herman bellowed, "You're training to be a matriarch."

Sara was unblinkingly loyal to Herman. She loved her "Hermie sweetheart." Says Holly Mankiewicz: "His needs and what he wanted and what made him comfortable and uncomfortable were the dominant theme in her life, always." Sara was also—and always—proud of Herman. In Sara's mind her husband was as good a writer as Ben Hecht and as handsome as any movie star in Hollywood. Her reports on Herman to friends so glowed that Margaret Sullavan once interrupted her, saying, "I don't think we're talking about the same man."

Herman expressed his own deep feelings when he wrote Sara, in the thirties, from New York. "I do miss you and love you so much," he said. "You will please, please believe, Schnucks, that you are the central object of my real thoughts always. Despite all my mishegoss [craziness], I can't help but see clearly—nor can you—that I am never happy except in your approval of me and miserable in your disapproval."

"In the Mankiewicz family you never really hug," says Joe's son Tom. "You caress each other with a one-liner." Every day of their marriage Herman wooed Sara with his own particular Mankiewicz tenderness. Sara saved a sheaf of telegrams he sent during her trips East to her parents: "Missing you and loving you—stop—everything as it was ten years ago only the kids are feeling fine." Or: "You must come out here sometimes, the climate is great and am sure you'll find quite a few old friends and former Broadway and Baltimore acquaintances. Guess who."

He continually reassured her: "After slow start, finally getting more rapid tempo of 'My wife's gone to the country, Hurray' technique. Thus last night had dinner at home, saw Cleopatra at studio, had Ovaltine at Brown Derby. Would appreciate Christmas gift of one gross candles for burning at both ends. Love. Pretty Boy."

It was a marriage-long signal of affection when Herman signed his letters and cables with a gallery of mind-bending names: Karel, Matchboxes of Cholly, Julian, Maurice, Old Subscriber, Stinnes, Giovanni, Luigi, Abelard, Gaston, Knarf, Columbus, Ambivalent Max, Maecenus.

A number of times, as Sara traveled back to California from the East, Herman quietly journeyed to Gallup, New Mexico, and got aboard the Super Chief. Without warning he knocked on Sara's compartment door. "It was a shocking thing," says Sara. "He'd come in, get undressed—naked—and get into my bed. It was the most indecent thing that could happen to a person. And I must say, I loved it."

Behind Sara's back, especially to women friends, he talked warmly of her: "Sara feels . . . Sara says. . . ." If he joked about her, it was self-mocking: "Sara doesn't understand about my drinking." Frank remembers that there was a sweetness in his father's remark: "I have this terrible swelling on my eye which is getting worse and worse, but your mother, the doctor, does not wish me to seek medical help elsewhere. And of course, she knows best."

One of Herman's important offerings to Sara was his tolerance of her Jewish devotion and kosher household. He insisted that they observe the dietary laws at home; he went outdoors to smoke on the Sabbath, always led the Seder ceremony, and insisted the boys be bar mitzvahed.

But Herman never pretended religious devotion. When Herman and Sara gave Frank and Holly their wedding, Holly was moved by the rabbi's words and went glowingly to Herman. "Wasn't this beautiful?" she enthused.

"Yessiree," Herman answered. "But I could have done without the witch doctor and the mumbo jumbo." Then he kissed Holly on the cheek so her feelings would not be hurt.

On the other hand, Jewishness was good ground for ridicule. Standing in his room, Herman watched Sam Jaffe pass in the street below, clad in a dazzlingly white tennis shirt and shorts, and carrying his tennis balls in a little white reticule. "Behold the outdoor Jew," Herman said.

When the writer Barney Glazer, a Jew, divorced his plain wife and married his mistress, Herman sent the newlyweds a cable on their wedding night aboard an ocean liner. He quoted the line in the Seder ceremony: "Wherefore is this night different from all other nights?"

Herman scorned the hypocrisy of those who pretended to be only partly Jewish. He defined a half-Jew as "somebody whose mother and father were Jewish." But until his marriage Herman's Jewishness had been unimportant in his life. However, particularly at the time of Hitler and Mussolini and the approaching Holocaust, Herman hated being set apart from humanity, one of a scorned and persecuted minority. He wanted to be purely an American.

In the late 1940's, after Israel had been recognized by the United States, Herman at a party presciently attacked the concept of a Jewish homeland based on religion and at the expense of the Arabs. He forecast permanent turmoil and advocated other countries providing asylum. The brutalities against the European Jews were evoked, and a young Jewish writer, Arthur Ross, reminded Herman of his own vulnerability as a Jew. "What makes you think the same thing isn't right around the corner here?" Herman looked at Ross for a long stricken moment, left the house, stood brooding by the swimming pool for a half hour, and went home.

*　　*　　*

Herman did love Sara. But to be endured, to be cleaned up after, even to be loved in that all-protective way chafed that part of Herman which agreed with his friend Charlie Lederer, who said, "Sara was a pain in the ass, always the eternal woman being done wrong to by Herman."

And Sara herself, looking back on her marriage, wonders whether, perhaps, she was actually bad for Herman. "Maybe," she says, "if *he* had been the one to say to *me*, 'For Christ's sake! Did you *have* to go out and get drunk last night; did you *have* to spend this money! You had no right to. . . .' But I was always so concerned and disciplined. I was such a goody-goody. I don't know why he didn't hit me. Years later when I read *Of Human Bondage,* the artist explains why he left his wife and says, 'She was a good woman, Goddamn her!' I understood what he was talking about."

Conflagrations could be sparked by very little. Sara would want to refuse an invitation, knowing it would end in trouble. Sometimes she declined without telling him. "But I never did anything heinous he could pin on me," Sara says. "So he had trouble working up a legitimate anger."

There were occasions when Herman systematically created a crisis, an excuse to slam out of the house and go drinking. He would provoke her into saying, "Herman, that was wrong of you. Why did you . . . ?"

And Herman would say, "Can't you *once* in your lifetime be on *my* side? You haven't heard the whole story, and you're already on the *other* side."

"No, Herman," Sara would answer, her voice full of sarcasm, "I'll never be on your side. I'll *always* take Sam Jaffe's side *every* time."

One evening Sara avoided every issue with such saintly compliance that Herman was frantic. Finally, Sara mentioned a dinner engagement the next day, Tuesday. "Tomorrow is Wednesday," Herman said.

Sara dropped into the trap. "No," she said, "Tuesday."

"WEDNESDAY!"

"Herman, it's Tuesday. I'll get a calendar."

"Oho! The Delphic oracle! By God, that's enough. I do not wish it to be recorded in the pages of history that . . . to hell with. . . ." And out the door he went.

Whenever Herman engineered one of those exits, Sara would listen to the car careen out the driveway. "Then I was a wreck," she says. "I'd call up my sister and get awfully busy with the children, see that they were bathed, put them to bed. Then the real, horrible worry would set in."

Sometimes Herman was simply circulating among friends. Eddie Knopf remembers the evening when he and Mildred were just finishing their dessert, chocolate pudding. The doorbell rang. Herman walked in, wordlessly pulled a chair up to the table, and said to the maid, "I'll have a plate, please." He took a liberal helping, topping it with whipped cream. "Would you bring me a small glass of whiskey, please?" he asked the maid. She brought a glass and a bottle of scotch. She started to pour it. "I'll pour it," Herman said. He filled it to the brim, finished the pudding and the scotch.

Then he said, "What did you have for dinner?"

"Corned beef."

"I'd like some corned beef." He took a generous helping, refilled his glass. The Knopfs sat silent, watching the performance. Consuming the beef and the whiskey, Herman said, "Okay, now I'm ready for a little dessert." When the second dish of chocolate pudding was gone, he said to Eddie Knopf, "Okay, I came down to play some gin with you." Knopf said all right. Then Herman turned to the maid, "Do you have any bicarbonate of soda?" She brought it to him with a glass. "I don't need any glass," Herman said. He filled a spoon with the bicarbonate, dumped it onto his tongue, and chased it with another glass of whiskey. "Then," Knopf remembers, "there came forth from the bowels of Herman a burp the likes of which the world had never heard."

They played gin rummy, Herman drinking more scotch and periodically repeating the bicarbonate of soda and the burp. At eleven-thirty he said, "Well, I've got to go home. Big day tomorrow. Do you have any sleeping pills?"

Knowing Herman was forbidden them, Knopf said, "No, I'm sorry."

Herman insisted, "I want those little red ones. Seconal."

"I don't have any," Knopf said.

"Okay," Herman replied. He walked up the stairs and into Mildred Knopf's bedroom without knocking. She was in bed, reading. From her he got two Seconal.

Downstairs he poured another little glass of scotch and washed down one of the pills.

Knopf said, "For God's sake, Herman, don't do that. Wait till you get home."

"Now listen," Herman said. "I know myself. This way I will just be going to sleep as I come into my driveway—and I'll take the second one just as I go to bed. It works absolutely like a charm."

Sometimes Herman's nocturnal escapes took him to Chasen's. Dave Chasen had been a vaudeville performer. Partially financed by Harold Ross, he parlayed a sparerib joint into a small, luxurious Beverly Hills restaurant that had become virtually a Hollywood club.

One of Herman's frequent companions at Chasen's was the young Irish actress Geraldine Fitzgerald, whom he told, "They'll never see you as the central figure; you'll always be the one who's combing the heroine's hair."

"Unsay that. Unsay it," she cried out.

"All right," Herman said. "I won't say it."

Geraldine Fitzgerald remembers: "I wasn't a bit afraid of Mankiewicz. Being Irish, I recognized him. I knew he had that terribly Irish thing: that inability to confess to a genuine concern for another person. The Irish are cursed by this gift of mockery, which includes self-mockery. And this mockery is just another name for self-destruction.

"I took Mankiewicz to be a very good man with a thin

veneer of cynicism—like people in Ireland I grew up with who were witty and creative and very special. It was an absolute given that they were decent people who were against everything evil—not pro-child labor, not anti-Semitic, not antiblack. Since they were 'good citizens,' they were then permitted any sort of outrageous ironic observations. And their propriety was never questioned. And when I met Mankiewicz, I found exactly the kind of Irishman I most admired."

Once at 2 A.M., after Chasen's closed, Geraldine and Herman stopped to buy the early-morning edition of the Los Angeles *Times*. Across the front page was the banner headline "Rumanians Kill Jews." Herman handed the paper to the newsboy. "No," said Herman. "I don't want that one. I want the one that says, 'Jews Kill Rumanians.'"

Herman often drank without getting drunk, and there were friends, like Geraldine Fitzgerald, who never saw him even befuddled. Nevertheless, after different companions, there were early mornings when he would come home wobbly and belligerent. Sara, waiting up, would hear his car turn in from Benedict Canyon. She would quickly snap off her light, get into bed, and feign sleep. He would come stamping up the stairs, talking loudly to himself or singing: "Nobody knows the trouble I seen. . . ." Often, to see if he had managed to awaken her, he would go out on the balcony and peer through Sara's window.

Eventually he would march into her room. "Schnucks?" He would turn the light on in her face. "Get up. I want to talk to you." ("Very peremptory," Sara says.) Or while she lay there, he would tell her a funny story or an anecdote from the evening, watching her closely to see if she was angry or still crying. He would return to his own bedroom, sit in his chair, and yell, "Come in here!" ("I could have killed him.")

She would sit on the edge of his bed, exhausted from worry and desperate to return to bed but afraid to enrage Herman further for fear he would go out again. "Now look, honey," she would say, "you have an early-morning appointment." ("I'd be very factual.") Let's call it a night. You've done enough damage. Let's just. . . ."

"Sit here while I smoke this one cigarette." So Sara would sit a half hour or more, trying to talk on safe subjects: the children, gossip, when the script he was writing was due ("He didn't want to talk much about that"). Finally, he would say, "If you sit here while I undress, then you can go." While she waited on the edge of the bed, Herman would get under the covers, kiss her tenderly, and say in a mock New York accent, "You're not mad on me anymore?"

"No, Herman, I'm not mad on you anymore."

"Promise that you're not going to be mad on me from now on?"

Once, on a day she was to leave to visit her parents, Herman decided they should get a divorce. "Now look," he said, "it's silly for us to go on like this. You're going to Washington anyway, so you see your lawyer there, and I'll see mine here."

"Herman, if you want a divorce," Sara said, "maybe you'd be better off. ("That was the phrase that got him. I could see a shadow pass over him.") But what do we need lawyers for? What are we going to divide up? Your debts? I know whatever money you make you're going to give me. So why are we seeing lawyers?" ("And suddenly if we couldn't have lawyers and conferences and consternation, the glamour went out of a divorce, and he lost interest.")

But Sara never thought of herself as Poor Sara. She says emphatically, "The scales were weighted on the side of happiness and achievement and joys, rather than hardship. I know that I have been blessed. I don't know any other wife who's reached such heights of real glory. Nobody in my family . . . I wouldn't exchange one day for any of their serene lives."

Herman often managed weeks and months of complete

sobriety, drinking only ginger ale. "Everything was glorious," Sara says. "The future looked rosy." Their son Frank, in part protected at home by closed doors and being whisked out of the way, remembers only a father who came home sober, ate dinner, went to bed just like everybody else's pop. Throughout the 1930's, says Frank, he had no idea that his father had either a drinking or gambling problem.

When Herman did drink, it was during the day and as secretly from his family as he could manage so that his family would not see him in such a state. Nunnally Johnson once pointed out to Helen Hayes that Herman had shot glasses concealed throughout the Tower Road house, in vases, behind books. While Sara was out in the garden, Herman quietly filled them with his day's surreptitious supply. In his early Hollywood years, when he had to dry out, Herman tried to keep that a secret, too. The wife of a childhood friend Carlton Coombs went to a Los Angeles hospital to have her baby. There on the obstetrics floor, getting well in the last place anybody would look for them, were Laurence Stallings and Herman Mankiewicz.

Sara, however, had few illusions. She also had some sub rosa stratagems of her own, pouring half a bottle of scotch down the sink and filling it up with water. Sara insists Herman's drinking was an antidote to trouble and fuel to meet the pressure to perform and be funny. Joe Mankiewicz believes it was Herman's way of hitting back at Sara, his father, the Establishment, Louis B. Mayer. Herman's psychiatrist friend Dr. Fred Hacker says, "He had a very domineering, masterful, assertive father. I would think he tried to identify with his father, while at the same time there was a very strong competition, which he knew he would lose, for the affection of his mother. Therefore, his drinking was probably a surrender gesture, an attempt to play forever the role of an infant, a total falling apart, an inability to handle himself, total reliance on other people, particularly his wife, a real return to the womb."

Herman believed he drank because he was neurotic. In 1937 he began going to the psychiatrist Dr. Ernst Simmel, an eminent German refugee who had been a close friend of Freud's. Psychiatry was fashionable then in Hollywood, and several of Herman's friends were also seeing Simmel. Herman suggested they all wear sweat shirts emblazoned with a huge *S*. Moss Hart had the appointment preceding Herman's. As Hart came out of the office, Herman teased him so mercilessly, Hart finally switched appointments. Another of Herman's copatients was George Gershwin. He came to Simmel after a series of other psychiatrists had been ineffective in treating his cataclysmic headaches. Simmel immediately told Gershwin he had a brain tumor. By then it was inoperable.

Under analysis, Herman at first enjoyed a rush of optimism, stopped drinking, and announced, "The days of the week are only a goy attempt to establish a difference where there is no difference. Each one is just a twenty-four-hour slice of life, surrounding a nine A.M. to ten A.M. visit to the Viennese *Obermacher*." He called Simmel "my caretaker," and when Sara argued back or reprimanded him, he would say, "Oh, you're going to get it tomorrow."

At one point Simmel decided the treatment required several weeks of rest away from the temptations and strains of his Hollywood life. Simmel suggested a tiny psychiatric rest home in Alhambra. Herman telephoned Sara and said he was being put away in a booby hatch. She was satisfactorily shocked but rallied and asked what she should pack for him. "Oh," said Herman, "just my cocked hat, my picture of Josephine, and a little birdseed."

The sessions with Simmel lasted two years, and ultimately the psychoanalysis failed. There was less pain for Herman in remaining his neurotic self than in changing. He self-defeatingly kept Simmel laughing. Herman began using his new smattering of psychiatric analysis to excuse his behavior and eventually started ridiculing analysts who believed that "if your mother locked you in the closet when you were a child, you're going to hate closets." To his card-playing friends he would deride Simmel, "Great analyst. He couldn't stop my gambling, but I know why I gamble." The two men agreed to end the sessions. Herman exited with a joke. After two years of talking about himself, Herman paused at Simmel's door, turned, and said, "Incidentally, I wanted you to know— I don't think I ever told you—I have a sister and I hate her."

Sometimes, when the pressures were more than he could bear, Herman took himself into isolation. With a load of books, quite sober, he would hole up in a third-rate hotel on Santa Monica Boulevard. After three or four days he would call Sara: "Come and get me." When she arrived in his little room, he would give his two-fingered salute and go silently out to the car while she packed his things. "It was heartbreaking," Sara remembers.

Sometimes he would go to New York. "His father was there," Sara recalls, "and he could get more solid help. They had a wonderful relationship—like doctor and patient, but with love." These trips were always followed by the promises that punctuated Herman's life. Returning by ship via the Panama Canal and working on a script, Herman wrote Sara in 1933:

> I have, of course, been doing a lot of thinking about myself and I've come to the conclusion that I want nothing so much as to get home and prove that I'm aware of my responsibilities to you and the kids and anxious to make good on them. We're going to be happier than we ever were, Schnuggles. I've gotten my mishegoss completely out of me. When next you see me, I'll have been almost fourteen days on the wagon—and that's the way I'm going to stay. I've been pretty bad, darling, but I'm going to be what you want me to be. I love you terribly, Schnuggles. Please wire me and tell me you love me.

Early in that year of 1937 Irene Selznick, who lived at the top of Tower Road, received an urgent summons from Sara. The two women started walking and met halfway, in a bend of the road. They stood there and chatted. Sara, at age forty, was pregnant. Should she have an abortion? She was profoundly embarrassed. A woman her age. How would she face people? The boys were just reaching the age when . . . economically it was . . . they hadn't planned . . . it was certainly going to be a boy. And, Sara said to Irene, "I'm telling you, it will just be another screaming Mankiewicz, another of those big bruising men. I don't need another penis around the house. The Aaronsons, they don't exist."

"But, Sara," Irene said, "maybe it will be a little girl."

"Think of Erna," said Sara.

Herman and Sara decided to have the baby. They swore each other to secrecy and promptly spread the news. Herman told George Oppenheimer and threatened to kill him if he failed to show surprise when Sara informed him. Much later Oppenheimer took her to a movie, and Sara announced she was pregnant. Oppenheimer feigned such amazement he almost drove off the road. At home afterward Sara told Herman, "George was so cute about my having a baby. He was so surprised."

"The damned hypocrite," Herman said. "I told him two months ago."

Sara, feeling strong movement inside, still feared the baby would be a boy. And so in her mind she willed the image of a little girl with golden braids. On the back of a section torn from a handbill for *Mother Goose,* the story of Mack Sennett, Sara tried out names for girls: "Maria Mankiewicz, Ellen Mankiewicz, Mary Mankiewicz." She made a red line opposite "Johanna Mankiewicz," the name of Herman's mother.

On September 30, 1937, the pains began. Sara immediately entered the hospital. Nothing. False labor. The next morning Herman and the boys arrived. Still nothing. "There was great consternation that I might do this thing that afternoon and they couldn't go to the football game," Sara recalls. But luck held, they went to the game, Washington beat USC, 21 to 7, and they returned, Sara remembers, "smelling of hot dogs and full of football talk and not paying much attention to me." The children went home, and Herman and Sam Jaffe went out to dinner. At 12:01 A.M. the baby was born.

At 4 A.M. Sara regained consciousness and was told, "Mrs. Mankiewicz, you have a beautiful little girl." The baby was brought to her, a small shape in a pink blanket. All Sara could see was golden hair, "like a halo," she says. She telephoned home, and Herman answered. "Herman, we've got the most beautiful little girl."

"Yes," Herman said, "she is the most beautiful thing I have seen in my life." And they both cried.

The next day Herman arrived at the hospital carrying a tiny French embroidered silk handbag and a little parasol.

Irene Selznick came with tears streaming down her face. And Sara asked, "Did you see what I saw?"

"Sara," Irene said, "it's not a Mankiewicz, but it's not an Aaronson either. How in hell . . . whose baby is it, Sara?"

In the *Hollywood Reporter* the Rambling Reporter announced, "The Herman Mankiewicz's baby is soooooo beautiful." George Jessel's wife, Norma Talmadge, was "as excited as if I had given birth to her myself" and presented little Johanna with a pearl necklace. The Hammersteins gave a pink chair; George Cukor, a brown teddy bear; Mrs. Irving Berlin, bath towels; the Harpo Marxes, a white bassinet; Louis B. Mayer's mother, a high chair. Moss Hart wired Herman, "Congratulations. Tell Sara I'm having an opening on Monday, too, and give her my love." Professor Mankiewicz wired, "Welcome thrice welcome, you gracious gift of God, may you be a blessing to yourself and all the family."

Flowers overwhelmed the room from Ben Schulberg, Gregory Ratoff, Ernst Lubitsch, F. Scott Fitzgerald. Fitzgerald's bouquet bore a bon voyage card, printed with a picture of a ship. On it he wrote, "This isn't the correct card, Sara, but I refer to the daughter's journey on the sea of life."

"Nobody had such a baby," says Irene Selznick. "If you put her in the window of. . . . It was as though it didn't matter what Sara had gone through or suffered, because the gods knew and they rewarded her. And Herman and Sara started over in a curious way. The magic."

Herman would slip into the baby's room and stand looking down at her, on his face a mingling of tenderness and introspection. If somebody came in, he said, "Have you ever seen anything like this?"

"Johanna had a strong resemblance to Mank," Geraldine Fitzgerald says. "I think his persona didn't fit what he would have wanted it to be. And here was his child as beautiful outside as he'd like to have been."

Herman watched his daughter grow up as though monitoring a slow-motion miracle. In a letter to Don at Columbia, Herman said the truth about Johanna was impossible to write:

> I might, with more chance of success try to put into words a picture of a moonbeam, Luckman passing sixty yards for a touchdown against the Green Bay Packers in the final four seconds of play, a mystically translucent cloud in a perfectly conceived aquamarine heaven, individually prepared French fried onions, the primary silence upon a peak in Darien, and a sailor's face as Columbus states flatly that it *is* land and not a mirage—all, of course, added to a Ziegfeld first night in the early 20's.

Herman called Johanna Miss Viking and decided that she had accepted him "much the way one gets reconciled to baldness." Each morning he awaited her knock and her entrance "full of simulated surprise and pleasure." They would cross to Sara's room, where Johanna began "a ten-minute routine that includes sex, impishness, a slow-breaking smile of eternal wisdom, and hair-breadth escapes from cracking her skull against the bottom of the tea table." In time she augmented this with another ritual, carrying everything from Sara's dressing table piece by piece to her mother's bed, while Sara watched "with an expression closely duplicating the look on Mrs. Sarah Roosevelt's face as she watched her son being inaugurated."

Herman enjoyed making gentle fun of Sara's pride—and indirectly his own. He wrote Don at college:

> If you care to believe the story your Ma will tell you that Johanna has said 'Choo-choo' and 'I've been wondering when you were going to take me East to see my grandparents, my brother at Columbia and the scenic beauties in and around Washington, D.C., to say nothing of the historic buildings in the nation's capitol itself'—it's perfectly all right with me. I won't even say flatly that Johanna didn't say those things. All I can say is that I didn't hear them.

Each milepost of progress was duly announced by her father. When Johanna emerged from diapers, he reported that "her Ziegfeld farmerette trousseau has been enlarged and she now has overalls of different colors." He noted "the emergence of dainty and pearly masterpieces of the dental art." For her first birthday party Sara trimmed her "super Ann Harding hair" and carefully stored a blond lock in the pink book "Our Baby's First Seven Years." It was the first of all those backyard parties around the pool: posed pictures of a fluffy princess in little white shoes never scuffed, white frocks and hair ribbons, Dutch girl outfits, black velvet dresses and patent leather shoes, Sara bending over Johanna and straining to look up at the camera.

To Herman, so profoundly aware of his own failings, Johanna was perfection achieved. In his mind she was beauty unalloyed, a person he could love without ambivalence, a blessing nobody else possessed, not Joe Mankiewicz, not Louis B. Mayer. She was his resident "rosebud," symbolizing the hope that his abilities could still flower in a wide-open future.

CHAPTER

Strip away the phony tinsel of Hollywood
and you find the real tinsel underneath.

—OSCAR LEVANT

IF A DISEASE COULD PARADOXICALLY KEEP A MAN ALIVE, THAT
would have been Hollywood for Herman. The scholar and
historian in him knew exactly what he had bought and sold
when he remained in the movie industry. Yet he continued to
survive on the hope that outside forces would somehow break
his inner patterns and his career would suddenly soar. Hollywood was the right place to hold onto such expectations.
Optimism was the breath of life, a necessity for facing the
thousand nerve-grinding complexities of moviemaking. Moreover, the industry was indeed a place of overnight transfigura-
tions. As in the movies it produced, Hollywood had rainbows
and jackpots.

At the same time careers capriciously died. The under-
side of optimism was fear. But reality in Hollywood was like
the movie sets, its painted face toward the actors and its
ramshackle rear safely out of sight. Whatever Herman's ter-
rors may have been, he lived literally in a dreamworld devoted
to replacing anxiety with make-believe. The fantasy those
men and women put on film to distract the public permeated
their own private lives.

Bennie Thau, a Metro vice-president, stood at lunchtime in
the middle of the studio commissary, demonstrating a golf
grip. In his mind there was nothing fantastic about saying to
a passing waitress, "Gimme a putter." Not even the Hollywood

money seemed real. "It was like snow," said Dorothy Parker, "and melted in your hand."

At night the fantasy took on three dimensions at huge costume parties. Herman and Sara attended these extravaganzas, which nostalgically used as themes the elemental values which had been appropriated for the movies but discarded in Hollywood private lives. Basil and Ouida Rathbone converted the Victor Hugo restaurant into a papier-mâché cathedral. Kay Francis made the Vendôme restaurant over as a ship. And she once gave a barn dance with real pigs, chickens, rabbits, and geese. At the Raskins's Christmas party, the ground was covered by artificial snow, and in the California heat, carollers wearing wool mufflers and earmuffs sang under fake lampposts. The Countess di Frasso sponsored the ultimate flight of fantasy, a come-as-somebody-you-would-like-to-be party. Herman went dressed as W. C. Fields playing the part of Mr. Micawber; Sara, as David Copperfield.

In counterpoint to the costume balls, Hollywood pursued another spurious reality with come-as-you-are parties, sudden invitations that brought matinee idols with shaving cream on their faces and glamour queens in hair curlers. These began with young Charlie Lederer's spur-of-the-moment invitation to F. Scott Fitzgerald, while still in his heyday. "Come as you are," said Lederer on the phone, and Scott and Zelda turned up in pajamas. Eventually Zelda removed hers and danced nude. "I never showed my amazement," Sara says.

All Hollywood gathered at the elegant balls at the Ambassador and Biltmore hotels, including deeply tanned beauties in white chiffon and ermine capes, from which slipped bottles of bootleg booze that smashed on the marble floor. At tables around the dance floor were the Mayer enclave, the Hearst enclave, the Schulberg enclave, where Herman and Sara sat with Humphrey Bogart, Gary Cooper, Carole Lombard, the Marx Brothers. When Garbo came with John Gilbert, she paused at the top of the ballroom stairs. There was a sudden silence, all eyes upon this mysterious recluse. In a delicate gesture of independence, she removed her shoes and descended the steps in stockinged feet.

In Hollywood Herman found a milieu so exotic that it could tolerate him for twenty-five years and even seek him socially. Just as hostesses invited Fritz Kreisler to dinner and said, "Please bring your violin," Herman and his wit were a star attraction, and never mind his fireworks. Says Joe Mankiewicz: "My brother was one of the all-time popular dinner guests. He was a guarantee that the party would not suddenly die. People who wouldn't hire him to write scripts would invite him to dinner. Even if he got drunk and individually and thoroughly insulted every guest, that would make your dinner party *the* conversation piece the following day."

Though Herman was a Hollywood celebrity in his own right, there was a slightly self-demeaning quality to this role of performer. Gottfried Reinhardt was then in Hollywood, along with his father, Max Reinhardt. "Herman in Vienna or Berlin," says Gottfried, "would have been a famous star of the coffeehouses. He could actually have made a legitimate career of it. In Europe the great writers, usually not brilliant talkers, were jealous of a man like that. They didn't say, 'Oh, he's just a talker.' But in America a wit at parties is not particularly respected."

Herman never refused an invitation and was immersed in that opulent world he ridiculed as "the Florence of the Western Hemisphere." He told an actress weighted down by rings and bracelets, "Several Central American republics could go on a permanent war footing with your left arm as security." Joseph Cotten was very proud of his new Utrillo and had it hanging in his living room. "Look, Sara," Herman said in earshot of Cotten, "do you realize that we are the only Jews west of the Mississippi who do not own a Utrillo?"

Christmastime, the quintessence of Hollywood vulgarity, was a period of despondency for Herman, lasting until the season was safely past. Gift giving was by lists, and competitive: who could afford the most expensive jewelry, Rolls-

Royces, furs, gold knickknacks. Margaret Sullavan required three days to open her presents, which included lavish gifts from fans. Marion Davies took close friends to a table spread with diamond bracelets, necklaces, and rings and let them pick. Herman maintained it was a holiday invented by people who hated children. The reality could not possibly match the fantasy built in their minds. He would show his sons the ads of perfect families with the perfect dog receiving the perfect gifts. In actual fact, he would say, "two of the toys would already be broken, the dog would be shedding his hair and stepping on the electric train, the father's new shirt would be too small, so not only is it impossible to wear, but he is reminded that he is gaining weight." Herman's depression lasted at least until New Year's Eve, when the Jaffes came over for mulled wine, which he hated. Sara always turned the thermostat way up in hopes that the heat would make Herman sleepy and he would not go on to Charlie Lederer's all-night party.

In this feverish Hollywood society, a bubble being treated as permanence, salaried men spent like millionaires, actors believed in their glamour, magazines and columnists worked full time pumping consequence into minor daily events. Seemingly no minutia was exempt:

> Herman Mankiewicz sponsored a stag backgammon party at which every player chipped in $10 for the prize, a silver ice bucket.

> The Knights of the Round Table in their daily meetings at the Embassy have ribbed Herman Mankiewicz to take over the part of the author for a single performance in *Once in a Lifetime*. Mank's one condition is that no person will be permitted to throw bouquets, in any form, onto the stage.

> The diminutive Mrs. Mankiewicz' merry soirees will be missed for a while. She left New Year's day to join her distinguished husband in New York.

Sara had become a dexterous hostess, and an invitation to

Tower Road was prized. But Herman sneered at the idea that friendship with the famous was some kind of achievement or even satisfaction. He told Sam Jaffe's wife, Mildred, "You see this finger? Put yours in a telephone dial, and you can get anybody in Hollywood to come to a party. Just give them food and liquor. It's as simple as that. It means nothing." That was true. But even so, there was a vicarious glamour in hobnobbing with romantic names. Herman and Sara felt it. That was part of the glue that kept them both in the West.

"I always felt that I was terribly privileged," Sara says. "I never got over the wonderment of everyday life here." Sara sporadically kept a guest book for dinner guests. Carl Sandburg wrote: "Tomorrow will never catch up with Yesterday because Yesterday started sooner. Thus spake Potatoe Face." Harpo Marx wrote: "A tochas no painter could paint," and signed, "Harpistically, Adolph Marx." John Gilbert wrote: "For the Sweet 'Manks.' Because of so many years of ups and downs (ins and outs) and silly times—a compliment—I love you."

The friendship with Gilbert began soon after Herman and Sara arrived in Hollywood. In the late twenties they were included in one of the movie colony's most exclusive rituals: Sunday tennis and buffet lunch with John Gilbert and Greta Garbo.

Gilbert was an effervescent, unreflective man, immaculate in light-gray suits and black Oxfords. With his pencil-thin mustache, he was then the preeminent lover in silent movies. American women swooned and their husbands were forever trying to punch him at restaurants. He was worth $10,000 a week to MGM, but the Mankiewiczes's unimpressed German cook delighted Herman by always saying, "The *Schauspieler* [playactor] is here."

The first Gilbert-Garbo movie, *Flesh and the Devil* in 1927, made Greta Garbo into a major star and the two of them into America's most famous lovers. A movie magazine breathlessly quoted the film's director as saying, "They are in that blissful state of love that is so like a rosy cloud that they imagine themselves hidden behind it, as well as lost in it." Garbo was already pathologically shy, and the group at Gilbert's house was limited primarily to Herman and Sara, the director King Vidor, writer Barney Glazer, Helen Hayes and Charlie MacArthur, producer Arthur Hornblow, Jr., and stars Edmund Lowe and his wife, Lilyan Tashman, a trend-setting arbiter of chic who kept her figure svelte by deliberately vomiting after dinner.

During tennis games Garbo often sat by the court and read Swedish newspapers, while Herman noisily entertained, expounding, for instance, on the theme of Jews as athletes. Garbo listened appreciatively to the banter. But, says Sara, "there was never any real conversation with her—a few jokes." She liked Herman. And when she laughed—melodiously, beautifully—at some raucous American joke, Herman would teasingly say, "You don't understand one word. What are you laughing at?"

Garbo would laugh some more, protesting, "I *do*. I *do*." And she would try to explain the joke in her broken English, while everyone roared.

On the tennis court Herman was a lunging, burly figure, whose style featured far more shouting and joking than grace but whose untutored, two-handed strokes were surprisingly effective. Garbo held her racket in the middle of the handle, wore a tennis visor, and rolled her socks down to the tops of her low sneakers. She played says Hornblow, "no relation to any tennis you've ever seen." But she was one of the best, running fast, hitting hard, and getting the ball back. Her net game was particularly ferocious, though wearing sunglasses, she stood so close to the net that opponents were terrified a ball might damage this immensely valuable woman. She played tennis often with the star Aileen Pringle, who beat her regularly. Garbo never said, "You played well." She would say, "I played badly today."

An extra reason for the exclusivity was to guard the secret

that Garbo lived at Gilbert's house. "We go there for social intercourse," Herman insisted, a grin in his eyes. "If there's any other kind, I don't know about it." So elaborate was the hugger-mugger that from behind a sliding panel in Gilbert's bathroom wardrobe, a secret stair led down to Garbo's bedroom. "It added to the excitement," Sara recalls dryly.

Gilbert tried everlastingly to marry Garbo. When Eleanor Boardman, in 1927, married King Vidor at a wedding given her by Marion Davies, Gilbert asked that it be a double ceremony including himself and Garbo. Garbo never appeared. Gilbert glowered through the reception until L. B. Mayer, in the men's washroom, advised him, "Don't marry her; just screw her." Gilbert, drunk, hit the president of the studio and knocked Mayer sprawling.

On the morning of another Gilbert-Garbo wedding day, Gilbert presented his wedding present, a white Rolls-Royce. Garbo was ecstatically pleased and asked "to try it on." With liquid grace she slipped behind the wheel. Suddenly she started the engine and drove down the road. She did not return. It was the end of the romance. That night the police found Gilbert, drunk, on a balcony of Garbo's house carrying a gun.

While Gilbert was king of the silent movie lovers, MGM gave him a five-year million-dollar contract. Then Gilbert's punch made Mayer into an enemy. Herman always believed that when sound arrived in Hollywood, the vengeful Mayer allowed it to destroy Gilbert's career. Gilbert could act naturalistically, as in *The Big Parade*. But for talkies, Gilbert was not given training to lower his slightly treble voice. His first sound movie, ironically titled *His Glorious Night*, was an old-style flamboyant romance. So to the accompaniment of extravagant, silent movie posturing, Gilbert uttered his first words in a high tenor: "I love you. I love you. I love you." The audiences laughed. When Gilbert's ship from Europe docked in New York, a minor studio functionary came aboard to deliver the news. Gilbert wept. Summing up his friend's career, John Barrymore said, "From Garbo to limbo."

Thereafter, Gilbert was convinced that the MGM brass—Mayer, Mannix, Thalberg—were deliberately walking past him as though he was invisible. He believed they were trying to goad him into tearing up his million-dollar contract in a fit of bravado. Instead, he holed up in his house and drank. Sometimes he issued forth at night in order to be talked out of suicide by friends like Herman and Charlie MacArthur. Finally fed up, MacArthur told Gilbert, "Bon voyage," and shut the door.

One night on his own rounds Herman arrived at Eddie Knopf's house just after Gilbert had left. A dinner party was in progress. With horrified excitement, the guests described Gilbert, villainously drunk, shouldering into the house, sitting down at the table, putting a loaded revolver in front of him. Herman listened courteously to everybody's fear and outrage. Then, exasperatedly, he interrupted, "Oh, come on! How much can a gun eat?"

Gilbert succeeded in drinking himself to death in 1936.

The most celebrated and legendary social set that welcomed Herman and Sara was headed by Marion Davies and William Randolph Hearst—small dinners at which Chaplin entertained for hours, white-tie Mayfair balls, Brobdingnagian costume birthday parties: Hearst as a riverboat gambler, Hearst in shorts, lederhosen and Austrian hat. Now, after all his dinner dissertations on Hearst and Tammany Hall, Hearst maneuvering to be governor, ballot boxes floating down the river, Hearst in the Brooklyn Academy campaigning with free concerts, Herman Mankiewicz was next to the man himself.

For the first time Herman's Hollywood pleasure merged with his political scholarship. Studying Hearst first hand, Herman was fascinated by the Olympian power and waste of Hearst's money, by the man's obsessive will as Hearst worked to make Marion Davies the new Mary Pickford and himself the supreme movie mogul. He saw Hearst as "a finagling, calculating, Machiavellian figure." But also, with Charlie Lederer,

Marion Davies's nephew, Herman was one of the men who wrote and had printed parodies of Hearst newspapers to amuse the publisher and Marion. "Herman never had any trouble finding time for that," says Sara.

A faked front page of Hearst's *Herald-Examiner*, kidding Marion's stutter, had the banner headline "D-D-D-Davies Returns." A subhead read, "Star Sails from England; British Fleet Mutinies. 'Lawdy! Lawdy! English Folks is Sho' 'Nough Quality, but I'se Pow'ful Glad to Be Home,' Declares Actress as She Lands." And the story began, "So spoke dainty Miss Marion Davies as she was pulled from the platform of the Chief early this morning by thousands of hungry mouths."

There was a photograph of Herman captioned "Believe it or Not" and one of Sara titled "Poor Sara." Herman supplied a column called "Last Minute News" and by-lined Arthur Membrane, a takeoff on Hearst's lieutenant, Arthur Brisbane. It carried such items as: "Sam Goldwyn wants story for Vilma Banky. So did last three Vilma Banky pictures," and "Irving Thalberg celebrated twenty-sixth birthday with bigger celebration than last year's twenty-sixth birthday celebration. Plan bigger twenty-sixth birthday celebration next year."

A takeoff on the Los Angeles *Evening Express* marked Hearst's sixty-eighth birthday with the headline "Great Tribute Paid to Rising Young Publisher." In the accompanying mock interview Hearst was asked if he thought American wrestlers were better than European. "I'm against foreign entanglements," the publisher answered. A box outlined in black announced, "A special prize will be awarded to anyone present who can spell Mankiewicz's name—the prize being Mankiewicz."

A letter to the Embarrassing Moment Editor, signed William Randolph Hearst, read: "I arrived home from Europe and declared that I had nothing to declare. Imagine my embarrassment when the customs officials went through my trunks and found Rheims Cathedral in my soiled linen, Leonardo da Vinci's Madonna among my collars, seven Spanish carved altars among my suits and The Tower of London in my derby. I really mean, imagine my embarrassment."

Like a Medici gone mad, Hearst was then bankrupting himself building the ultimate in make-believe, San Simeon, his composite medieval castle in the mountains near San Luis Obispo. From his empire of newspapers, New York real estate, mines, paper mills, Hearst's personal income was $15 million a year, but he was outspending that. His warehouses were stuffed with $25 million worth of European plunder, including an entire monastery from Segovia, shipped over in 14,000 crates. He imported 30,000 trees and spent $12,000 on a single planting of daphnes. When Cecil B. De Mille bumped his head on the limb of an ancient live oak, Hearst, instead of having the limb cut off, ordered the entire tree transplanted a dozen feet back from the path. To Hearst, convinced that he would die when he stopped adding to it, San Simeon was his talisman keeping old age at bay.

There were two castes in Hollywood, those who had been guests at San Simeon and those who had not. Herman and Sara went several times. A limousine picked them up at Tower Road on Friday evening and delivered them at 8 P.M. to a special train car at Union Station in downtown Los Angeles. There were usually eighteen to twenty guests, such as the director George Fitzmaurice, Aileen Pringle, Lederer, Norma and Constance Talmadge. They ate, drank, laughed, played backgammon, arrived in San Luis Obispo at 2 A.M., and transferred to a long file of black Buick limousines. Through air scented by vineyards, they rode for an hour and a half along the coast until suddenly bursting above them in the blackness was a mountaintop blazing with lights. "I honestly thought I was dreaming," Sara recalls. "It was like an allegory in which we were all playing roles and I wasn't Sara and he wasn't Herman."

At the castle, after champagne and sandwiches, Herman and Sara were always ushered to the same medieval Florentine apartment in La Casa del Monte guest cottage. "It was like

Herman moved to Hollywood and Paramount Pictures in 1926. Among the first of the Broadway wits and journalists to travel West, he was an immediate writer of importance. This migration was so new, the studio used it for a gag publicity picture of four ex-newspapermen interviewing actress Florence Vidor. Above, left to right, are: Herman; Vidor; E. H. Griffith, director; Clive Brook, actor. When sound came to movies in 1929, Herman, experienced in dialogue, was even more valuable and got producing assignments. That year he produced a classic, *Laughter*. Below, on the set, he poses with, from left, Diane Ellis, Nancy Carroll, and Fredric March.

B. P. Schulberg, all-powerful production chief of
Paramount and literate ex-newspaperman, was
Herman's mentor. When Schulberg was fired in
the early 1930's, nobody in Hollywood would help
with a job. His descent was so steep, he was in a
few years approaching Herman for small loans.

The men who bossed Herman at MGM, most of whom he considered fools and cretins, were the likes of, from left, Irving Thalberg, vice-president, and Louis B. Mayer, production head, and, far right, Harry Rapf, Mayer's longtime assistant and Herman's favorite target. Third from left is Will H. Hayes, the industry's moral watchdog who helped block Herman's anti-Hitler movie, *The Mad Dog of Europe.*

As a birthday present for Schulberg at Paramount, Ben Hecht made a ribald movie short. Here Herman plays the part of an all-thumbs waiter.

With the advent of sound Paramount sent Herman to New York to find dialogue writers. Above he posed with two of them, Bartlett Cormack and John V. A. Weaver, a Round Table member.

When Herman left Paramount, David O. Selznick (left) immediately hired him as a right-hand man at MGM, sitting in on meetings—here with Walt Disney.

Consummately convivial, Herman often made lunch the high point of his day, turning the meal into an impromptu party and entertaining a rapt and laughing circle till long after other diners had left and waiters were resetting tables. Sometimes Sara materialized to take him home to sleep off the drinks.

At Paramount Herman was producer on two Marx Brothers movies, *Monkey Business* and *Horse Feathers,* and was fired from a third, *Duck Soup.* The four brothers and their father, Sam "Frenchie" Marx, signed a picture for Herman. With an arrow pointing to himself, Groucho wrote in the margin, "The only Marx who can spell Mankiewicz."

During the filming of *Horse Feathers,* Herman works with Chico in the football sequence. The limit of Chico's talent, believed Herman, was his Italian accent.

Everybody's favorite Marx was Harpo, who for this joke picture dressed up as William the Second while Herman donned all the brothers' costume props—Chico's hat, Harpo's wig, Groucho's glasses and mustache.

The Mankiewicz/
Aaronson clan as-
sembled for Don's
bar mitzvah. Stand-
ing, from left, are:
Don M., Ruth
Aaronson Chase,
Olga A., Estherlea
A., Johanna M.,
William Chase,
Emanuel A., Erna
M., Mattie A.,
Frank M. Seated:
Sara M., Naomi A.,
Professor M., Her-
man M., Reuben A.

Enjoying Hollywood, Sara created her dream bedroom—a feminine bower of lace, cream satin, and butterfly wallpaper. Herman had his separate, masculine bedroom.

Herman's permanent home on Tower Road in Beverly Hills was rented for many years and then finally purchased.

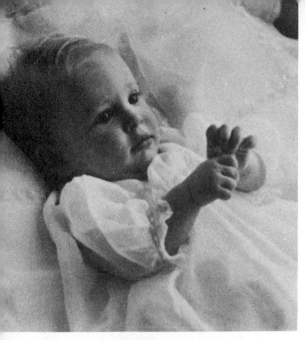

In 1937 a third child, a girl, Johanna, ful-filled every fantasy—particularly for Sara, who had been terrified it would be another shouting Mankiewicz man.

For Herman, Johanna was the repository of his disappointed dreams. In his bedroom reading chair, they would go through *The Little Auto* together, Johanna pointing to the pictures.

In his Beverly Hills house, redolent with success, Joe Mankiewicz poses with his wife, Rose, a former actress, and his sons, Christopher (standing) and Tom. Rose later committed suicide. Joe remarried and late in life fathered a little girl, much as Herman had Johanna.

a little castle of our own," Sara says. Their bags were already unpacked, nightwear was laid out, and the canopy bed—golden gilt headboard carved with a shouting face, red velvet brocade side curtains—was turned down.

Sara saw little of Herman on those weekends. He was up and out early, energized by the excitement of the place and the company. Sara slept late. She marveled at the room: the coffered gold ceiling, the sixteenth-century Italian marriage chest, the seventeenth-century French walnut cabinets, the deeply carved Italian stone mantel topped by a Madonna and Child terra-cotta. On her way to breakfast in the central two-towered castle, called Casa Grande, Sara followed stone paths past other guest cottages and perpetual gardens: foxglove, orchids like purple bells, groves of tree roses. Through gaps in the foliage were flashes of statues and fountains which filled the air with the gentle sound of water. On the mountain slope Sara could see zebras, giraffes, buffalo, elk, camels, moose, elands, emus, and ostriches. A serpentine vine-covered pergola one mile long wound around a nearby ridge. And far beyond the horizon stretched the Hearst duchy—275,000 acres—only slightly smaller than Rhode Island. Sara remembers, "I used to feel as though I were walking on air, not ever hitting the ground, tremulous with excitement."

Once called a cross between the Palazzo Uffizi and the Hippodrome, San Simeon was actually a resort hotel beyond imagined extravagance. Marveling at the dimensions of the Hearstian ego and whim, speculating on the Hearstian need to be a twentieth-century Lancaster or Burgundy, Herman and companions strolled the private zoo and laughed at the story of Jerry, the chimpanzee, throwing his defecation at the steamy romantic authoress Elinor Glyn. Herman browsed in the library of first editions and swam in the Neptune pool surrounded by marble colonnades, and with a Greco-Roman temple at one end. He went horseback riding and fell off. He ruefully complained that while he lay in the dust testing his arms, legs, and head, everybody was shouting, "Get the horse."

Herman played tennis, while Marion sat in the bleachers, calling out to poor players, "D-d-doing better, honey. V-v-very good." Sometimes the games did not reflect the castle's museum atmosphere. Herman once played doubles with actress Billie Dove, Harry Crocker, who was Marion's closest confidant, and a French count. The count was struck in the eye by a hard-hit ball, and as he bent over in pain, he kept saying over and over, "Oh, *mon Dieu*, nevair again to see the beautiful tits of Billie Dove."

Sometimes Hearst organized a command performance "picnic." The file of Buicks delivered the guests to some distant point where they were served a sumptuous luncheon, a scene reproduced in *Citizen Kane*. Then this potpourri of paunchy newspaper editors, hard-drinking moviemakers, tender, pampered actresses, many of whom had never even thought of a horse before, were hoisted into saddles and taken up and down mountains by Hearst. Some women, terrified and in pain, would sob, and men would dismount to lead their horses. Marion Davies dulled the agony by sneaking sips of gin from a flask, and sometimes two men rode on each side to keep her upright. Hearst would implacably continue forward. "He was a bit of a sadist," says the director King Vidor. At dusk they arrived at a campsite to find elaborate tents erected over wooden floors, singing cowboys, Spanish dancers, tables spread with food, a bonfire, a songfest.

Marion Davies was a hopeless, cheerful alcoholic. Hearst first saw her in the chorus line of the *Ziegfeld Follies of 1917*, at which he purchased two seats, one for himself and one for his hat. Marion was a blond, 118-pound beauty, joyous, wildly sentimental, generous, and a born comedienne able to make the dour Hearst laugh out loud. At San Simeon, where Hearst imposed stern limits on all drinking, Marion was in constant connivance to outwit "sourpuss," as she called her benefactor. She would say to a trusted friend like actress Eleanor Boardman, "Your suitcase is coming on Tuesday."

"I brought everything . . . no . . . my suitcase isn't . . ." Eleanor would begin.

"Y-y-yes, h-honey, your suitcase is coming." When it arrived, it would be full of gin bottles. "J-j-just keep it under your bed," Marion would say. She hid bottles in the brook on the way to the tennis court, in the pine trees near the stables, in the water tanks of toilets. But there was a fair exchange; to keep instantaneously in touch with his minions, Hearst had telephones concealed in similar crannies throughout the grounds.

Hearst was a tall, large, aloof, lonely, and elusive man, who terrified Sara. He had a coldness in his gray-blue eyes. His mouth was thin-lipped in a long face whose nose jutted straight down from his forehead. He spoke reluctantly and in a disconcertingly high-pitched voice. Before dinner, when guests assembled in the Great Hall, Marion Davies would say to Sara, "H-h-honey, you come over here and sit," and they would work together on the elaborate picture puzzle perpetually under way. Marion's closest friends who got to know Hearst liked him. "He was half elephant, half sheep," says Eleanor Boardman. Not very deep inside Hearst was a gee whiz adolescent. When Robert Benchley's son, Nat, in 1937 edited a *Harvard Lampoon* parody of Hearst's *Cosmopolitan* magazine, Hearst sent Nat a congratulatory note with the comment "Gee, I wish I could be back fifty years or so and with the *Lampoon* again where 'good fellows get together with a stein on the table.' Darn it. Beer only makes me sleepy now."

Dinner at San Simeon was served in the vast refectory under ranks of Sienese family flags and a 400-year-old monastery ceiling. Down the center ran the long refectory table with two dozen wooden Dante chairs. Set among the extravagant silver service were paper napkins, plain bottles of ketchup and mustard, symbols of Hearst's conceit that San Simeon was his "ranch." Hearst sat at the center with Marion opposite. Everybody at the table kept an eye on W. R. If he laughed at something, it was all right to laugh. Herman, expected to stimulate conversation, was seated near Hearst.

The publisher was interested in this ex-newspaperman who was so knowledgeable about politics. Hearst invited Herman to his private office, a Gothic-arched, starkly medieval room from which Hearst presided over his empire like some plainclothes Pope. From there he sent telegrams beginning. "The Chief suggests. . . ." And in that room Herman mingled with the Hearst editors and columnists: Walter Winchell and Arthur Brisbane. Says Sara: "He was a guest who meant something to Hearst."

Herman had respect for Hearst's knowledge, and he admired what the publisher had been until presidential ambitions derailed his ideals. When Hearst died in 1951, at age eighty-eight, Herman correctly pointed out: "Until he was about forty, Hearst was among the greatest fighting liberals. He fought for the forgotten man and the underfed one-third of the nation before the rest of the country knew what it was all about."

After dinner Marion usually disappeared into the powder room to sit on the counter between the gold-fauceted washbowls and hold giggling court, gossiping with friends. "She was one of the dearest minxes you can imagine," Sara recalls. "Fun, kind, a simple, loving girl."

Later the guests assembled in the movie theater, early Roxy, with red brocade walls on which wooden Greek caryatids held electric torches in outstretched arms. Herman and Sara sat up front with Marion and Hearst. Although Hearst always held Marion's hand, Sara felt they were more like father and daughter. Nevertheless, Marion Davies did desperately want to marry Hearst. She once told Eleanor Boardman, "I started out as a gold digger, and I ended up in love." Herman was sorry for Marion Davies. He felt she was not very smart and that her life with Hearst was miserable, basically "dull, dull, dull."

*   *   *

By 1936, after his return from England, where he wrote a romantic film called *Love in Exile*, Herman was no longer a part of the Hearst circle. Because Hearst hated the habit in Marion, he would not tolerate heavy drinking around him, and Herman had become an increasingly hazardous guest. Alcohol worked more and more rapidly in his system. He told Geraldine Fitzgerald that after years of steady drinking, "the fire is laid and a single match will touch it off."

Herman was often, for him, exemplary. Nevertheless, when Sara received an invitation, she would say, "You've got to remember that Herman can be unmanageable sometimes, and if you want to ask him for dinner, you'll have to bear the consequences." To recoup himself with a hostess after some atrocity, Herman concocted a satiric form letter of appreciation. It was set in ornate type, and he would fill in the appropriate words.

Dear   ,

    I want to thank you for the lovely   I spent at your home. Particularly do I appreciate the little thoughtfulnesses that characterized your reception of me. How, for example did you know that the   you served on   evening was my favorite   ? And the   ! Yummy!

    Thank you again, dear   , and remember me to your charming   .

Yours,

In addition, Herman's political arguments made him more and more difficult. "Mank saw himself as an arbiter of the truth," says actress Geraldine Fitzgerald. "It can be very destructive to keep going after the truth." Moreover, Herman had always regarded himself as marooned on an island populated by political idiots. At a party actress Florence Eldridge was expounding her views to a group that included Herman. When she stopped for breath, Herman said in a low, distinct voice, "Go away." She looked startled and went on with her semilecture. A moment later Herman's voice, quiet, persistent, sounded again. "Go away." She did not go away. She continued. He continued. "Go away."

At another party Florence Eldridge recounted this experience, and looking fondly and forgivingly at Herman, she finished, "Of course, he was a little tight."

"I was stone sober," Herman said.

"Mank," said Nunnally Johnson, "was our answer to Dale Carnegie."

Herman habitually asserted his superiority by contesting whatever was the prevailing opinion in the room. In 1936 politics became fashionable in Hollywood. Amateur pundits were now debating Herman the political scholar, a man who knew, for instance, that the Senate's failure to allow the United States to join the League of Nations was related, in part, to the character and views of Thomas Riley Marshall, Woodrow Wilson's Vice President. In Herman's judgment, if his antagonists had even heard of Wilson, they thought he had founded a high school in Glendale. Such minds, which he considered not entitled to hold *any* opinion, were overnight experts on Hitler and Franco. He would rail, "If you spent half the time reading history that you spend knowing the name of Franco's foreign minister who tortured children in Madrid. . . ."

What further inflamed Herman, a violent anti-Communist, was his conviction that many of these know-nothings were getting their new beliefs from somewhere else, like the suddenly fashionable *New Masses*. It was bad enough that to him they were manipulated fools. But the final push toward apoplexy was the fact that they were preempting many of his positions.

For example, partly on the basis of his insights in the twenties in Berlin, Herman had been a very early anti-Nazi at a time when there was an appealing loneliness to that role. In 1933 he originated and fought for a project which by movie-industry standards was prescient and courageous.

In 1933 he wrote his scenario for *The Mad Dog of Europe*. It was essentially a newsreel account of Hitler's ascendancy, with special attention to the Nazi brutality toward the Jews. Herman argued then, "There is great danger that the just indignation and fury of the world will die out gradually as new concerns present themselves for its attention. For example, in Los Angeles, the German murder of civilized thought, which was streamer headlines news, has gradually become inside page stuff for even the most important items."

No studio would touch it because they feared such a movie would destroy the market in Germany. Prominent Jews were afraid that the film would intensify anti-Semitism in both Germany and America and refused to bring pressure on Hollywood. Herman was willing to give up his job at MGM to make the movie. Only at the last minute did he abandon the idea of a full-page ad in *The New York Times* asking for contributions with 50 percent of the profits to go to the relief of German Jews and Catholics. The obstacles were too great. The sole outcome of the project was an order by Dr. Paul Joseph Goebbels banning all films bearing Herman's credit from being shown in Germany.

Then, in 1936, Herman's position was usurped by the detested Communists. The Hollywood Anti-Nazi League was formed to counteract Fascist propaganda and influence. Herman saw immediately that the leadership was following the party line. His old Algonquin friend Donald Ogden Stewart was president. Stewart recalls, "I got to hate Herman because he hated me so much."

After the Berlin-Moscow pact in 1939, the pro-Stalin faction of the League became antiwar, again intolerably in agreement with Herman. An isolationist in the liberal tradition of Robert La Follette and Hiram Johnson, Herman believed that war permanently undermined freedom. The federal government, big business, the military—all vastly and perhaps permanently increased their power. And the war, Herman believed, would actually be waged to pay off the munitions makers, pull England's imperial chestnuts from the fire, and preserve colonialism in India.

Herman was also convinced that the United States would lose a war with Germany. "I am an ultra-Lindbergh," Herman declared, insisting, "The strength of the so-called Rome-Berlin Axis is so overwhelming as to make the thought of conflict the work of a madman. I suggest that the American public return to its worries about the World Series, the chance that the Goldbergs will really be able to pay off their mortgage, and schemes for getting the government, or the state, or the city, or the township, or the ward, to pay them one thousand dollars every Monday, Wednesday, and Friday."

Arguing with Charlie Lederer, who never forgave him for such seemingly unpatriotic talk, Herman demanded, "Would you go into the ring with Joe Louis?"

"And I was a useful ally," says Lederer, Herman's pipeline to Hearst and Marion Davies.

Herman's systematic contrariness stemmed partly from conviction—but also from his determination to prove that he was the one person in ignorant Hollywood who knew the how and why of Hitler and the true situation in Germany. He saw himself as an outpost of "clear thinking uncomplicated by the emotional reactions which are the particular object of my nausea." This led him into curious and damaging dogma.

Eleanor Boardman, the former silent film star, by then married to Herman's friend Harry D'Arrast, returned to Hollywood from her husband's home near Biarritz in 1940, when the Nazis were already in Paris. She was telling Herman and Sara of the terror in France. Herman interrupted to protest that Hitler was right. "All the doctors, lawyers, and professional men in Germany were Jews," Herman said, "and they were getting too strong a hold."

The more Herman believed that communism was mobilized in Hollywood, the more outrageous he became. The more he was counterattacked, the more he was egged on into binges of perversity and extremism. There were bitter arguments with people whose ideologies were as strong as Herman's. At the directors' table, in friends' living rooms, Herman, his sweat-soaked shirt sticking to his back, would yell, "You jackass you! What the hell do you know?" And he would say, "Idiocy is all right in its way, but you can't make it the foundation of a career!" Friends began to flee him. Ernst Lubitsch, the director, once ordered Herman to leave his house. And Sara's sister Mattie Fox remembers guests stalking out of her dinner parties, saying, "I'm not taking it. I'm terribly sorry, but don't invite me again if. . . ."

In actual fact, Herman was a passionately patriotic American. When not fighting verbal donnybrooks—and secretly enjoying them—the lover of flag and country was campaigning to keep friends from sailing to Europe on German liners. He became the official sponsor for hundreds of German refugees and took responsibility for total strangers fleeing to America. Sam Jaffe protested that he could not possibly fulfill these obligations. Herman continued to sign a stack of affidavits and said, "Yes, but the government doesn't know that." When war became inevitable, he tried to rejoin the Marines but was rejected for bad kidneys. Both Don and Frank enlisted.

But Herman continued to infuriate people. He never endorsed America's participation in the war. He continued to declare around Hollywood, "There's nothing in the Constitution that stops a citizen from making a separate peace." After FDR called on the nation to become the arsenal of democracy, Herman began referring to America as "The horse's arsenal of democracy."

Even in Hollywood, that citadel of make-believe, Herman's careless life eventually had to founder on reality. By the end of the 1930's, and on the threshold of *Citizen Kane*, Herman's orbit was smaller, his word carried less weight, his reputation was increasingly "Ho, ho, here comes crazy Mankiewicz." In

1939, while he was talking importantly about making a better deal at another studio, MGM did not renew his contract, and Herman was grateful to remain on a week-to-week basis. And that September another financial crisis ended up in the office of Louis B. Mayer. There was again an advance against salary and an even more abject promise never again to gamble. The very next afternoon Herman was in a poker game in the studio commissary. As he leaned forward to make a bet, his gaze lifted and locked with the eyes of L. B. Mayer across the room. Herman got up from the table, returned to his office, collected his ritual parcel of pencils and stationery, and left the studio lot. The next day he was officially fired.

CHAPTER

10

□ □ □

There but for the grace of God goes God.

—HERMAN MANKIEWICZ
on Orson Welles

IN TRUE HOLLYWOOD STYLE HERMAN, DOWN AND OUT, suddenly fulfilled his potential. For once, his knowledge, intelligence, and anger were used on a single creative effort, the screenplay for *Citizen Kane*. In 1962 *Kane* was voted the best film in motion-picture history by seventy critics from eleven nations. Even in the 1970's, when film had replaced the novel as a major artistic force, a group of American producers and critics chose *Kane* and *Gone with the Wind* as the two most significant movies in U.S. film history. Orson Welles was *Kane*'s producer, director, star, and dominating force, but the movie would never have existed without Herman Mankiewicz.

The writer's credit reads "Herman J. Mankiewicz and Orson Welles." However, the authorship of *Citizen Kane* has become one of film history's major controversies. And the question of who did what and how much opens up an extraordinary subdrama of jostling egos. The question was raised by critic Pauline Kael in her 1971 *New Yorker* article titled "Raising Kane." She stated that Herman wrote virtually the entire script and that Welles systematically usurped the credit. Though he admits he had important help from Herman, Welles indignantly insists that he was the primary author not only of the script but the original idea. John Houseman, Welles's onetime partner and Herman's editor on the first draft of *Kane,* has written a memoir called *Run Through.* While describing his work with Herman, Houseman strongly implies that he himself was a crucial influence in the creation of *Kane.* Speaking vociferously from the grave, Herman claims sole authorship. For example, in a letter to his father after *Kane* opened, he said, "There is hardly a comma that I did not write."

Pauline Kael calls *Kane* "a shallow masterpiece" but nevertheless "an American triumph" which "manages to create something aesthetically exciting and durable out of the playfulness of American muckraking satire." The story of Charlie Kane is told by the interlocking recollections of the five witnesses, presented in interviews and dramatized flashbacks. The episodes are arranged independent of chronology, moving back and forth in time. Gradually, like parts of a puzzle fitting together piece by piece—here, there—these memories complete a mosaic portrait of Kane, a man destroyed by wealth and the inability to love. Perhaps no movie script has ever been so complex, yet such a marvel of engineering which meshes its ideas, action, techniques into a satisfying and consistent whole.

The critic Andrew Sarris sees the themes of *Kane* as "the debasement of the private personality of the public figure, and the crushing weight of materialism." Welles himself says, "The essential story of *Kane* is of someone who is raised without love or even human attention, and inherits an incredible fortune, and spends it—having himself no talents."

The saga of the *Kane* script, searched out like another rosebud in a thicket of claims and contradictions, begins with an ironic fact. The conception and creation of *Citizen Kane* depended entirely on a series of failures and fiascos. And Mankiewicz, Welles, and Houseman all came to their various involvements with *Kane* because of an accident, a piece of tragicomic bad luck in the disorderly downward progression of Herman's life.

The day Herman was fired from MGM and discredited at

all the studios, he optimistically recited to Sara the wonderful movie and play ideas that were going to resuscitate him. Perhaps fate had at last freed him from pernicious Hollywood. He talked about going to New York to find a job and move east permanently. Perhaps Kaufman would collaborate again. He said that a young screenwriter named Tommy Phipps, the nephew of Lady Astor, was driving to New York and had invited him to ride along. Sara agreed. The next day, September 8, 1939, carrying some cash borrowed from Joe, Herman climbed into Phipps's Buick convertible, and they departed.

Shortly thereafter Sara opened the financial statement Herman had left behind. He was badly overdrawn at the bank and had no income. He had a Morris Plan loan of $4,200, a loan on his furniture, and numerous personal debts. Joe took charge: Sam Jaffe lent money, Professor Mankiewicz sent $500, and Erna $1,000, and the Aaronsons contributed.

While Joe and Sam and a lawyer were conferring, Herman and Tommy Phipps were whizzing through the California sunshine toward the desert leg of their journey. Phipps was also leaving Los Angeles because of a catastrophe, a severed romance with a girl named Ethel. One could argue that it was Phipps's broken heart that brought about *Citizen Kane*.

Ethel had sent Phipps a departure present accompanied by the tantalizingly unpunctuated note: "Take good care of yourself always Ethel." That first day on the road was dominated by the word "always." Herman sat listening to Phipps's monologue debate on what "always" meant: whether or not it was a clue that after all, Ethel loved him. "And I was to remember," Herman recounted, "that she was not the kind of girl who could lightly write 'always Ethel.' If she meant just 'Ethel,' she would write 'Ethel.' The second day was dominated by the word 'good.' I should understand," Herman said, "that if a cultured girl like Ethel wanted to say, 'Take *good* care of yourself,' then that was what she would write and not 'take *care* of yourself' because if she meant 'take care of yourself,' she would write 'take care of yourself' and not 'take *good* care of yourself.' "

That evening, driving in the rain, Phipps turned on the radio. Every tune reminded him of Ethel. "Little White Lies" was the song an orchestra had played the first night they met. Songs evoked fights and reconciliations, their first dance, anniversaries, even a miserable time away from Ethel. In the passion of his torment the teary Phipps was driving faster and faster. The car skidded on a curve, hit a culvert post, plunged over an embankment, turned over.

Phipps, unconscious, had a broken collarbone. Herman was pinned under the car, his leg broken in three places, a deep cut extending from above one eyebrow to the back of his neck. And Herman always swore that as the car rocketed from the road, he saw written in letters of fire across Tommy Phipps's forehead, "She'll be sorry when she hears about this."

Returned to Los Angeles, Herman lay on his back for a month in the Cedars of Lebanon Hospital, his leg elevated in traction, "somewhat," said Herman, "in the posture of a lower-class Klondike whore." From the professor Herman received, by letter, a dose of advice and inspiration:

> *Kopf hoch* [head high]—I am not going to quote for you the proverbial saying of the silver lining which every cloud has, of the sunshine which follows rain, of the promise that every road has a turn—but I say this to you: Let the past bury the past, and let it be buried so deep that there is no chance of a resurrection. Eyes that do not turn backwards do not see any neurosis. There is a future of promise ahead of you.

Among Herman's visitors was a friend from New York, Orson Welles. They had met at lunch at "21" when Welles was the wonderboy of Broadway, staging in partnership with John Houseman one adventurous hit after another. Houseman remembers the day that Welles met Herman in the late 1930's

and told about "this amazingly civilized and charming man."
Houseman adds, "I can just see them there at lunch together,
magicians and highbinders at work on each other, vying with
each other in wit and savoir faire and mutual appreciation!
Both came away enchanted and convinced that, between them,
they were the two most dashing and gallantly intelligent gentlemen in the Western world! And they were not far wrong."

When Welles found Herman in the hospital, both physically
and financially prostrate, he decided to help him. Welles
offered Herman a job adapting literary classics for his *Mercury
Theater* radio show. Herman would get no credit; as a publicity device all the radio shows were billed as written, produced, directed by Orson Welles. But Herman would receive
$200 a script. Welles recalls, "I felt it would be useless, be-
cause of Mank's general uselessness many times in the studios.
But I thought, 'We'll see what comes up.'" What did come
up, eventually, was *Citizen Kane.*

Herman was immediately demanding and impatient about
the radio job, while Welles handled him with consummate
and disarming charm. He assured Herman by wire that the
sponsor had not yet approved the books for dramatization.
"I can cover a couple of days with a neat alibi about a
grounded plane and a washed out track," Welles cabled. "But
even I shrink from attempting a wholesome explanation for
my conduct and whereabouts since I solemnly promised six
days ago to let you hear from me in twenty-four hours. I give
you my oath the only thing I could have done before this
is keep up the decencies. Surely this is too much to ask. Much,
much love to you. Orson."

Herman began on the *Mercury* scripts in October, when he
left the hospital and returned to Tower Road. To cool Herman as he lay incarcerated in a cast that was "like a boulder
holding me down from my navel to my toes," Margaret Sullavan had his room rigged with a makeshift air conditioner.
She delivered long sticks for scratching under the cast. To

facilitate the writing, Joe Mankiewicz brought around the lap board he himself used. Herman said, "What the hell do I want with that?"

One day Herman's work was interrupted by a delegation of MGM writers who assembled at his bedside. They presented him with a large silver cigarette box engraved with all their names and the words "From Manky's pals." But to him it was like a gold watch given an old man when he retires. Herman wept after they left.

Herman wrote weekly *Mercury* scripts for *Huckleberry Finn, Rip Van Winkle, Vanity Fair, The Murder of Roger Ackroyd, Dodsworth.* "He was useful," Welles says, "particularly with Houseman," who was the editor on all the radio scripts and remembers editing Herman "rather harshly." Herman grew a mustache and wrote his father: "One way or another, the Lord or the opposition—I am a little mixed up myself as to who has been keeping his eye on me of recent years—will provide. We are all in reasonably good spirits, though we are not down on our knees in a halleluiah chorus all day long, y'understand."

To obtain income, Sara rented the Tower Road house and moved to southern Beverly Hills, where she rented a small house owned by the actor Laird Cregar. Orson Welles was a regular visitor there, coming in the evenings to enjoy Herman and confer on the radio scripts.

Welles was a stirringly handsome, flamboyant man, slightly rumpled, six feet three and a half inches tall. He had the same ravishing, irreverent charm as the young Charlie Kane. Geraldine Fitzgerald recalls, "We used to say that Orson had a 'God's-eye view,' that he saw in you all the things that other people didn't see, all the wonderments and brains and beauty and wit you had. But what was disturbing about this beautiful light was that it was rather like a lighthouse. When the beam turned, then somebody else was illuminated, and you were back in the darkness."

At the tiny Roxbury house, Sara's bed was the only place

in the bedroom to sit while visiting Herman. She was usually propped up on pillows, reading. Welles would say, "Move over," and lie down beside her. As he and Herman talked, goading each other with sarcasms, laughing uproariously, Welles would reach over and massage Sara's neck. "He was fun," Sara says. "Magnetic, absolutely."

Though Herman's 1939 accident was the immediate event that delivered Welles to the Roxbury room—and to *Citizen Kane*—Welles's route to Hollywood began in the fall of 1937. The hit of that season was a one-act bare-stage version of *Julius Caesar,* directed by and starring Orson Welles, who then was only twenty-two. It launched a rampage of innovative successes by the repertory Mercury Theater, which Welles and John Houseman had founded.

Welles, working twenty-hour days, had the production ideas, designed sets, discovered actors like Joseph Cotten, directed all the plays, and starred in most of them. John Houseman contributed a superbly organized intelligence. A British- and French-educated Armenian and former London grain broker, Houseman raised the money and was the tasteful, practical enabler for Welles's flashing imagination. Along with the stage productions, Welles and Houseman were creating their weekly radio dramatizations. "The War of the Worlds," broadcast in 1938, panicked much of America into believing the Martians were landing in Grovers Mill, New Jersey.

There was, of course, a flash flood of publicity, including a Welles cover on *Time* magazine captioned "Marvelous Boy." These stories all detailed his wunderkind credentials. His mother was a gifted musician, his lighthearted father a dissipated inventor who eventually committed suicide. At three Welles was reciting Shakespeare, at nine, performing magic, and at ten, discovering theater at the progressive Todd School, where he directed and starred in thirty Todd Players productions. At sixteen he acted a season with the Abbey Players in Dublin, Ireland, and at eighteen toured with Katharine Cornell. At twenty-one, he was ubiquitous on radio, doing the voice of Chocolate Pudding and historical characters in *The March of Time* and creating that invisible nemesis of evil the Shadow, hissing, "The seed of crime bears bitter fruit."

But in the 1938–39 season Orson Welles's success machine ran away with him. The last two Mercury productions, *Danton's Death* and *Five Kings,* were disasters. The latter was a grandiose telescoping of five Shakespeare histories into one play. Time and money ran short. Hopelessly unready, *Five Kings* closed in Philadelphia. During the production a simmering disaffection between Welles and Houseman boiled over. Welles accused Houseman of sabotaging him. Houseman complained that Welles's commitment was desultory, while his consumption of liquor, food, and women was awesome.

From this bitter failure, twenty-four-year-old Orson Welles traveled west in August 1939, the same month as Herman's accident. Houseman came also, but much reduced in importance, and working mainly on the radio shows. Welles had an RKO contract that paid him $100,000 a year to write, direct, produce, and perform in four movies, one per year. The subjects were to be chosen by Welles and filmed without interference from RKO executives. But by September, when Welles went to visit Herman in the hospital, the Hollywood adventure was already turning sour.

The movie industry regarded Welles as a puffed-up wise-acre who deserved deflation. His contract enraged veteran filmmakers who could only dream of such carte blanche terms. Their irritation was further inflamed by Welles's widely quoted remark during his first tour of RKO: "This is the biggest electric train a boy ever had." When Welles invited the important names of Hollywood to a party, nobody came. An actor cut off Welles's necktie at the Brown Derby. After Dorothy Parker, screenwriting in Hollywood, was introduced to Welles, she said, "It's like meeting God without dying." An actor named Gene Lockhart composed this doggerel:

> Little Orson Annie's come to our house to play,
> An' josh the motion pitchurs up and skeer the stars away,
> An' shoo the Laughtons off the lot an' build the sets an' sweep
> An' wind the film an' write the talk an' earn her board-an'-keep;
> An' all of us other acters, when our pitchur work is done,
> We set around the Derby bar an' has the mostest fun,
> A-listenin' to the me-tales 'at Annie tells about,
> An' the Gobblewelles'll git YOU
> Ef you DON'T WATCH OUT!

By November 1939, when Herman had begun writing *Mercury* radio scripts, Welles's first movie project, Conrad's *Heart of Darkness,* had already been shelved by RKO as too difficult, too expensive, too uncommercial. Welles switched unenthusiastically to the less ambitious English thriller *Smiler with a Knife.* Welles wrote his own script but, not satisfied, hired Herman to doctor it.

Smiler put Welles on Herman's own turf. For Herman, a self-destructive personality who worried that he was a washed-up hack, the chance to deflate this boy wonder proved irresistible. According to Welles, despite their genial relationship, Herman set out "to show that writing a film script was one thing I couldn't do and also one thing I had better come to him for. He destroyed my confidence in the script, sneering at everything I did, saying, 'That will never work.' "

By late December 1939 Welles was desperate. *Smiler with a Knife* was stalled, and his boy-wonder balloon was sagging down on top of him, to the delight of a grinning Hollywood. Welles began scratching for a new project. Both Hollywood outcasts, Welles and Herman had remained friends. They were already talking movie schemes and notions, that half fantasizing habitual to filmmakers. Now the brainstorming became a serious search for a plot idea—"just the two of us," says Welles, "yelling at each other not too angrily"—while

Herman fretfully poked his sticks under the cast, smoked, cursed, hollered needlessly for Sara, made Welles maneuver the bedpan, and writhed uncomfortably within his jungle gym of traction supports and exercise bars. Arguing, inventing, discarding, these two powerful, headstrong, dazzlingly articulate personalities thrashed toward *Kane*. Nobody knew who thought of what. To each man, everything seemed his own, perhaps because, like most great conceptions shared by two people, many of the basic elements already existed in the brains of both Mankiewicz and Welles.

For example, according to Welles, the initial, germinal idea for *Kane* was the movie's plot device: creating a posthumous portrait of a man through the memories of his survivors. Welles says it was his idea. Geraldine Fitzgerald testifies that she planted it in his head. Waiting for her husband to join her in Hollywood, she was living at Welles's house. One evening he was despondent over the abandonment of *Smiler*. So Geraldine Fitzgerald suggested the technique of telling a story from many points of view, a scheme for a play which had been in her mind for years. Soon after *Kane* was released, she said to Welles, "You know, that's taken from that idea I gave you."

"I don't want you talking about it," Welles said.

Geraldine Fitzgerald remembers: "I was so amazed because I thought he'd say, 'Yes, isn't it grand, the way it's turned out?' "

However, Herman, who was forever hustling old, pet ideas to new audiences, had already used the multi-point-of-view device in the mid-1930's. In the first act of his unproduced play *The Tree Will Grow,* news of Dillinger's death is brought to the gangster's family. The play is a complex and contradictory portrait gradually accumulated from the recollections of mother, father, friends, minister.

According to Herman, *Kane* was not triggered by the multiview idea. Herman once explained: "We discussed an unusual technique which was to show an actual guy in a *March of Time* and then find out about the guy." Whether or not *Kane* originated with the newsreel thought, it was undoubtedly Welles's contribution, a bonus of his two *March of Time* years, dramatizing the news to the pulse of "This week, as it must to all men. . . ."

Once they were launched, the two men began hunting a subject for their plot idea. They considered an industrialist, a soldier, even the life of Dumas. Herman said, "Then I told Welles that I would be interested in doing a picture based on Hearst and Marion Davies. I just kept on telling him everything about them. I was interested in them, and I went into all kinds of details."

Suddenly Herman's career had arrived at the center of his being. All that abstruse political reading and his whatnot shop of obscure Hearst lore merged with his movie professionalism. Says Don Mankiewicz, "I have always thought of his Hearst idea as a coin Pop carried around in his pocket, and then he finally spent it." Welles himself does give Herman grudging, lukewarm credit for suggesting Hearst: "I suppose I would remember if it had been me."

But, again, the thought was waiting in the heads of both men. Hearst was no stranger to Welles either. His father and Hearst had been young roisterers together. The Hearst friend and theater critic Ashton Stevens, eventually the model for the character Jed Leland, had been a sort of uncle to Welles. And in Hollywood of the 1930's everybody, including Welles, was steeped in the wonders of the Hearst-Davies household.

The Hearst idea took various shapes. Welles wanted the individual recollections about the newspaper publisher to be radically different, exactly like the later Japanese film *Rashomon*. Several long sequences would be repeated exactly but acted differently so the same events and dialogue would give conflicting images of Kane. Herman, says Welles, wanted to build the movie around the mysterious shooting of Hollywood pioneer Thomas Ince aboard the Hearst yacht. The theme would be the examination of a murderer.

Herman himself said that he wanted to do a love story between a publisher and a girl. The publisher was to be patterned not only on Hearst, but on other tycoons who had similar relationships with women: Brulatour and Hope Hampton, McCormick and Ganna Walska, Samuel Insull and Gladys Wallis. In fact, this plan would have been a rudimentary version of the final *Kane* script.

Mankiewicz and Welles were developing exactly the explosive, convention-busting movie that Welles needed to restart his stalemated career. But Herman, apparently finished in Hollywood, was hardly a choice to salvage anybody else's fortunes. Welles hired him anyway. "But," he says, "I had no intention of Mank being the coauthor. None. Rightly or wrongly, I was still without self-doubt in my ability to write a film script. I thought Mank would do that anecdotal kind of thing about Hearst, give me a few ideas, fight me a little—and mainly would be as destructive as he had been in *Smiler with a Knife*. But I didn't know how *not* to let him in since the essential idea of the many-sided thing had arisen in conversations with him. Of course, now I'm enormously grateful he existed."

But as they hammered at the details of the plot, often disagreeing, everything that was best in Herman emerged and Welles was doubly trapped. "Mank took off and became extremely constructive, even where I didn't agree, either at first or later," Welles says. In late January 1940, more than a month after the initial idea, their arguments were becoming less and less creative. Welles decided that Herman should start writing. Herman agreed, but on one condition: He must have as editor John Houseman, who had broken with Welles and the Mercury Theater and retreated to New York. Welles flew to New York, and Houseman, excited by the idea, returned with him.

In Hollywood the three men had several long script conferences, thoroughly discussing everybody's ideas. Around February 1, 1940, a two-car caravan set off, carrying Houseman, a secretary, a German nurse, reams of paper and source material, a bottle of pills supposed to combat Herman's alcoholic thirst, and Herman himself, excited and groaning cheerfully in the rear of a limousine. Their destination was a vacation retreat called the Campbell Ranch, a group of low Spanish adobe buildings on the desert flat near Victorville, California. Herman and Houseman shared a two-bedroom, living-room guest cottage. No liquor was allowed at Campbell Ranch. "That appealed to me," says Sara, who chose the place.

In that desert limbo Herman found the perfect circumstances in which he could function. He was quarantined from everything that had always plagued and immobilized him. Trapped in his cast, he could not go drinking. Studio ignoramuses were not degrading him. His family was not riddling him with guilt. There was little to do except write. Disputations and dissipations were not draining his energies and concentration. Herman was at peace.

The creativity in Herman was released. His self-doubts were eased and his confidence was bolstered by the presence of John Houseman, a challenging, analytical, perceptive man. Welles's enormous abilities almost guaranteed success. And in Welles and Houseman, he finally had creative intelligence he could respect.

The opportunity to use that banked-up political-historical expertise and excitement, hitherto useless in Hollywood for anything but conversation, must have galvanized Herman. And he was psychologically charged to make his great effort. The car accident had been a brush with mortality, a reminder that pulling himself together could not be postponed forever. Lastly, he was powerfully motivated by the very circumstances which made his *Kane* pinnacle almost incredible. Herman was at rock bottom. This screenplay was almost certainly his last chance.

The secretary Sara found to work with Herman was a tall, handsome English girl named Rita Alexander, who lent her name to Susan Alexander in *Kane*. She had already been asked by Sara not to drive Herman to local saloons. And on her first visit to his room after lunch, Herman, in bed in his cast, said, "Mrs. Alexander, one of your duties is of a kind that I hesitate to ask of you, but we might just as well get down to it from the beginning." He instructed her exactly on how to spoon bicarbonate into his mouth. After he had washed it down with water, he said, "You'll excuse me if I have a little belch. That's part of it." And the belches rocked the room, while Rita laughed and he grinned sheepishly and offered courtly apologies.

Rita Alexander was the only dispassionate witness to the events at the Campbell Ranch. The routine she experienced included little of Houseman. "Mank was so on top of what he was doing," she says, "that Houseman sort of ended up riding herd." She and Herman began each day around ten in the morning with a horrendous decision. Should the dictation take place indoors with Herman in bed? Or now that Herman could hobble on crutches, should he sit in the arid, sunny little patio with his leg up on a stool? In either spot, Herman still contrived to procrastinate. Mrs. Alexander, taught by her father, was expert at cribbage, and Herman would interrupt the dictating with bouts played for small stakes. When, as usual, he kept losing, he suggested upping the stakes to recoup. But he still lost as he entertained Rita with anecdotes about Hollywood and the Round Table.

Herman's main period of work was at night, after dinner, when he would dictate until midnight or 1 A.M. Rita would type up the pages immediately and return them to him before going to sleep. She asked how the story was going to turn out. "My dear Mrs. Alexander," Herman said, "I don't know. I'm making it up as I go along."

The movie had needed a device to knit together the series of reminiscences into a plausible story line. Welles unenthusiastically offered a long quote from Coleridge. Herman substituted the search for "rosebud"—the sled young Kane was riding in a blizzard the day his mother bound him over to the bank executive, the symbol of the parental love denied to both Charlie Kane and Herman.

Recollections of his boyhood winters in Wilkes-Barre had been kept on the surface of Herman's mind by a present Sara gave him, a glass ball paperweight containing a minute and wintry Swiss chalet and tree fixed forever in fluid. Herman would sit in his bedroom chair at Tower Road reflectively shaking the ball and watching the snow swirl up inside and settle down on the tiny scene. When Kane intoned, "Rosebud," he held just such a ball, which then rolled from his lifeless hand and broke.

Out of some private corner of Herman's memory came a gentle passage in the script, a moment of purity recollected which he gave to Kane's factotum, Bernstein. "One day, back in 1896," says Bernstein, "I was crossing over to Jersey on a ferry and as we pulled out there was another ferry pulling in . . . and on it there was a girl waiting to get off. A white dress she had on—and she was carrying a white parasol—and I only saw her for one second and she didn't see me at all— but I'll bet a month hasn't gone by since that I haven't thought of that girl." It is Welles's favorite passage in *Kane*, and even he says Herman wrote it.

Orson Welles's need for maximum credit for the *Kane* script has always been intense. At the time of the movie's release in 1941, it was his vindication. The movie silenced the sneers and proved that he was indeed a boy genius. But the presence of Mankiewicz, a discredited, production-line writer, tarnished the triumph, harmed the symmetry and credibility of the Welles creative package described by *Photoplay* magazine: "A master craftsman who writes, produces, directs, acts." It was the self-image which has been the cornerstone of the Welles ego. In time, Welles began dismissing Herman, telling interviewers, "Mankiewicz wrote several important scenes."

Orson Welles specifically denies that Herman did the basic script for *Kane*. According to Welles, he himself wrote the first script, a mammoth, 300-page version, mainly dialogue, which Herman actually took with him to Victorville. "Though everything was reworked throughout, that contained the script as it developed. But apparently Mank never showed it to anybody."

Welles had never before mentioned that massive piece of preliminary work. Hitherto he always based his claim of primary authorship on a very different story. That one has him writing his own, original screenplay, not *before* Victorville, but in parallel with Herman *during* Victorville. When the two scripts were finished, Welles combined them both.

It would have been strange if Welles had *not* put his *Kane* ideas on paper before Herman began writing. Moreover, he had chunks of Herman's script to work on during Victorville. At least once, midway in Herman's labors, Welles drove out and picked up all the pages to date. Reading them on the trip back to Los Angeles, he was outspokenly critical and began editing in the car. But as for an original script by Welles, there is only his word. Both Richard Wilson, his production assistant, and Richard Barr, the young aide-de-camp who ran his households and his errands, do not remember Welles, either before or during Herman's stay in Victorville, working the number of weeks that such a writing job requires.

To evaluate Welles's version of events, it is fair to consider him through the eyes of several men who worked on *Kane*, including Herman himself, who once wrote a treatment for a movie whose main character was Orson Welles, thinly disguised. "It is a real genius that he has," wrote Herman, "and not any particular talent or collection of talents that have become fortified and outstanding through training. He is no Meglin Kiddie or premature Quiz Kid. And he provokes a hero worship that makes it possible to react to his bad behavior as if somebody else were guilty of it. You really have to excuse and forgive him. Why, God knows."

The sound technician on *Kane*, James Stewart, remembers: "I'd work all day, and he'd make an appointment for eight o'clock at night to run rushes. Bob Wise, the cutter, and his assistant, Mark Robson, and myself were supposed to sit there and wait. He'd show up at midnight. No apologies. Just 'Let's get going now.' And we'd work till three or four A.M. He'd have a jug of whiskey, but no offering it to anybody else in the room. Just for Orson. I don't remember ever asking him for a favor. And I don't think it would have occurred to anyone else.

"And I remember Bernie Herrmann—he composed the music for *Kane*—once slammed open the door to the dubbing stage and began telling us what he thought of Orson's manners and methods. Then he slammed out again, and we all sat there a little stunned. Then the door burst open, and Bernie stuck his head in and said, 'Remember, I'm not talking about Orson the artist.'" Stewart adds, "If Orson called up tomorrow and asked me to make a picture, I'd know I'd learn something. I'd say, 'I'm with you.'"

Herman has written about Welles's relationship to the truth. "He has a large number of genuine incredible experiences, but he also has an enormous assortment of lies. And the terrible thing is that anyone who believes he has caught him in a fantastic lie is apt to find that the fantastic story is the truth. And some simple unimportant statement, like just having bought an evening paper a half hour ago, is the lie."

Paul Stewart, in addition to being the rehearsal director of the *Mercury Theater* radio shows and the actor who played Raymond, the butler, in *Kane*, had a social relationship with Welles. Stewart says, "Orson will say anything anywhere to anybody and look them straight in the eye. I remember when Orson was married to Rita Hayworth and we were sitting in the Cub Room of the Stork Club, and he says to me, 'Will you do me a favor? Tell Rita how I jumped out of a plane and parachuted into Chicago when we were late for a broadcast.'

"And I said, 'My God, I'd forgotten that,' as though you could forget such a thing. And I went on, 'The only thing is, I'm hazy on the details. I remember I was scared to death when I saw you do it.' See, I'd done this number with him before.

"And Orson goes on to tell how we're flying from New York to Chicago—you had to do it then in hops with small planes—and we stopped to refuel in Buffalo, and we refueled in Detroit and flew on to Chicago. And he tells Rita, 'I was so late, I said to the pilot, "Circle Lincoln Park. I'm going to parachute in. I know I can make it." '

"And I looked at Rita," Stewart says, "and she had *some* beautiful eyes and they were *this* big. And my wife—she knew. She kicked me under the table. He lies in other . . . in important things, too." But Stewart also says, "With Welles he's *so* brilliant, and he has a way of complimenting you and needing you. He phoned me personally in New York in September 1940 and asked me to play a part in a movie he was making. I said, 'Sure.' Didn't even ask what the part was. I was so pleased to be friends with him again. I'd missed him in my life because every day with him was a day of last-minute preparation and plunging ahead and creating."

While stating that Herman wrote the script and that he himself was only an editor, John Houseman nevertheless manages to claim a major role in the creation of the *Kane* structure, plot, and characters. In his memoir, *Run Through*, he describes a partnership of coarchitects:

> We started with the image of a man—a giant, a tycoon, a glamour figure—we asked each other how this man got the way he was . . . we discovered what persons were . . . we learned what he did to them . . . we found the dramatic structure of the film gradually asserting . . . we reduced the number of principal witnesses to five—we were creating a vehicle suited to the personality and creative energy of a man only slightly less fabulous than. . . .

And the gospel according to Houseman describes a rigid routine which kept him astraddle the project but does not square with Rita Alexander's memory. He tells how in the early morning he edited the previous day's pages. Later in the living room-office he and Herman loudly argued about changes with Mrs. Alexander present and planned that day's writing. Houseman wrote: "Once Mank had come to trust me, my editing, for all our disagreements, gave him more creative freedom than his own neurotic self-censorship." By midafternoon Herman would retire for a nap, and Houseman and Rita Alexander would review her notes. After dinner, according to Houseman, they worked together until around ten, and then he went to bed while Herman continued dictating. Houseman's impact on Herman's thinking was undoubtedly important. But *Run Through* leaves the impression that Herman was in part a conduit for Houseman's creative powers.

His need to claim a share in *Kane* is also great. In the Mercury Theater in New York, Houseman must ultimately have been galled by his role as Welles's clear-eyed catalyst. He must have grown sick of subordinating his ego while believing, perhaps, that he was making the wonder-boy career possible. As one of Welles's assistants once said, "There was only one umbrella, and that was Orson. You either enjoyed the shade or got out."

And then in Hollywood Houseman was drastically demoted by Welles. *Run Through* diminishes Welles's contribution to the Mercury Theater. The *Kane* script becomes Houseman's proof that he was always a creative contributor in his own right, perhaps even the key to Welles's great accomplishments. Welles says, "I have only one real enemy in my life that I know about, and that is John Houseman. Everything begins and ends with that hostility behind the mandarin benevolence."

In a letter to Alexander Woollcott about *Kane*, Herman once said:

> I feel it my modest duty to tell you that the conception of the story, the plot, the characters, the manner of telling the story and about 99 percent of the words are the exclusive creations of
>
> Yours,
> Mank.

In 1948 Herman, Welles, and RKO were sued for plagiarism by Ferdinand Lundberg, the author of *Imperial Hearst*. The suit was settled out of court. In a deposition Herman testified, "I would say I wrote a good 98 percent of the picture."

Herman's need for sole credit was overwhelming. *Kane* was proof that he was a major dramatist capable of a work of art. It was his shot at self-respect. In the Mankiewicz household, the fact of Herman's authorship was irrevocably taken for granted.

But in the overall, historical puzzle of who did exactly what, Herman's percentages seem implausible. Houseman, a fluent man of intellect, must have made valuable input. It is impossible to imagine that the protean Welles at the height of his powers was merely an admiring spectator. Moreover, Herman's version ignores some five weeks of preliminary script discussions. Undoubtedly both Herman and Houseman arrived at the Campbell Ranch crammed with Welles's ideas and wishes.

Nevertheless, Herman's pride of authorship was justified. There is no corroborating evidence of early drafts by Orson Welles. Herman endured the writer's special agony and faced the blank pages. Selecting from the ideas of Welles and Houseman, exercising his own imagination and knowledge, applying the experience of a decade of screenwriting, Herman assembled in his mind the roots and trunk of *Kane*. What Herman created in Victorville contained all the characters, nearly all the scenes, and more than 60 percent of the dialogue in the finished film. Herman Mankiewicz wrote *Citizen Kane*.

In Victorville Herman finished the first version of *Citizen Kane* in twelve weeks. As Houseman chooses to put it, "We were done." The manuscript was titled *American*, an ironic jab at Hearst who wrapped himself, like many extremists, in the mantle of Americanism. Despite Houseman's description of himself and Herman paring every excess out of *American*, it was 325 pages long and outrageously overwritten, even for a first draft. Houseman blandly ignores this fact. He implies that *American*, with only the conventional amount of polishing, was what was filmed. Moreover, Houseman departed for New York just four days after delivering *American* to Welles.

Three months—April 16 to July 16—were required to cut *American* by half from 325 pages to 156 pages. Herman, too close to the work to be objective and always proprietary about every line, must have found such ruthlessness difficult. One of his later producers, Bert Granet, once said, "Herman would rather talk for three days than change two innocuous lines of dialogue. Before you knew it, Plato, Kant, and Mencken were involved in whether the leading lady should open or shut the door."

On the other hand, Orson Welles was primed for the job. Houseman, before he left Hollywood, noted that Welles was "working once again with a concentrated, single-minded intensity that I had not seen since the first year of the Mercury." Welles was attacking ground already broken by Herman, and within *American* the nucleus of *Kane* was sound, the surrounding fat clearly visible. Welles, both the producer and director, made all final decisions. Always brilliantly articulate and perceptive, Welles was confident of his ability to write, or rewrite, dialogue. In fact, after *Kane*, he wrote the screenplays for all but one of the movies he directed—though none were commercially successful or celebrated for their scripts. Most have been judged more or less flawed, often because of Welles's excesses or irresponsibility. But in 1940 his genius and ego and determination were still in equilibrium.

Moreover, his great gift has always been the leap of his imagination, the exciting boldness of his innovations—augmenting, revising, rearranging, transposing—imprinting his personality on whatever he controlled. He would not have restrained himself in the case of Mankiewicz and *American*.

Mankiewicz provided Welles with the blueprint of a masterpiece. Then Welles, with solid help from Herman, added important enrichments and refinements and lifted the script the final distance. "I know Orson touched every scene," says Richard Barr, Welles's assistant, who later became a Broadway producer and president of the League of New York Theaters. "And I don't mean cutting a word or two. I mean some serious rewriting, and in a few cases he wrote whole scenes. I think it's time history balanced this situation."

For example, Welles remembers writing the confrontation between Kane and a drunk and moralistic Leland: "The truth is, Charlie, you just don't care about anything except you." Welles says Thornton Wilder's *Long Christmas Dinner* inspired the breakfast scene depicting the deterioration of Kane's marriage. "Open plagiarism, confessed to at the start," says Welles delightedly.

But, adds Welles, "I didn't come in like some more talented writer and save Mankiewicz from disaster." There was an intermediate script marked "Welles version" and a later one marked "Mankiewicz version." Revised pages were passed back and forth between the two, Welles changing Herman, who changed Welles—"often much better than mine," says Welles.

They fought over cuts and additions. Welles wanted the characters talking about Kane to disagree and their versions of the man to be radically different. Herman had softened this approach. Eventually Welles concurred. Herman argued against the farcical quality in the early newspaper scenes— and lost.

In *American*, Susan Alexander had a young lover at Xanadu who was murdered by the sinister butler, Raymond. Welles insisted that this was too sensational; it would throw the film out of balance. Herman, arguing, said, "But if we keep it in, we'll never have any trouble with Hearst!"

They disagreed about the scene re-creating Herman's drunken failure in 1925 to finish his *Times* review of Insull's wife. In the scene Jed Leland falls asleep by his typewriter as he annihilates Susan Alexander's operatic debut. But Welles decided that Kane should finish Leland's scathing review. Says Welles, "I always wanted Kane to have that sort of almost self-destructive elegance of attitude which, even when it was self-regarding and vain, was peculiarly chic. Mank fought me terribly about that scene: 'Why should he finish the notice? He wouldn't. He just wouldn't print it.' Which would have been true of Hearst. Oh, how Mank hated my version!"

Herman said about Welles, "It never occurs to him that there is any solution other than his own. Despite yourself, you find yourself accepting this notion." And indeed, Sara remembers no serious unhappiness over the surgery he and Welles were performing, which is also testimony that Welles never wrote a parallel script. "This was as good a time as Herman had in his career," she says. "He didn't drink at all and grew very expansive, was able to enjoy the boys, enjoy Johanna. If Orson had brought in his own script, Herman would have screamed and yelled, 'Jesus, you should see what he's got!' Never."

Sara had moved the family back to Tower Road, and she has a mental image of meetings in the green-cushioned reed sofa and chairs out near the pool. She remembers clipboards on laps, secretaries, Herman going up to his office to type out a page. Sometimes members of the cast, Mercury actors like Joseph Cotten, joined the sessions. She has movies of barbecues she put on. "We went to Mank's garden and sat around reading the script and making suggestions," says Cotten, who played Jed Leland. "What Herman was most concerned about was that we might let Poor Sara know that the man who came by every day was *not* cleaning the pool. He was a bookie."

Welles, however, remembers Herman at that time only as an antagonist and rejects the possibility of any such sociable backyard meetings. "There was great work done at this time," says Welles, "but it wasn't as happy or useful as it might have been. I have always conceived of Houseman's main role in Victorville as that of arousing Mank's latent hatred of anybody who wasn't a writer—and directing it at me. When Mank left for Victorville, we were friends. When he came back, we were enemies. Mank always needed a villain."

Orson Welles has his own views on Herman's contribution to *Citizen Kane*: "Without Mank it would have been a totally different picture. It suits my self-esteem to think it might have been almost as good, but I could never have arrived at *Kane* as it was without Herman. When we were together in New York, Mank was absolutely beside himself with delight over the banker Richard Whitney, who was sent to Sing Sing, a perfect J. P. Marquand type. The head of the stock exchange with stripes on. God, how he loved that. And I think Kane was a WASP boogeyman to Mank. A suitable topic for jokes. And Mank's spleen was given a marvelous direction by that; it gave energy to his writing.

"There is a quality in the film—much more than a vague perfume—that was Mank and that I treasured. It gave a kind of character to the movie which I could never have thought of. It was a kind of controlled, cheerful virulence; we're finally telling the truth about a great WASP institution. I personally liked Kane, but I went with that. And that probably gave the picture a certain tension, the fact that one of the authors hated Kane and one loved him.

"But in his hatred of Hearst, or whoever Kane was, Mank didn't have a clear enough image of who the *man* was. Mank saw him simply as an egomaniac monster with all these people around him. So I don't think a portrait of a man was ever present in any of Mank's scripts. Everybody assumes that because Mank was an old newspaperman, and because he wrote about Hearst, and because he was a serious reader on politics, then that is the whole explanation of what he had to do with *Kane*. I felt his knowledge was journalistic, not very close, the point of view of a newspaperman writing about a newspaper boss he despised.

"I don't say that Mank didn't see Kane with clarity. He saw

everything with clarity. No matter how odd or how right or how marvelous his point of view was, it was always diamond white. Nothing muzzy. But the truths of the character, Kane, were not what interested him.

"Mank was only interested in very personal terms in the all-devouring egomaniac tycoon. So the easily identifiable, audience identifiable reasons for what happened to Kane were part of Mank's contribution—and what made the picture finally popular. I think if I had been left to my own devices, we would have had to wait another fifty years.

"My *Citizen Kane* would have been much more concerned with the interior corruption of Kane. The script is most like me when the central figure on the screen is Kane. And it is most like Mankiewicz when he's being talked about. And I'm not at all sure that the best part isn't when they're talking about Kane. Don't misunderstand me! I'm not saying I wrote all of one and Mank wrote the other. Mank wrote Kane stuff and I wrote . . . who knows.

"I don't suppose that authors ever agree on how much they did when they finish. In their secret selves they all think they wrote what they didn't. I'm sure of that. I'm sure I do. My recollection can be just as. . . ."

There is one postscript to Welles's remark. Herman, unaware that his attitude toward Hearst would ever be important, answered a 1943 letter from Harold Ross asking for help on a profile on Hearst. Herman answered with his usual dash of self-satire:

> I happened to be discussing Our Hero with Orson, and with the fair-mindedness that I have always recognized as my outstanding trait, I said to Orson that, despite this and that, Mr. Hearst was, in many ways, a great man. He was, and is, said Orson, a horse's ass, no more no less, who had been wrong without exception, on everything he's ever touched. For instance, for fifty years, said Orson, Hearst did nothing but scream about the Yellow Peril, and then he gave up his seat and hopped off that band wagon two months before Pearl Harbor.

* * *

In July 1940, with the script haggling finished, the two men had another argument over the title. Nobody had been able to think of one. Welles offered a $100 prize to anybody who did. His secretary, Katherine Trosper, came up with one which still moves Welles to delighted laughter. She proposed *A Sea of Upturned Faces*. It was the RKO studio head, George Schaefer, who suggested *Citizen Kane*. Herman fought hard against it: "They'll all think it's because it's Cain and Abel that you want to call him Kane."

"Do you suppose anybody's ever thought of that?" Welles asks. "How could you? Kane. *K*. Nice Irish name. With a *K*. You never fail with a *K* in a name."

Then Herman and Welles argued over the casting of Dorothy Comingore as Susan Alexander. At her screen test, Herman told Welles, "Yes, she looks precisely like the image of a kitten we have been looking for." Welles hired her. Then they learned she was three months pregnant. Herman, worried about physical changes, fought, futilely, to remove her. He finally wrote Welles a letter: "I feel it my duty to express my opinion again —and for the last time, you will be pleased to hear. It is simply incomprehensible to me that with the start of production two weeks off. . . ." He signed it "Yr obd't svt."

The shooting of *Citizen Kane* began on July 30, 1940. On the twenty-ninth the entire *Citizen Kane* company—actors, grips, camera crew, the music composer, film cutter, etc.—met for breakfast at 1105 Tower Road. And like the first day of rehearsal for a stage production, the cast read the script aloud from the first to last scene. Welles generously kept Herman and Houseman on the Mercury payroll at $1,000 a week, though both were now largely extraneous. Houseman had had almost no connection with *Kane* since the delivery of *American*.

Nobody remembers Herman's presence on the shooting set, where Welles regarded him as "a visiting enemy." Herman would refer to Welles as "the boy wonder's boy wonder" and joked about "Orson's descent upon Hollywood and his production of the first full-length motion picture completely with-

out film!" At the Campbell Ranch, Herman and Houseman
had taken to calling Welles "Maestro, the Dog-Faced Boy,"
and once at RKO, nodding toward Welles, Herman remarked,
"There but for the grace of God goes God." Later when Sara
bought a dog for Johanna, Herman named it Orson. Perhaps
Herman, pouring into *Kane* his vitriol against all bosses, *had*
to hate Welles, too. Anger was his one completely unstifled
passion. "I wonder whether rage wasn't the best thing Mank
had," says Welles. "But there was nothing secret about Mank's
hate. I think hatred, to be truly useful, had better be partially
secretive."

Herman did see occasional rushes of *Kane,* but he was not
privy to Welles's cinematic vision which lifted the script beyond anything Hollywood imagined. Herman once vigorously
criticized the work in progress. There were not enough standard
movie conventions being observed, he said, including too
few close-ups. And there was too little "evidence of action," so
Kane was coming out too much like a play.

But Herman was primarily occupied once again by his
broken leg. It healed at last. The cast was removed. To cele-
brate, he went to Chasen's. He celebrated so thoroughly that
when he got up to leave at 2 A.M., his crutch slipped and he
fell and broke his leg again. There were more months in a
cast in bed—and his left leg remained permanently shorter
than his right.

Once the filming of *Kane* was under way, the question of
writer's credit began to loom. There are two diametrically opposite versions of what happened. One of them has Welles
battling to be listed as the sole writer, removing Herman. This
version begins in Victorville when Herman mentioned almost
casually that it was turning out to be a good script; too bad he
wasn't going to get credit. Rita Alexander felt a rush of indignation: "How could you agree to such a thing?" Herman
explained that he needed the money and that this was part of
his deal with Welles.

Eventually Herman was assured that he would get cocredit.

But on his return to Tower Road, Sara thought he deserved sole credit. Herman kept blandly telling her not to worry, he would get credit. She must understand that Welles had to get cocredit as part of "written, produced, directed, and performed by Orson Welles." Anything less would break his contract. "Herman was acquiescent about it, far too acquiescent," says Sara. "At the time I was not myself. I was Pollyanna. I kept thinking right would win out—which it never does—and that Orson would finally say, 'Oh, Christ, I'm not going to take any credit; you've done it all.' "

When *Kane* was roughly a month into production, Houseman talked to Herman by phone and, says Houseman, "I had to listen to his ambivalent ravings about 'Monstro,' his latest name for Welles, whom he alternately described as (one) a genius shooting one of the greatest films ever made, and (two) a scoundrel and a thief, who was now claiming sole credit for the writing of *Citizen Kane*."

Herman lodged a protest with the Screen Writers Guild. According to Welles's assistant, Richard Barr, this was a battle Welles set out to win. "I believe," says Barr, "that Orson didn't want anybody's name on that script but his own." Herman made angry phone calls to influential friends. He asked Sara, "If Welles offers me money to take my name off the credits, should I accept it?" Sara said, "Are you out of your mind?" An offer of $10,000 was actually made, believed Nunnally Johnson, and Hecht advised Herman to "take the money and screw the bastard."

But then Herman withdrew his guild arbitration request, according to a Welles biographer named Roy Fowler, who did his research in the early 1940's, when memories were fresh and all the participants alive. Herman was afraid of retribution from Hearst, says Fowler, and decided not to be a writer of record on *Kane*. Then Herman vacillated. Should he or should he not protest to the guild? In January 1941 Herman was awarded his credit anyway by RKO, says Fowler. The routine guild credit form listed Welles first, Herman second. Somebody—Richard Wilson, his production manager, says Welles did it—circled Mankiewicz with a pencil and drew an arrow putting him in first place. So the official credits read "Screenplay by Herman J. Mankiewicz and Orson Welles."

The second version is the Welles story. He regards himself as permanently vilified. "I hate to think," Welles has said, "what my grandchildren, if I ever have any, are going to think of their ancestor: something rather special in the line of megalomaniac lice." These are Welles's facts: "When Mank turned into the real writer, it was immediately understood between us that he would get first billing since he was a distinguished screenwriter. And I've always said that his credit was immensely deserved. But then Mankiewicz persuaded himself that he was the sole and only writer. He wanted his name to be the only name. He wanted mine off. I didn't want mine off. And I tried to persuade Houseman to put his name on, since he'd been working all this time. But Houseman was more interested in mischief than glory. And there wasn't any way of discussing it with Mank. I felt that some kind of awful magic mirror had been placed between us."

Welles adds, somewhat plaintively, "Certainly anybody who was around then can . . . maybe Wilson can verify that." But Richard Wilson does not remember any credit battle at all. The director Peter Bogdanovich, Welles's friend and defender, wrote for *Esquire* an elaborate rebuttal to Pauline Kael's pro-Mankiewicz article in *The New Yorker*. But he had no evidence supporting Welles's version of the credit dispute. Welles says that preparing for a possible guild arbitration, he had his secretary assemble all the pages he alone wrote, and copies were sent to Herman. But even Welles himself was unable to extract this memory from the secretary, though she remembers typing many script pages for Welles. "There went my best case," he bewails.

Screenwriter and director Frank Pierson (*Cool Hand Luke, Dog Day Afternoon, A Star Is Born*) sits on the guild arbitration committee. It is Pierson's personal opinion that if Welles wrote original material during the cutting of *American,* the changes made at that time were more than enough to earn him a second line credit—signifying that Welles was not co-author but did make significant contributions. Considering the two men involved and the probabilities, the existing credit seems fair.

In the first days of January 1941, a little more than a year after those sessions in the Roxbury bedroom, the filming of *Citizen Kane* was completed, and almost immediately Louella Parsons precipitated the Hearst counterattack that Herman had feared. The Hollywood of Herman's era was summed up, in a sense, by the fact that gossip columnists like "Lolly" Parsons, and her prime competitor, Hedda Hopper, wielded serious power.

Originally hired by Hearst because of her friendship with Marion Davies, Louella wrote columns of prattle that were an unimportant mix of cat's claws and sentimentality. Nothing existed but Hollywood. While Herman had been in Victorville, Europe was moving toward war, and her column reported: "The deadly dullness of the past week was lifted today—when Darryl Zanuck admitted he had bought all rights to Maurice Maeterlinck's *The Blue Bird* for Shirley Temple." And Hollywood could never decide which was a more frightful punishment—to be banned from Lolly's column or be the target of her spleen. Furious at Nunnally Johnson, she wrote of his wife: "I ran into Dorris Bowdon last night. She used to be such a pretty girl before she married."

Tough, fat Louella so worshiped Hearst that when hard-drinking Dr. Harry Martin proposed marriage in 1930—she called him Dockie-Wockie—Hearst had to give his blessings before she would accept. To his endorsement, Hearst later added a wedding present of a $25,000 necklace. And he always made it clear that a quarrel with Louella was a quarrel with the entire Hearst empire.

That was the fight she started after she saw *Kane*. Herman, in his letter to Alexander Woollcott, told what happened:

Dear Alec:

It is my opinion that Mr. Hearst, who is smart at these things, would have ignored *Citizen Kane,* positively and negatively, had he been given the chance. But this behavior was denied him chiefly because of an idiot named Louella Parsons and a very smart woman named Hedda Hopper.

The general subject matter of *Citizen Kane* was a matter of public knowledge for months to everyone connected with the picture industry, except Miss Parsons, its most comprehensive and authoritative reporter. In fact, just a few weeks before the scandal broke, she had called Orson and asked him to confirm or deny, on his sacred word of honor, her exclusive scoop that *Citizen Kane* was about Communism. Orson denied this.

When, for publicity purposes, Orson assembled the picture and arranged to show it in a very rough form to *Life* and *Look,* Hedda forced her way into the showing. At its conclusion, I am told, she got to her feet, screamed magnificently that this constituted an outrage against a great American, and proceeded to call the great American at San Simeon to tell him what she had just seen. (Hedda has for some time been letting it be known that she would be much better in Louella's job than Louella is, which is true, and it is not impossible that her call was connected with her ambitions.)

Whereupon, Mr. Hearst called Louella and told her about the picture. Louella, every ounce of her suet apoplectic, summoned two Hearst lawyers from downtown Los Angeles, demanded and received an immediate showing of the picture, and at once started telephoning young Bill Hearst, in addition to all the other Hearst executives she could get hold of. She also called George Schaefer, President of RKO, and she told him she would run him out of the business.

An immediate order was issued, banning all *Citizen Kane* publicity, plus all mention of Welles, myself and others connected with the picture from the Hearst papers. Mr. Hearst himself got in touch with Louis B. Mayer and gave him a calm and unexcited version of the situation as it seemed to him.

To wit: Mr. Hearst had no specific attitude as to whether the picture should be released. He thought this was an attitude the industry should determine. But personally, if he was Mr. Mayer or the Warner Frères, he would be violently opposed to the release, by any company, of a picture that could be considered offensive to anybody, like Mr. Hearst, who had always been such a great friend of the industry. Then Mr. Hearst casually gave them a hundred examples of unfavorable news—rape by executives, drunkenness, miscegenation and allied sports— which on direct appeal from Hollywood he had kept out of his papers in the last fifteen years.

General observations were made—not by Mr. Hearst himself but by high placed Hearst subordinates—that the proportion of Jews in the industry was a bit high and that it might not always be possible to conceal this fact from the American public—with the further fact, which is true, that a number of German Jewish writers, who cannot talk English, have been provided with affidavits and contracts for Hollywood employment at a time when many noble, honest American born writers in Hollywood didn't know how to pay their rent.

It quickly became difficult, through Mr. Mayer's efforts, for RKO to get bookings for the picture. The Music Hall in New York, for instance, which had the picture scheduled for release on February 14, found that previous bookings made it impossible to keep that date and that there seemed to be little chance to set a new date for months and months and months to come. Harry Warner, who controls an enormous number of theaters, told RKO he would be delighted to have *Citizen Kane* play his theaters but that, since there were so many rumors about possible law suits involving many penalties and even jail sentences for local managers, he thought it only a matter of ordinary business precaution to ask RKO to provide him with a $5,000,-000.00 indemnity bond. In RKO's present financial situation, a $50.00 indemnity bond would be funny. The Loew theaters, controlled by M.G.M., were obviously out of the question.

Herman always believed that Hearst knew in advance about *Kane* and chose not to act. Before shooting started, Herman had given Marion Davies's nephew, Charlie Lederer, a final version of the script. Concerned about hurting Marion, who had been a generous friend, worried about his future in Hollywood, Herman wanted Lederer's opinion on her reaction. Lederer remembers thinking, "This book is noteworthy for dullness." He told Herman not to worry; Susan Alexander bore no resemblance to Marion.

This act of Herman's was astoundingly ingenuous. Or else he was terrified of success, of creating future expectations he feared he could not satisfy. Lederer, no longer a friend of Herman's, would have had good reason to take the manuscript to Hearst, who, before production began, could probably have stopped the movie. Lederer, who is noted for his honesty, has always denied showing the script to anybody. But on its return to Herman, pencil lines marked every conceivable reference to Hearst, the tracks, perhaps, of Hearst lawyers.

Also mysterious was a confrontation Herman had at a dinner party soon after *Kane* was completed and when it was being shown to select audiences in RKO screening rooms. A woman fresh from a week at San Simeon attacked Herman for a sequence in the movie in which a President of the United States is assassinated immediately after inflammatory attacks by Kane's newspaper, an echo of Hearst's campaign against President McKinley. This episode, however, was not in the film, had not been in the script Lederer saw, and had occurred only in *American*.

As the offensive to quash *Kane* gathered momentum, Nicholas Schenk of Loew's and MGM told Schaefer at RKO, "Nobody'll ever see that picture," and he offered Schaefer the cost of *Kane*, $800,000, to burn the negative. Louella telephoned Nelson Rockefeller, a major creditor of RKO, which was in receivership, and threatened an ugly story on John D. Rockefeller. She phoned David Sarnoff, president of RCA which controlled RKO, and promised him an unfavorable personal article. The Hearst papers were refusing all RKO advertising, while belaboring Schaefer and Welles. A sycophant to L. B. Mayer, agent Frank Orsatti, circulated the rumor that Schaefer was anti-Semitic. Louella Parsons called the local draft board and demanded to know why Orson Welles, a young man of draft age with no dependents, had not been called into the service. The Hearst chain tried to label Welles a Communist. "It looked like I had a dead duck on my hands," says Schaefer.

But RKO continued to back Schaefer, and he showed *Kane* to the chief Time Incorporated libel lawyer, who felt RKO was safe after one minor change was made. Welles's lawyer, Arnold Weissberger, assured him that in order to sue, "Hearst is going to have to say, the reason I know that SOB is me is because I'm that SOB, which he is not likely to do."

RKO opened *Citizen Kane* without repercussions at its Palace Theater on Broadway on May 1, 1941, followed by openings at RKO and rented theaters in other major cities. And publicity programs were printed with photographs of Welles, the one-man band, directing, acting, and writing. "I'm particularly furious at the incredibly insolent description of how Orson wrote his masterpiece," said Herman in a letter to his father. "The fact is that there isn't one single line in the picture that wasn't in writing—writing from and by me—before ever a camera turned."

Now that Hearst had failed to take action, Schaefer threatened an antitrust suit against Warner Brothers, which relented, followed rapidly by the Paramount chain and Loew's. But though *Kane*, made by Welles for the extraordinarily small sum of $746,000 did not lose money, it was too unorthodox for the forties audiences and was a commercial failure.

Nevertheless, few motion pictures ever received reviews equaling *Kane*'s. Howard Barnes, in the New York *Herald Tribune*, opened his with the sentence "The motion picture stretched its muscles at the Palace Theater last night to remind one that it is the sleeping giant of the arts." The New York *World-Telegram* announced that "Orson Welles' *Citizen Kane*

is a Masterpiece of the Cinema." *PM* called it "A Truly Great
Picture." Archer Winsten, in the New York *Post*, called the
film "a great work of art" and said, "Citizen Kane will be a
film which is important in the history of American motion
pictures," while the *Hollywood Reporter* trumpeted: "Mr.
Genius Comes Through; 'Kane' Astonishing Picture."

Only one critic, Eileen Creelman in the New York *Sun*,
called *Kane* "a cold picture" and echoed Welles's own misgiv-
ings. "Its faults live with me," says Welles, who considers his
1966 *Chimes at Midnight* by far his best film. *"Kane* was made
in the most wildly fun-and-games kind of way. But from the
very beginning I felt it had a curious iciness at its heart. It has
moments when the whole picture seems to me to echo a bit.
I was always conscious of the sound of footsteps echoing in
some funny way—a certain effect made by proportions of
certain chemicals. And that spirit was very strange. Very
strange. It disturbed me and still does."

Following the reviews, Welles wired Herman:

Dear Mankie. If you haven't seen all the papers I'll be glad to
send them on. In the meantime feel you should know that a lady
named Miss Closer has been phoning me claiming to be your
rosebud. She says she has written her own libretto and some day
you will have to hear her sing. She tells me to tell you this. Please
advise. Love—Orson.

Herman's answer was from Sara: "Report to me, the only
original authentic rosebud, on all of Herman's rosebuds you
meet giving full details including what kind of spectacles, how
many pimples, and so forth. Isn't it wonderful about the picture? Love, Sara."

Citizen Kane was nominated for an Academy Award in
every possible category, including Best Original Screenplay.
Herman insisted he had no chance to win, though the *Hollywood Reporter* had given the film first place in ten of its
twelve divisions. The fear of Hearst, he felt, was still alive. And
Hollywood's resentment and distrust of Welles, the noncon-

formist upstart, were even greater since he had lived up to his wonderboy ballyhoo. The Academy Awards dinner, broadcast on radio, was held in February 1942. Welles was in South America filming *Carnival*. Herman refused to attend. "He did not want to be humiliated," says Sara. "He thought he'd get mad and do something drastic when he didn't win."

The night of the awards Herman turned on his radio and sat in his bedroom chair. Sara lay on his bed. As the screenplay category approached, he pretended to be hardly listening. Suddenly from the radio, half screamed, came "Herman J. Mankiewicz." Welles's name as coauthor was drowned out by voices all through the audience calling out, "Mank! Mank! Where is he?" And audible above all others was Irene Selznick: "Where is he?"

Herman was in his bathrobe and slippers doing a dance with Sara, stumping around on his bad leg. Olga Aaronson was at Mattie's house, and still in their nightgowns, the two women drove right over. And Olga, holding up the long skirt of her gown, danced with Herman.

George Schaefer accepted Herman's Oscar. Except for this coauthor award, the Motion Picture Academy excommunicated Orson Welles. John Ford was best director for *How Green Was My Valley*. Gary Cooper won for *Sergeant York*. The Best Picture was *How Green Was My Valley*. But as Pauline Kael put it, "The members of the Academy . . . probably felt good because their hearts had gone out to crazy, reckless Mank, their own resident loser-genius." When his Oscar was sent over by George Schaefer with "congratulations and best wishes from a high-priced office boy," Herman was unashamedly proud of it. He put it on his bureau in his bedroom, then said to Sara, "Would you like to take it down to the living room?"

For a birthday present Johanna painted a crude Oscar on a blue tie—and Herman wore it everywhere. He figured out the acceptance speech he should have made if he had been at the Academy Awards dinner: "I am very happy to accept this award in Mr. Welles's absence because the script was written in Mr. Welles's absence."

A small patter of congratulatory wires came in from B. P. Schulberg, from Moss Hart ("I am proud to know you"), Herbert Bayard Swope ("I hope it means money in your pocket"). Herman sent out answers, joking that it had been a sympathy vote: "I am frankly pleased to have won the award, but I don't look forward to much more success in this direction, because the right leg won't stand any more breaking, and that leaves only one leg left."

"But," says Sara, "I think Herman was a little disappointed at both Ben and Rose Hecht's reception of *Citizen Kane*. They never said anything about it."

From Rio de Janeiro, Orson Welles wrote:

Dear Mankie:

> Here's what I wanted to wire you after the Academy Dinner:
> "You can kiss my half."
> I dare to send it through the mails only now that I find it possible to enclose a ready-made retort. I don't presume to write your jokes for you, but you ought to like this:
> "Dear Orson: You don't
> know your half from a
> whole in the ground."
>
> *Affectionately,*

"God, if I hadn't loved him," says Welles, "I would have hated him after all those ridiculous stories, persuading people I was offering him money to have his name taken off. . . . That was the kind of thing he enjoyed for mischievous purposes, moving aside from the facts if it would make a little fuss and entertain everybody. He was not wedded to the truth. And I swear to you, we used to sit around and laugh and say, 'There goes Mank.' Wouldn't you know that having succeeded in . . . here we had a fine movie . . . that he would be carrying on like this, denouncing me as a coauthor, screaming around. You know, he just couldn't relax. Imagine a man who could command not friendship; you felt an emotion for him that's different from friendship to such a point that even I, feeling as I did, never for a moment felt the slightest change in my affection for him. You felt this fondness, though you knew that if he had a chance, he would cut you off at the knees. Not because he would dance on your grave, but because he wanted company down there himself!"

Herman Mankiewicz and Orson Welles, willful, egocentric enemies of anything established, both chose their purgatories. Though the two worked in vastly different leagues, Joseph Cotten could have been talking about either one when he said of Welles, "I don't know how far he could have soared. He never has a conventional thought; that's what keeps him alive. He has a constant fear of conformity, and I suppose he felt if he accepted one grain of discipline, it would destroy his genius."

When Welles talks about the waste of Herman, he is talking, too, about the waste of Orson Welles. "I think," he says, "that Hollywood is more stupid and cruel than anybody has ever said, the history of the way really gifted people have been treated. And the gifts were there in Mankiewicz. Mank was certainly one of the real victims. That he might have found another source of persecution is beside the case. He did, truly, find it in Hollywood. He was given nothing, no encouragement of confidence, that *everything* he needed to be a happy writer. The system was totally against him. But it's against talent."

Taken as a whole, of course, *Citizen Kane* was overwhelmingly Welles's film, a triumph of intense personal magic. Herman was one of the talents, the crucial one, that were mined by Welles. But one marvels at the debt those two self-destroyers owe to each other. Without Welles there would have been no supreme moment for Herman. Without Mankiewicz there would have been no perfect idea at the perfect time when all was possible for Welles and perhaps no fully resolved film to confirm his genius.

And one marvels, too, at the thought of two men so empty of self-restraint—and the sane Mr. Houseman—combining on a script better than any of them knew how to write. Neither Welles nor Houseman ever proved to be a gifted screenwriter. When in 1955 Welles wrote his own unsuccessful rehash of *Kane*—*Mr. Arkadin*—one critic said it "demonstrated only too clearly the coarsening of his showmanship." The *Citizen Kane* script was true creative symbiosis, a partnership greater than the sum of its parts.

Orson Welles is correct when he says, "Mank was a unique kind of person. If you're in the presence of talent, you recognize it. Finally in his life, Mank was given a filmmaker who was prepared to use the best of his work and get it on the screen, use those enormous gifts which should have been used on many *Kanes*."

And Herman once wrote about Welles: "When he has walked among men, they loathe his guts. But they miss him more than they would somebody they loved."

CHAPTER

11

Ah, the Whirligig of Life!

—HERMAN MANKIEWICZ

Citizen Kane WAS HERMAN'S SECOND CHANCE. HE WAS AGAIN a man of stature with entrée into saner, more satisfying worlds beyond Hollywood. Like a jumper, weightless at the peak of his leap, he was momentarily released, free to choose his life, to vitalize that serious, ambitious Herman Mankiewicz lost in detours and dead ends. Outside of the movie business, he could still have been a galvanic teacher, drawing upon the political historian, the collector of first editions, the erudite son who worshiped his professor father. Perhaps he could still be a coruscating, witty political columnist, a combination of Broun and Pegler.

Herman's phone began ringing with offers from studios. George Kaufman invited him to collaborate on a screenplay. "*Kane*," said Herman, "has restored a knowledge of my talents that seemed sadly forgotten." He savored his triumph and stayed in Hollywood. He wrote a friend:

> I seem to become more and more of a rat in a trap of my own construction, a trap I regularly repair whenever there seems to be danger of an opening that will enable me to escape. I haven't decided yet about making it bomb proof. That would seem to involve a lot of unnecessary labor and expense. And then every now and then people put such shiny new silken bows on the sides of the trap, and re-furnish and air-condition the whole thing so charmingly and efficiently. How do I know I would like it in the great world, anyhow?

Herman's deterrents were deep. If he had somehow entered the arena of the intellect, he would have met his father face-to-face. "Herman's father was his main competitor and at the same time his model," says the psychiatrist Dr. Fred Hacker. "The father was a real intellectual, and one of Herman's big conflicts was that he emulated intellectuals, but in his own mind believed he could never quite measure up." And self-destruction brought a kind of satisfaction. It was both a form of revenge on his father and a fulfillment of the professor's predictions.

Moreover, Hollywood suited a sardonic wit who fed on recognition and excitement. The hive of a studio teemed with targets for ridicule, and audiences were endlessly at hand. Whether his listeners laughed or cursed, they confirmed Herman's self-image as a wasted genius, an enfant terrible, a legend in the glamour center of America.

Herman did make a pact with himself. He would continue the formula of Victorville: no drinking; intense, regular work. He would parlay his refurbished reputation into more *Kanes* and into satisfaction right in Hollywood. At his first job at Fox he hired Rita Alexander, his *Kane* secretary, and paid her salary himself, a favor to Rita and a good-luck talisman for himself. And indeed, Herman was now a better screenwriter. He had more pride and less contempt for the medium. His fists were not so defensively cocked.

He was proud of many of his 1940's successes. For Fox there was *Rise and Shine* in 1941, a mad, profane satire on the hypocrisies of high-pressure college football. And there were others: *Pride of the Yankees*, the life story of Lou Gehrig, starring Gary Cooper; *Enchanted Cottage*, a romance between a disfigured war veteran and an ugly girl, played by Robert Young and Dorothy McGuire; *Christmas Holiday*, a Maugham short story and an attempt to broaden the image of the fading singer Deanna Durbin. The film historian William Everson considers that movie "one of the most interesting of the 40's film noir cycle, and much under-rated."

The producer of *Christmas Holiday*, Felix Jackson says, "Mank was very erudite and knew what to do with material. And believe me, that is a rare distinction. In Hollywood you could get a hundred years of colloquial writing, but it was very difficult to get stuff that was really written."

The Hollywood fun also continued: the hilarious dinner parties at Tower Road, the lunches at Romanoff's, full of what Nunnally Johnson called "first-class conversation." But in 1941 there came a series of shocks. A major one occurred during *Pride of the Yankees*. After the years of fruitless aspirations, Herman in *Kane* had achieved his vindicating triumph. Now, however, he was working, not with Orson Welles and John Houseman, but for Sam Goldwyn, a prototype mogul, a man who once exploded at a balky Bert Granet, "Fuck ethics! Who's paying you!" Herman rediscovered that after all, Hollywood was still "the cesspool." He began drinking again.

Sam Wood, the director of *Pride of the Yankees*, wrote a note to Herman: "I dismiss Goldwyn as a loathsome person, something you would expect to find under damp logs when you roll them over. If he had been where he belongs, making buttonholes, we would have had a better picture. Anyhow, Mank, we know how much we contributed to that bastard picture. But if he has his way nobody else will."

One of the indignities Herman suffered was a young writer named Richard Maibaum, secretly hired by Goldwyn to write a parallel script. One afternoon Goldwyn spotted Herman suffering the effects of his bonhomie at the Cock and Bull restaurant, the place Herman called "the Mother Church." Goldwyn summoned Herman, lectured him about drinking, and climactically produced Maibaum's pages, proclaiming, "This is what I mean by *screenwriting!*"

Herman sourly read through the pages and placed them

back on Goldwyn's desk. "He should drink," said Herman.

The movie was eventually written in collaboration with a constructionist, Jo Swerling, and received excellent reviews: "a resourceful script which has accomplished something of a dramatic miracle." It was voted the box office film of the month, and the script was nominated for an Academy Award. Once again Herman did not attend the awards dinner. "He had no false hopes," says Sara.

In November 1941 Professor Mankiewicz retired from City College of New York and arrived in California to settle permanently. The very next morning, out for a walk to buy fruit, he suffered a cerebral hemorrhage and soon passed into a coma. Herman sat hour after hour beside the professor's hospital bed, holding his hand, stroking it. Occasionally Herman would bend close and call out, "Papa. Papa." Erna Mankiewicz flew out and left after a few days. Joe came and went. At home Sara worried that Herman might have a breakdown as he paced the house, saying, "Oh, please, God, just six months more. Please. Just six months."

Joe remonstrated, "Herman, if he's not going to recover, why?"

"I just want to be able to talk to him," Herman said.

Joe replied, "After six months, it isn't going to be any easier than it is now."

"I just want to be able to talk to him," said Herman.

Professor Mankiewicz lived eight days, one of them his sixty-ninth birthday. He never regained consciousness. Herman never received or spoke any final, reconciling words of love.

The professor's body was returned to New York by train, and Herman and Joe were aboard, imprisoned together in a compartment. Joe was dispassionate. Herman had brought a supply of whiskey. He talked endlessly and half-coherently about his stolen boyhood bicycle. At the funeral Herman was very sober, very controlled. It was held in a funeral parlor, crowded with the professor's friends and colleagues. Afterward, riding to the airport with Erna and Joe, Herman was quiet. "Nothing worse can happen to us now," he said.

When Herman's mother died in a Connecticut nursing home in 1943, he did not travel East for the funeral.

Following his unhappy experience on *Pride of the Yankees*, Herman decided to exploit his renewed luster in the East among the Algonquin group. George Kaufman had invited him to work on a movie script, and in the spring of 1942 he settled, resoundingly, at the Kaufman farm in Holicong, Pennsylvania. Beatrice Kaufman, speaking to a friend, described Herman entering the living room "emitting sounds from every orifice."

While at the Kaufmans', Herman received an invitation from Alexander Woollcott to visit him on his island in Lake Bomoseen in Vermont. But Woollcott had to enter a hospital, and the visit was canceled. Herman later wrote Woollcott, "An operation for gallstones seems to me to be a very high price to pay for the privilege of not seeing me while I was in the East, but I suppose you know your values. The highest price ever paid in this connection was George Sterling's suicide in San Francisco the night before Mencken was to arrive to visit him."

Kaufman shelved their collaboration, titled *Sleeper Jump*, on the advice of David Selznick, who felt the script was too slight for Kaufman's debut as a screenwriter. The disappointment was another kick down the slide which started in 1941. "Heartbreak, heartbreak," says Sara. "I saw it in his face almost every day the last ten years."

Herman was now working at a series of studios on a succession of projects, most of them eventually abandoned. By the time he was hired for *Christmas Holiday* in 1944 he was well into a period of drinking. One day, not drunk, not sober, he walked into the office of the producer Felix Jackson, a man he liked. "Well," said Herman, "my psychiatrist finally cleared everything up. It is not Herman Mankiewicz who is drinking;

it is the little kid in me. So if the little kid is drinking, Herman Mankiewicz is not an alcoholic. Is that true?"

"Yes," said Jackson gently. "That's true."

Midway through the script, two top executives saw Herman drunk on the lot, and he was fired. At Universal there was a writer Herman scorned, named Dwight Taylor, son of the actress Laurette Taylor. Herman, a week after his dismissal, marched solemnly into Jackson's office. "Felix," he said, "don't you think Herman Mankiewicz drunk is still better than Dwight Taylor sober?" Jackson laughed and rehired him. Herman remained sober.

Jackson was an émigré from Germany and was self-conscious about his heavy German accent. During the picture Jackson became a United States citizen. "I know what you're thinking," Herman said to the new American after a little celebration. "You're thinking that there are too many goddamn foreigners in this country."

During *Christmas Holiday*, Herman stopped one day after work for drinks at Romanoff's. As he drove home up Benedict Canyon Drive toward Tower Road, his car drifted over the center line and collided head-on with a small station wagon containing Lee Gershwin, her secretary, and her maid. Lee Gershwin was the wife of George Gershwin's brother, Ira, called "the wrong Gershwin" by Herman. She suffered a three-stitch cut on her forehead and a case of "dashboard knees."

The accident happened in front of the deluxe bungalow that had once been Marion Davies's dressing room at MGM. Now it was Hearst's private quarters on her Benedict Canyon estate. At the moment of the collision Hearst was entertaining William Curley, publisher of the New York *Journal-American*. Hearing the crash, Curley investigated and discovered the unlucky coauthor of *Citizen Kane*. With the eyes of the Hearst press on them, the Beverly Hills police gave Herman a drunk test—walking a straight line—which he flunked. He was taken to the Beverly Hills police station and booked for drunk driving, in this case with bodily injury involved, a felony carrying a jail sentence. He was held for five hours without a lawyer. The arresting officer in his report described Herman as "insulting, sarcastic, impolite, and talkative."

Hearst's newspapers and his International News Service began a vendetta so flagrant that *Time* magazine ran a story on it as an abuse of the rights of a free press. Every successive detail of the traffic accident and trial received almost daily coverage in the Hearst chain. Herman said, "Dragged from the obscurity of the police blotter I was promoted from a middle-aged, flat-footed, stylish-stout writer into Cary Grant, who, with a tank, had just drunkenly plowed into a baby carriage occupied by the Dionne quintuplets, the Duchess of Kent, Mrs. Franklin D. Roosevelt, and the favorite niece of the Pope."

His friend John Gunther wrote Herman, "I read with bitter indignation the calumnies that fill the papers." Herman wrote back, "Hearst, I'm told, is going crazy trying to make up his mind whether to use the type size he was saving for Armistice Day—which is a slight consolation."

The trial was held in May 1943. Herman hired Jerry Geisler as his lawyer. "He's the same man who got Bugsy Siegel off," said Herman, "so we have hopes." Geisler argued that Herman's unsteady walk in the drunk test was due, not to liquor, but to the fact that one leg was shorter than the other. On the witness stand Herman pulled up his pant leg to show the scars from his operations. Orson Welles, who testified as a character witness, remarked, "That's the first time I've ever seen such an ugly leg used to influence a jury."

Dr. Saul Fox, husband of Sara's sister Mattie, also testified. That weekend his office was broken into, and the "M" drawer of his records ransacked. On top of the heap left behind was Herman's file. Dr. Fox has always assumed it was a fishing trip by the Hearst interests.

There was a hung jury, and the case was dismissed. Lee Gershwin and the secretary sued for $51,275 in damages.

They collected $3,216. One evening, weeks later, Herman was overheard at a telephone, in Romanoff's restaurant shouting, "Tell Mrs. Gershwin to stay the hell off the street for the next twenty minutes. Herman Mankiewicz is on his way home."

Herman once said to Margaret Sullavan, "You would be amused how quickly you get the idea that your phone must be out of order when you are unemployed." Herman had no work from January 1944, when *Christmas Holiday* was finished, until August. Herman entertained his friends with his predicament. He wrote George Oppenheimer: "You see, I have finally achieved that delicate balance I have been looking for all my life, where I won't work with fifty percent of the producers and the other fifty percent won't work with me. Of course, this makes for a good deal of hanging around the house during the day time, which leads Sara to holler on me, or to acquiring a package at Romanoff's, which leads Sara to holler on me."

Herman had always told himself that his old job in journalism would be a profession of last resort, an escape hatch if he ever did decide to leave Hollywood. Now in 1944, desperate for employment, Herman decided to fall back on what he called "printer's ink." He began writing satirical magazine pieces and expected a cordial reception at his old habitat, *The New Yorker*. But after three submissions, he wrote his friend Harold Ross a letter:

Dear Ross:

There's a serious situation in connection with the "New Yorker," to which I feel I should call your attention. To wit, somebody is intercepting mail addressed to you, returning manuscripts as "Editors of the New Yorker" and, on at least one occasion I can prove, forging your own name.

More specifically, during the past five weeks I have sent you three pieces to be printed in the New Yorker. They were all different, of course, but each one by itself was a perfect synthesis of Max Beerbohm, Katherine Mansfield, Frank Stockton, Bret

Harte, Maxim Gorki, Anatole France and—to an extent of about ninety percent—myself. When the first of these pieces was returned to me, with a note of apology from your "secretary," I thought nothing of it. Here, clearly, was a clerical error, over which we would both laugh in the days to come, to the accompaniment of one of the rare bottles of 1944 Ruppert's brought up from your cellar for the occasion.

The return of the second piece to my premises gave me for a moment to think. ("Gave me for a moment to think" is a mannerism, derived from my habit of writing indiscriminately in French and English, of which I must free myself.) There was with it, to be sure, a personal note, ostensibly from yourself, but despite its illiteracy I began to have my doubts. Then a few days ago, the third piece came home to rest with me.

The conclusion is obvious. Somebody is getting your mail before it reaches you and attempting to ruin you by returning all worthwhile contributions. (The reverse is also true. The same enemy or friend, as any issue of the New Yorker shows only too clearly, is facilitating the delivery to you of nothing but tripe and bilge.)

The situation has little importance for me. I have but to place in the mails the pieces to which I refer, to have them printed by "Pearson's" or "Everybody's" or "Ainsles's" or "Transition." I am trying to be of help to you. You will know how to plug the leak, if you truly desire.

Accept, my dear Ross, my sentiments true and cordial, while I remain,

Affectionately

Thereafter Herman received his rejections from Ross personally, and one of them said, "You've got enough effort and power in here to float the *Normandie*, but this is too weird a piece. It is overweighted because you are living in California, wasting the best years of your life."

Herman wrote back: "I took a chance, like Richard Whitney, that's all. Did he get pins stuck in him by mail Up the River?" Finally, one satire was published in the *Saturday Review of Literature*.

Herman traveled to New York to do an abortive collaboration for Jed Harris on a play called *Tucker's People* on the New York numbers racket. Before returning to California, Herman was in a high-stakes poker game. He lost $9,000. He wrote out three postdated bad checks.

Back home Herman flogged Hollywood for a job. He called his friends. He called Joe at MGM. He called all the agents he knew. Important names were still happy to come to Tower Road for dinner. But professionally, the impetus from *Citizen Kane* was fading.

A 1944 book, *The Pictorial History of the Movies*, co-authored by Deems Taylor, an old Algonquinite, made no mention of Herman in connection with *Kane*. "Did the actors make up their lines?" Herman raged. "Did Orson, directing, say, 'You cross from behind that chair, and while you're doing it, suppose you say as follows'? Or did Gregg Toland holler, 'Let's have a lot of lights on the left foreground, and while we're about it, I think I'll put a sled called Rosebud there to supply a little thread of story'?"

But even for Herman the *Kane* episode had so dimmed—and his capitulation was so complete—that he actually wrote his onetime adversary Louella Parsons a note of congratulation on her fatuous memoir, *The Gay Illiterate*. And Lolly wrote back a gushy, illiterate thank-you: "Coming from a sophisticated intellectual like you is praise indeed."

Whenever Herman, out of work, finally did get a job, he would call up friends with the news and boyishly say, "They loved me. I charmed them." An Eddie Cantor movie was abandoned "after two weeks of shadowboxing." There was an abortive movie biography of Helen Morgan and an eventually canceled potboiler called *Tasker Martin*, whose producer was John Houseman. There was a musical version of *Alice Adams* and an anti-Nazi script for Nunnally Johnson, both stillborn.

Sometimes Herman was hired simply as an experienced presence to reassure an insecure producer. When RKO put

him on its costume spectacular *Spanish Main*, starring Paul
Henreid and Maureen O'Hara, there was already a complete
script written by a young man named Yates and accepted by
the studio. The producer was a Wall Street broker with no
previous movie knowledge but important holdings in Techni-
color. Herman called him "the camel driver." Every morning
Yates delivered his repolished pages, and Herman read them
along with his morning mail. Sometimes, before passing them
on, Herman folded in some adjectives. "Give them guff," he
told Yates. "You write too bonily. The camel driver likes
guff."

Herman told Joseph Cotten, "Listen, I have a contract that
says I have to come to work and write so many hours a day.
But it doesn't say I have to admit what I'm writing." There
was an oblique self-respect in committing as little of himself
as possible when the work insulted his intelligence. He would
sleep on his office couch in the morning, his false teeth on the
table beside him and the secretary at the window on lookout
for the producer. Some mornings, as soon as he arrived, he
sent his secretary for a Dixie Cup to hold a dollop of scotch.

When the writer Frank Davis apologized for replacing him
on RKO's *Fighting Father Dunne*, Herman said, "Frank,
that's great. You write me out of it, and then you find somebody to write you out."

At RKO he was under the wing of the studio head, Dore
Schary. Herman had twice saved him in Hollywood and had
the temerity one day to use this fact for leverage. Schary was
outraged at the suggestion that he owed his career to Mankiewicz. There was an angry argument. Finally, Schary said,
"OK, Herman, you go your way, I'll go mine. And what's
more, you'll never work for me again as long as you live."

"Promises, promises," said Herman.

That evening Herman said reflectively to ten-year-old Johanna, "Life is just a Dore Schary."

Though the story is part of the Mankiewicz family lore,
Schary denies it, and Herman did stay on at RKO. Schary

insists that he considered Herman a good, tough-minded screenwriter. Indeed, Herman was an extraordinary optimist, and when he respected a project, he could still rouse himself. Schary gave him a whodunit, *A Woman's Secret*, to write *and* produce. It starred Maureen O'Hara and Melvyn Douglas. Whenever Herman produced a movie, Sara regarded that as just another of Herman's schemes to avoid his real work, writing. During *A Woman's Secret* he inveigled Sara into visiting the set. Arriving at the appointed time, she found Herman reclining in a hammock while two Nubian slaves washed his feet, dancing girls performed, and Maureen O'Hara fanned him.

In the spring of 1948 Schary assigned Herman to a script on John Broderick, known as New York's toughest cop. He traveled east with Sara on a two-week research trip.

A stay in New York was a major event in Herman's life. All Hollywood, in fact, looked to New York as toward Mecca. The money that controlled the studios resided there. The industry's newly rich came there to buy paintings by old masters. Women bought clothes in Beverly Hills stores to wear into New York stores to buy New York clothes. Although success in Hollywood was nice, nobody felt truly *important* unless recognized and respected in New York.

In the 1940's a return to his Algonquin haunts was more than ever for Herman a sentimental journey to his origins. As the train approached the Hudson River, Herman, frantic with anticipation, would pace the aisles. At New York's 125th Street station, where the steam engine was switched to an electric engine for the haul down Park Avenue, Herman's eyes would fill with tears.

His New York visits were like a man waltzing with the girl he wished he had married. Exhilarated by the pulse of the city, surrounded by the hard-edged mental energy he missed in Hollywood, received as a visiting celebrity, Herman was both elated and wistful. Now Broun, Benchley, and Woollcott were dead. But there were lunches and dinners with

Hecht, Kaufman, Billy Rose, Ross, Swope, all of whom still treated him with respect. He spent days in Nyack with Charlie MacArthur and Helen Hayes, rarely stirring from the bar and periodically telephoning Sara in Hollywood to say reassuringly, "I'm right here with Helen and Charlie, and I'm fine." He was again part of the elite aura of the Broadway stage, still his fantasy first love, though he sometimes found himself in "21" with two tickets in his pocket long after curtain time. Kaufman and Moss Hart continued to ask him for advice on their plays—as in 1934 when *Merrily We Roll Along* was a disappointment. The first scene was the opening-night party for yet another hit by an extravagantly successful playwright. The mansion was superb, the wife gorgeous, the guests the counterparts of Dorothy Parker, Baruch, Gershwin, Maxine Elliott, Swope, MacArthur. The problem, pointed out Herman, was that the play went on to ask the question, "How did this poor son-of-a-bitch get into this jam?"

No matter how salubrious it was for a cerebral wit, New York could be hazardous for a man with declining tolerance for double scotches. Sometimes he missed dates, like lunch with H. L. Mencken. Herman blamed it on a daylight savings time confusion. Mencken replied graciously from Baltimore, "Down here the yokels stick with God's time; they are afraid that lightning will strike their barns if they monkey with it."

While those days were bliss for Herman, he knew he was no longer a genuine part of New York. He had become a man without roots. Sitting in "21," Herman said, "Oh, to be back in Hollywood, wishing I was back in New York." Sure enough, the moment he returned to Hollywood, Herman wrote Herbert Bayard Swope: "That noise you heard last Friday around 42nd Street and Madison was me, being hauled screaming, fighting, clawing, and fouling on board the Century. RKO, the legalistic bastard, found some small type in my contract, overlooked by me when I signed it, calling for me to do a little work in return for my salary—so here I am, back in this Goddamn Lotus Land."

*   *   *

To fill his time, his need to love, his drive to leave an imprint, Herman more and more made an occupation out of Johanna. Outwardly the fairy-tale flower girl was growing into an operetta princess. The broad Mankiewicz features were refined into delicate, smooth white-frocked blondness. And to crown Herman's satisfaction, under the bobbed hair and bangs was a nimble Mankiewicz mind. Herman set out to train it. He transferred to her the weight of his hopes, repeating what his father had done to him.

Johanna would search out Herman the minute she came home from school. "Just to be in the same room with him was wonderful," she said. "To have him talk to you was even more wonderful. And to be a little kid and have his full attention was . . . ." Herman loved to debrief her, both flattering and annoying her. "What did you learn?" he would ask. "Who said what? Did you lead the discussion? What did you say? And Sharon? What grades did they get? What did you get?" Johanna sometimes stole a look at her father, off guard. "I remember feeling his torture," she said, "even though I didn't know anything about torture."

Herman always took her fantasies seriously, including a decision to become a neurosurgeon. "You have only to decide what you want to do and then do it," he would say. "There is nothing you cannot do." When she painted a picture for him, he said, "There's no reason why you can't be another Rosa Bonheur, or better yet, just a wonderful Johanna Mankiewicz."

He shamelessly listened in on her telephone calls and forced her to keep a diary. "Have you written in your diary?" he would ask. Then he read it secretly. Whenever he located any sort of problem, he worked on it with her. "It was like he hadn't been able to make it," said Johanna, "but I could."

Even spinach was an occasion for education. At dinner he ordered her to eat it. She said, "I hate spinach."

"Young lady," said Herman sternly, "in this house you do

not *hate* spinach. You *dislike* spinach. You *hate* your mother and father."

Herman disliked the fact that Johanna was a typical teenager and at the same time enjoyed it. He railed at her for wearing too much lipstick, for talking too long on the telephone, for going barefoot. At night after a party, he wanted to know, "What did Mary Ann wear? What did Louisa wear? Was Mary Ann's dress prettier than yours? Who did the boys talk to?" She would assert her independence by saying, "My dress was completely out of place. I had nobody to talk to. I didn't dance at all." Herman would look hurt and stare down at the floor. Then Johanna would pet him and go get him some tea.

"You always had to be *it*," said Johanna. "You were the best, and you had to show it. You couldn't be second best; you couldn't come in close. And that was an enormous pressure, and it made me rebel. I had this tremendous desire to be loved, whether or not I had done something terrific. I think that was part of my father's problem. You have to feel loved before you can do anything that requires self-love."

She also strained for Herman's approval. Johanna remembered: "You had to be very, very fast in everything, any mental work at all, skip grades, have the retort out before the person was finished. Profundity was not rated half so high as speed. But I was the best I could be around him."

It was always a triumph to extract a laugh from her father, a sort of "heh, heh, heh. That's very funny." "It was as though he had found a pearl in the garbage," says Frank Mankiewicz.

But at Tower Road there was a backlash to the humor. "You didn't dare commit yourself to anything or anybody," says Sam Jaffe's daughter Judy, "because you knew Herman would make a fantastic joke out of it. Or Sara's sister Mattie would do an incredible imitation of you the minute you left the room. You always pretended that nothing really matters."

Herman created with Johanna a feeling of conspiracy

against Sara. As soon as Sara left the house, he would stop working and say to Johanna, "Let's go have a driving lesson." They would pick up the afternoon editions of the newspapers and then drive aimlessly around Beverly Hills. Sometimes, when he fetched her at school, they went to a movie house where smoking was allowed in the balcony.

They played practical jokes on Sara. One involved the prized and hallowed house in Mount Tremper, New York, bought by Professor Mankiewicz as a summer retreat and willed to Herman. Laughing at their ingenuity, father and daughter concocted two letters to Sara. One was from the German caretaker, informing her the house had been totally destroyed by fire: "We must needs be telling you with great sorrow in our hearts which are overflowing. . . ." The second letter was purportedly from the insurance company, saying, with regrets, that the policy on the house had lapsed. Sara, completely deceived, saw no humor in the prank.

At night, before going to bed, Johanna would come up behind Herman's chair, put her arms around him, and kiss the bald top of his head. Herman pretended that this was too much sentiment. Sometimes he complained of his tired eyelids and made her kiss those, too.

When Johanna began going out at night with boys, Herman became a jittery Victorian. Every swain had to pass a driving test. A year younger than her classmates, Johanna had a strict eleven o'clock curfew. "Oh, God," said Johanna. "I would be driven into the driveway by a boy who might have considered kissing me—might—until he looked up and saw in the darkness on the balcony, this moving figure bellowing into the night, 'Johanna! It's eleven o'clock. Out and in!' It really did not do much for my social life." She once overheard her father predict that she would be married three times. "Mark my words!" he said.

Herman did not want his daughter to attend a coed California high school. She was enrolled in the snobbish Westlake School for Girls. It was the feminine Beverly Hills version

In Hollywood Herman was a celebrity in his own right, and an integral part of the social swim he often ridiculed. Typical of the 1930's was the Countess di Frasso's costume come-as-somebody-you-would-like-to-be party. Herman chose W. C. Fields playing the part of Mr. Micawber. Sara went as his David Copperfield.

Membership in Marion Davies' envied social set was enjoyed by Herman and Sara in the early 1930's. At a 1931 Mayfair Ball in Marion's honor are, standing, left to right: Clarence Brown, Robert Z. Leonard, Jack Conway, Irving Thalberg, Adolphe Menjou, King Vidor, Samuel Goldwyn, George Fitzmaurice, Herman Mankiewicz, Dr. Harry Brown (Louella Parsons' husband), John Gilbert, Lloyd Pantages. Seated: Mona Maris, Mrs. Robert Leonard, Mrs. Jack Conway, Eleanor Boardman (Mrs. King Vidor), Mrs. Samuel Goldwyn, Marion Davies, Louella Parsons, Mrs. George Fitzmaurice, Mrs. Herman Mankiewicz, Catherine Dale Owen, Aileen Pringle, Hedda Hopper.

Herman and Sara were also part of the ultra-exclusive Sunday tennis and luncheon group at the home of John Gilbert (right) while he and Garbo were the world's most famous lovers. Here, during one of their torrid films together, the two lunch on location.

A premier social event in Beverly Hills was the annual tennis tournament, attended by Herman with his close friends, husband and wife Leland Hayward and Margaret Sullavan. Sullavan so adored Herman, their relationship approached a platonic love affair.

The birthday parties of William Randolph Hearst—many of which were attended by Herman and Sara—were always colossal costume parties with brobdingnagian birthday cakes—like that above, a replica of Hearst's five-house village in Wyntoon, Calif.

San Simeon, Hearst's castle on a mountaintop near San Luis Obispo, was built over decades from hundreds of millions of dollars of European art plunder. The cottage where Herman and Sara stayed is at left, center.

Not only did Hearst's reckless spending finally bankrupt him, but Orson Welles, age 25, and Herman, then 43, combined in the script of *Citizen Kane* to write a semi-portrait of Hearst and lightheartedly hang the publisher in permanent effigy.

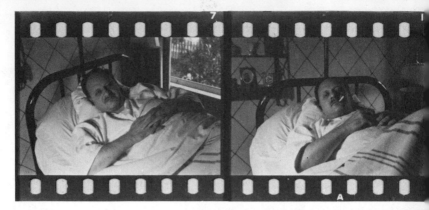

Herman and Orson Welles got together because an auto accident badly
broke Herman's leg. Welles visited
him at home, above, where their
conversations led to the *Citizen Kane*
idea.

When Welles commissioned him to
write a *Kane* script, Herman asked
that John Houseman, Welles' former
partner and Broadway producer, help
as his editor.

Herman's first draft of
Kane was done at a des-
ert guest ranch, dictated
to a secretary, Rita Alexander. Here, during a
lunch break, Herman
studies a snapshot of
Rita's while Houseman
looks on. In the loose-leaf
notebook is *Kane* in
progress.

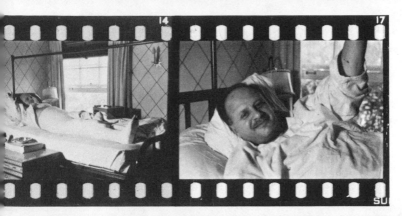

During the filming of *Kane,* a very young Welles confers with Joseph Cotten and Gregg Toland, the innovative cinematographer crucial to the movie. Welles sees himself in such pictures as "an uppish (vaguely poufish!) smart-ass."

During the writing of *Kane,* Orson Welles, left, visits Herman—who is having his brow wiped by his nurse. Houseman, right, holds pages of *Kane.*

Herman's personal "rosebud," the prototype of Charles Foster Kane's sled, was this bicycle. It was stolen during a boyhood misdemeanor and in punishment never replaced. The bike became a symbol of Herman's bitterness about his Prussian father and the lack of love in his childhood.

Rosebud, the sled, is the movie's symbol of Charlie Kane's loss of love and childhood, amputated when his mother signed him over to be raised by a bank executive.

In 1941 Herman won an Academy Award Oscar for the script of *Citizen Kane*.

In *Kane*, Joe Cotten passes out, drunk, while writing a review—as Herman once did on the *Times*.

Kane, dying, holds a Swiss snow scene paperweight—like one given Herman by Sara.

In New York, Herman also moved among the celebrated. On opening day, Mayor La Guardia invited him to the New York Yankees game.

In 1954, age 16 and class valedictorian, Johanna graduated from Westlake School. Sara's pride was solitary. Herman died in 1953.

Posing for a publicity picture, Herman promotes his second biggest success, *Pride of the Yankees,* the Lou Gehrig story. It earned him an Academy Award nomination.

Lou Gehrig was performed by Gary Cooper, and Babe Ruth acted himself.

Across the gulf of years and played-out expectations, the young, ambitious Herman of Columbia College eyes the final shrunken Herman the year of his death from kidney failure.

of his own Harry Hillman Academy. And paradoxically Herman fretted at the luxury of his daughter's life. He ruefully complained, "Johanna is cooperating wholeheartedly with our efforts to convince her that she's Barbara Hutton."

Johanna was the queen of her own clique, which included Walt Disney's daughter Sharon, Dore Schary's daughter Jill, and Sam Jaffe's daughter Judy. Margaret Sullavan's daughter Brooke Hayward was a close friend. All those girls inhabited homes that looked like movie sets.

Though Johanna's circumstances were by far the least lavish, she felt the most fortunate. "All that my friends had were screening rooms," she said. "And I had this tremendous father who could make us laugh any hour of the day or night, who knew everything there was to know about anything I needed to know. And my father was at home."

But Herman was also an embarrassment. He would appear in front of Johanna's friends in his habitual patched Viyella bathrobe, hairy legs disappearing into black socks and shoes. Picking up Johanna at Westlake School, Herman would emerge from the car in this outfit, and at school fetes he might be decked out in yellow or coral linen pants—with a green shirt. "He really thought he was a snappy dresser," said Johanna. And while daughters of the society wealthy did maypole dances in frilly white frocks, Herman would sit on the school steps holding a portable radio blaring out the news.

When her friends came to dinner at Tower Road, Herman thought nothing of removing his false teeth and putting them beside his plate without a pause in the flow of words. "But somehow," said Johanna, "you forgave him everything, if you just stayed in the same room long enough to listen to him."

A historical event the spring of 1948 compounded Herman's professional problems. Until then the studios had distributed their movies in theaters they controlled throughout the country. Theater owners had to exhibit all movies, no matter how mediocre. Even bad pictures usually paid for themselves, encouraging the prodigality and slack which Herman had always exploited. Now federal antitrust suits had stripped the studios of their distribution networks. Liberated movie-house owners could pick and choose and bargain and even conspire among themselves to keep fees down. Television was beginning to compete. Movie attendance was off. "It's not a papier-mâché panic," Herman said. "Those silly jerks have run out of money."

Wholesale layoffs and movie cutbacks were in progress at RKO, and Herman's sponsor, Dore Schary, was moving over to MGM as executive producer of all B pictures. There was no word on the Broderick project, "except from the barber in the second chair and a bus boy at Lucy's who admits he heard *something* about a Roderick, but it could have been Rod La Rocque."

Both Herman and the Broderick movie were dropped in the summer of 1948. Any payless time was a catastrophe in a household without savings and geared to earning $1,250 a week. Herman did not work again for a year. "Like show business," he said, "there's no business."

There were some misfires. A sleazy independent producer agreed to hire Herman if he was available cheap. On his way to the morning appointment Herman stopped by the Players Club for a few sips to dull his sensibilities. Then, when the producer made his cut-rate offer, Herman blistered him with scorn. And to complete the producer's punishment, Herman set out to humiliate him at gin rummy. Herman lost $5,000 and did not get the job.

In early 1949 Herman signed a contract to write the screenplay of Shaw's *Androcles and the Lion*. It was to be filmed in Rome, and Sara excitedly rented the Tower Road house and prepared to transplant the family. The producer was the extraordinarily flamboyant Gabriel Pascal, a Hungarian who had once been a dashing, resplendent young lieutenant in Vienna under Franz Josef. The movie's director, Harry Horner, was very satisfied with Herman's first draft script and found his suggestions stimulating. Pascal did not. Horner was ordered to fire Herman, who, protected by a contract, laughed uproariously. He sued Pascal and eventually won $20,000. The underfinanced project collapsed, and months later in the ultra-sedate Palm Court of New York's Plaza Hotel, Geraldine Fitzgerald mentioned Herman's name to Pascal, who instantly began yelling, "Herman J. Mankiewicz is a dagger in my rectum! Herman J. Mankiewicz is a. . . ."

Contacted by Nunnally Johnson, the producer Jed Harris got Herman a job writing the script for Tommy Dorsey's new radio show. Herman and Harris had lunch at the Brown Derby. "Never thanked me at all. No 'gee-this-is-great,' which I loved," says Harris, who asked Herman how he got into such a jam.

"For twenty years I made jokes about every son of a bitch in this town," Herman said. "Now they've locked the iron door on me. But don't think I wasn't canny. I knew this was coming. Right now at the Beverly Hills Branch of the Bank of America, I have over thirteen dollars stashed away against emergencies like this."

Herman despised the radio work and lasted at it only a few months.

Though it was against his nature, Herman tried unsuccessfully to retrieve some of the thousands of dollars he himself had lent through the years, writing men like producer Bernie Fineman, now gone from MGM and out of work. At the same time Herman was dunned by some old friends, down in their luck. Michael Arlen wrote, asking for "the five hundred dollars of our boyhood." "It would be very nice to see you," Arlen said. "Not quite as nice as five hundred bucks, perhaps, but nice all the same."

Herman promised to deliver the money "with a simple

ceremony: You utter the name of almost any American drink —a sidecar, say, and not too much sugar, please—but you preface it with the word 'double.' This may not be clear to you from my description, but you will catch on."

At the same time, no matter how low his financial ebb, Herman was as generous as always. He would buy Sara presents of a jeweled pin or watch, which she would stealthily return. Herman continued to give opportunity and encouragement and aid to far more people than had ever helped him. In 1948 Ben Schulberg, broke in Illinois, wrote Herman for enough money to get to Los Angeles to recoup. Herman sent $150, apologizing, "It's honestly the best I can do. Better than the best, actually. That may seem comic to you, but it ain't."

To help an indebted German refugee who was about to lose his house and furniture, Herman borrowed on his own furniture. It was a secret, until Sara came downstairs to find a strange man with a clipboard taking inventory of the contents of the house.

Throughout the 1940's, whenever the moneyless days continued month after month, Sara never lost her equanimity. She serenely continued her rituals: going to her manicure appointments, driving Johanna to her piano lessons. When the troubles were deepest, she would go to Elizabeth Arden's for a facial or sign up for French lessons. Once she had the dining room redecorated. "It's very necessary, like a hole in the head," wrote Herman to Sara's sister Ruth. "But I was occupied," says Sara, "I could exist." She was always sure everything would end happily. "Sara lived in a fantasy world," says Mildred Jaffe, "and that's what let her survive."

Sara also took practical steps. When absolutely necessary, she would rent the Tower Road house for $1,250 a month and move into an apartment costing $200, and the rent came to Sara. The two maxims Herman impressed on Frank were:

"Always pay your bills late (so creditors aren't nervous when you *have* to pay late)." "And always be out of the house when *they* move."

Sara's faith in events and people proved to be justified. Friends did eventually get work for Herman and did lend money. Herman managed some cash from the sub rosa practice of doing quickie, bootleg work for screenwriters who were overcommitted or missing their deadlines. He borrowed on life insurance and mortgaged his car. When checks bounced, he counterattacked fiercely. He wrote one creditor: "I find your communication unwarrantably insolent, and violating the established rules of behavior in a decent relationship." He berated another for using the phrase "apparently insufficient funds." "Funds are either sufficient," he wrote, "or insufficient."

Sometimes Joe Mankiewicz helped, though at Tower Road the word on Joe was: "He can't be counted on." Sam Jaffe always helped. But Sara turned especially to her own family, to Mattie's husband, Saul Fox, to Estherlea's Murray Silverman, to Ruth's Willie Chase, who says, "I'd send five thousand dollars, ten thousand dollars, whatever. I never thought anything about it. I just did it."

At Tower Road Sara kept the home running as steadily as a gyroscope. Meals were perfectly served. There was still a governess and cook. The vestiges of Herman's pride as a celebrated screenwriter demanded this Hollywood version of insolvency. But living even partially on the beneficence of people he considered inferiors must have been a humiliation, though, in his good years, Herman's purse had been wide-open for Aaronsons. Also, Herman still saw himself as a sort of flame at the center of Sara's family, giving off not only heat and light, but excitement and celebrity and even life. There was an A. E. Houseman poem Herman repeatedly declaimed, sometimes standing in front of the fireplace, a gleeful glitter in his eyes:

Good Creatures, do you love your lives
And have you ears for sense?
Here is a knife like other knives,
That cost me eighteen pence.

I need but stick it in my heart
And down will come the sky,
And earth's foundations will depart
And all you folk will die.

Sara's family was her solace, a warm and mitigating cave of relationships. Herman, too, cared deeply for his in-laws. "He could not have lived without their love," says Sara. During their frequent visits he was unstinting in his attention. He met their trains, took them to parties, made himself their attentive tour director who refused to start his day until he had planned their visits to movie sets and special restaurants. He once bought Estherlea a $300 gown so she could attend Irene Selznick's wedding. When Sara's brother Emanuel seemed doomed to take over the family box factory, Herman insisted he take up a profession and paid his way through dental school. For years he sent monthly checks to Naomi, an unmarried teacher in New York.

But Herman, endlessly ambivalent, also saw the Aaronsons as part of that gaggle of ducks nibbling him to death. He joked, fondly, about their seemingly constant presence. He claimed that Sara had a law barring anybody but a blood relative from eating at their table. He wrote Margaret Sullavan:

> If you are worried about any let-down in The Arrival of Relatives—don't be. Probably to stock up on relatives in case they get rationed, Naomi is due here next week and Ruth and Willie on August fifth. Estrellita is being held in reserve for September and we have just seen the last of three weeks of an added starter, a cousin named Janet. She's a very nice girl, I hasten to add. God damn it, they all are.

Herman increasingly vented his rage, his discouragement,

his unhappiness on those he needed and loved the most. Perhaps Herman considered the Aaronsons an extension of Sara, his Jewish mother and chief target. "Their closeness, their narrowness, the Jewishness drove my father crazy," said Johanna. Anything—a phone call from Naomi during dinner —could release a store of helpless anger. "You and your piss-elegant sisters," he would rave. "You bourgeois . . ." "This goddamn Jewish ghetto. . . ." An answering rebuke by Sara was more proof that Aaronsons considered themselves superior beings, more evidence that she cared for them, not him.

Herman, full of his own sense of self-degradation, seemed compelled to sully Sara and lower this proper matriarch. He detested the fact that she was proud of him and their life, feelings so opposite his own. Perhaps, somehow, she was a symbol of everything in his life that had come between him and what he would have liked to be. Herman would be conversing normally with some friend until Sara came into the room. Suddenly Herman's language would shift into such obscenities as "fuck Eleanor Roosevelt" and "that bleeding asshole Zanuck." If Herman had been drinking, he would lose all control, hurting Sara any way he could devise. Often in the final spasms of drunkenness, just before unconsciousness, he would cry out, "I don't want all this anymore."

After a ferocious scene with Herman, Sara would disappear in her car and stay away, knowing he would be wild with worry that she might not come back. Says Eddie Knopf: "Sara could be one of the terrible meek."

When she finally did return, perhaps not till the next day, she was remote and monosyllabic, the worst of punishments. "I didn't give in too quickly," says Sara. "I would never allow myself to be a doormat. I used to say, 'Herman, I'm human. I'm just a human being, and I lose control of myself, too, once in a while.' But he thought I never should. And productive it was not."

There were, of course, many serene times of tenderness

between Herman and Sara, and many kisses of apology. And no humiliation, even in public, dented Sara's dignity or her ultimate satisfaction with Herman. Her close friends never pitied Sara, though some suspected a streak of masochism. Joe Mankiewicz says, "It's hard to explain love in the sense that a Jewish wife loves the Jewish husband. In a good recipe, there has to be enough eggs to bind. And there has to be a certain amount of unhappiness to bind the Jewish marriage." Herman once said much the same thing: "Sara is well and happy and at the top of her misery."

When Ben and Rose Hecht gave Herman and Sara a festive and nostalgic twenty-fifth anniversary party at their house in Oceanside, Hecht affectionately pinned a huge purple heart medal on Sara. It was, said Herman, for "twenty-five years of uninterruptedly being wounded."

"Middle age," Herman would explain, "always is next year." But by 1949 Herman's health was finally giving out. His heart was enlarged. His blood pressure was high. The gradual failure of his kidneys brought chronic edema, and his ankles swelled hugely, engorged with water. He lived on a salt-free diet, taking a thermos of thin soup with him to Romanoff's for lunch. There were interludes in the hospital for tests and days of rest at home, seated in the sun near the pool. *Life* magazine did a long story on Joe Mankiewicz when in 1949 and 1950 he won four Academy Awards for writing and directing *A Letter to Three Wives* and *All About Eve*. *Life* writer Robert Coughlan interviewed Herman and found him sad and shrunken. "He seemed to know he was busted," says Coughlan.

Herman was eerily fulfilling one of those long-ago exhilarated courtship letters he wrote to Sara in 1919:

I prefer the photograph of you with the lean and hungry look. I'll save it—and years from now when the older children have gone to work and little Lucille has been thrown a ham bone to keep her quiet, and you complain that I'm not supporting you in the style to which you were accustomed, I'll drag out the photograph as proof that you were lean and hungry when I married you. All the photos I've let you have of me, you will notice, show me as eminently fat and prosperous. And years from now, when I look like the sad result of a year of Yom Kippurs, I shall upbraid you bitterly.

I love you, I love you.

Herman who loves Schnutz who loves Herman

But despite such a weight of difficulties, Herman did not give up. In 1949 he launched his weakening energies into a project he believed would be his second resurrection, a phoenix rising again out of a welter of unpayable bills and bad medical news—*Citizen Kane* recaptured but untainted by any debt to Orson Welles. It was a script titled *Woman on the Rock*, based on a book by Hector Chevigny, the fictionalized life of the evangelist Aimee Semple McPherson, who had died in 1944. Herman's plot device, a clear repeat of *Kane*, was a newspaper writer researching a retrospective story on the evangelist.

Aimee Semple was widely considered a fraud. She once disappeared for two weeks, then reappeared, claiming to have been abducted. Actually, insisted most newspapers, she had been in Mexico with the Foursquare organist. And Herman's version of McPherson, whom he renamed Ruth Church, was a sexy, dissolute dame.

When *Woman on the Rock* was finished, it was immediately in demand. Herman had the interest of William Wyler, Otto Preminger, Joe Mankiewicz, Joseph Losey and actresses Mercedes McCambridge and Evelyn Keyes. MGM and Fox both wanted it. Hedda Hopper had an item calling it "one of the hottest scripts of the year. Every top star in town is drooling to play it."

Herman's first problem was with the industry's Production Code, administered by Joseph Breen, who was described by Herman as "a devout Catholic layman and fathead." Breen judged the script detrimental to religion, and Herman was forced to make many changes. Then, as though once again success were unendurable and had to be sabotaged, Herman took the same stupid risk that he had taken with *Kane* and Charlie Lederer. Hoping to get support for the project, he gave the script to McPherson's daughter, Roberta, and thereby alerted her son, who had taken over as pastor of the Foursquare Church. This time Herman's subconscious wish was answered. The son threatened a suit for libel and invasion of privacy.

Herman retained Hollywood lawyer Greg Bautzer. When Bautzer spouted flowery legal phrases, Herman would yell into the phone, "For Christ sake, get off that nigger lawyer talk." But the moviemakers remained intimidated, and all interest disappeared. Herman sent the script to his friend Bennett Cerf at Random House, suggesting it be sold as a book. Cerf replied, frankly, no. And Herman wrote back: "I wanted a frank opinion; I always do. I'm beginning to wonder, however, why 'frank opinion' and 'not this time, Herm,' should always be synonymous." He gave the script to Orson Welles, who was unexcited by Herman's ideas.

In *Citizen Kane* a map of America sparkles with tiny lights which mark each of Charles Foster Kane's newspapers. When Kane goes bankrupt, the lights wink out one by one. "That's the way I think of my father," said Johanna. Herman worked sporadically during the early years of the 1950's; Eddie Knopf maneuvered him into a soon-abandoned vehicle for Red Skelton; Joe Mankiewicz, now at Fox, suggested Herman for *Pride of St. Louis*, the life of the Cardinal fastballer Dizzy Dean. The movie made money and earned some good reviews. Said the Washington *Post*: "One of the secrets for the success of this baseball film lies in the writing credit, Herman Mankiewicz."

Herman stayed on at Fox, writing an unproduced film, *The Number*, and with his old chutzpah counterattacked attempts to lower his $1,250-a-week rate, appealing directly to Zanuck. But the disappointment over *Woman on the Rock* had sapped the last of Herman's serious ambition. He began pressing the script into the hands of young writers at the studio, a small campaign to prove that *Kane* had not been a fluke.

"He was melancholy," says Sam Jaffe. "The jokes did not come as frequently. He kidded himself, but with a heavy sigh. And after a while it became 'Poor Herman.'"

Herman summed up his own classic fate. "When I came out here," he said, "I came for a few months. I don't know how it is that you start working at something you don't like, and before you know it, you're an old man."

In Hollywood, retrospection and depression often come early in life, when careers are shortened by the constant influx of young, fresh, vital successors, moving up fast. But Herman's predicament in the early 1950's was even more complicated and painful. He had long been the wit's wit, the conversationalist who could outtalk the famous humorists but could not put himself down on paper. Herman knew that his greatness was unpreserved, expended into the blank air during wit and carnage at movie producers' conference tables, at dinner and restaurant tables, at studio commissary tables, at poker and crap tables, at speakeasy tables and the Algonquin Round Table. And what was remembered was topical or dependent on tone of voice, timing, and exquisite turn of phrase. Lines which once rocked a room in laughter became pale when paraphrased in recollection. After he delivered a particularly flashing sally, Herman used to say, "You should write that down."

Somewhere in the mid-forties Herman's era had ended. The time of the adventurer wits was long over, replaced by a generation of men and women who thought of moviemaking as an art form. Now at the end of the decade Herman was a relic hung with legends, a semimythological figure on whom any outrageous story could be pinned. Young men at the studios sought him out—a new generation who reveled in listening to the flow of Herman's mind. These junior screenwriters evoked all the kindly paternalism in Herman, and he passed on the torch in the form of idiomatic maxims. "Get to the boobies! Get to the boobies!" he would insist, repeating an old burlesque catcall, which was to say, interest audiences right away. And Herman would advise, "Don't call the prince, he will call you," meaning, "Don't ask the producer about the script; that will only lead to trouble."

But Herman's own contemporaries no longer waited with anticipation for his arrival at the studio writers' table. As he sat down, most of the men just nodded and went on talking. A young admirer, D. M. Marshman, was mystified by this coolness. "I realized," says Marshman, "that Mank had worn out his welcome with them. There had been too many insulting wisecracks over the years, too many pukings on other people's dinner tables, too many conversations dominated and other people's achievements slammed. They were tired of him. Brilliant, often charming, but, on balance, more trouble than he was worth. If he had been enormously successful, he might have been able to get away with it. But a lot of his friends just walked away from him."

Herman was not the only product of the Algonquin era whose way of life led to a sense of exile, a disconnection from the people and ambitions that once sustained him. By 1943 Robert Benchley had become a Hollywood actor and stopped writing. He did continue his lifetime labor researching the Queen Anne period in England. But no word of the history play he planned ever reached paper. A Hollywood party in the early 1940's was struck silent by the sound of Benchley's voice shouting, "Those eyes! I can't stand those eyes looking at me!" Guests turned to see Benchley backing away from Robert Sherwood, by then the winner of two Pulitzer Prizes for dramatic writing. Benchley, pointing at Sherwood, went on, "He's thinking of how he knew me when I was going to be a great writer. And he's thinking, *now* look at what I am."

"Bob really hated himself," says a woman friend, Isabelle Davis. "He was very bitter and would tell you openly that he didn't want to live any longer." Benchley died suddenly in New York in 1945 of internal bleeding caused by alcoholism. In his Royalton Hotel apartment was a desk calendar with a page for each day. The pages were filled with reminders to himself, written ahead: dinner with so-and-so, get tickets for so-and-so, send allowance to Bob, etc. The page for the day of his death had the date circled in red, and every page after it was inexplicably and eerily blank.

When she was screenwriting in Hollywood, Dorothy Parker at a party at the Garden of Allah said, "I used to be a poet" —and burst into tears. Eventually she fled Hollywood to New York, where she confined herself in a cheap residential hotel she called "A Home for Unwanted Women." The loneliness, she said, "is no different from hanging, only you don't get used to it." She kept her liquor supply under the bed. Charlie Lederer isolated himself in his last years, contorted from arthritis, addicted to narcotics. Long before Ring Lardner, a heavy drinker, died in 1933 at age forty-eight, he had given up on living. Scott Fitzgerald called his death a prolonged suicide. Sometimes, when he was sitting alone, he held his face in his hands, sobbing.

Charles MacArthur died from alcohol in 1956. Helen Hayes says of her husband, "Charlie didn't ever get where he was heading. He didn't achieve a great deal. He had this terror of being shot down by that pack around him. They all had that fright, and they put on this 'I don't care' attitude like a bulletproof vest. But no writer is good when he doubts every word he puts down, when his nerve is broken."

The introverted, inhibited George Kaufman at the end became hooked on applause, appearing on television for a sort of celebrity fix. And even when he was ill and semiparalyzed from strokes, he dragged himself onto the *Jack Paar Show*. "I once owned a retriever who was very old and had arthritis," said Alexander King, who was there one of those nights. "He'd walk into the water up to his rump and with tongue hanging out would look into the horizon. He had once disported himself like a dolphin in these waters; now he was too sick, but still, he liked to have his belly wet. That was Kaufman."

During the late 1940's and early 1950's Herman had more and more times of depression, spent more and more hours alone in his bedroom. "It was like he was in Alaska," said Johanna, "getting the news of the world." The room seemed always in twilight. Wrapped in his bathrobe, his back to the window, Herman listened to baseball and football games on the radio, read every edition of every newspaper, every magazine, every new book. Sara or Herman went weekly to Hunter's bookstore and returned with a load of detective mysteries, many of which he had already read. "What he was concerned with," said Johanna, "was leaving a permanent mark. And if you have almost total disregard for the movies and that's the only mark you leave, then what are you living for?"

To raise money, Herman's library had to be sold. When the men came to appraise it, Herman stayed up in his room, and Sara got the figures.

He was cheered by the fascinated friends of his children who loved to listen to him talk. And any slight hope of an assignment could rouse Herman and get him dressed and ready to go. When the job collapsed, the despair was even deeper.

Herman's needs for alcohol and gambling excitement had long been drained away by drugs and ill health. "He looked ninety," Mattie Fox remembers. "But he was never more tender or sweeter, so dependent on each of us for love and affection. He wanted Sara always in sight." When Frank and his wife, Holly, moved to Berkeley—Frank was entering law school—they were no longer available for dinner and "discussion" afterward. One night Herman, sitting in the living room, said, "I miss the kids," and burst into tears.

Herman took radioactive iodine for his liver and returned from the treatments complaining that he felt like a vegetable. It affected his blood circulation; his nose turned white, and his hands were permanently cold. "I console myself," he said, "by remembering the early Christian martyrs."

Herman continued reporting for work at Fox studios, but there were times when he was too weak and in pain. His cough was deep and hurting. Irma May Templar, the ex-wife of Louis Weisenkorn, a neighbor in Wilkes-Barre, dropped by and found Herman in bed, frightened. Quietly they talked about Wilkes-Barre, about the Susquehanna River. They reminisced about the little Pennsylvania towns, like Pottstown, which they both knew. He thanked her when she left. Later Herman asked Sara for the scrapbook he had kept during his Columbia student years. But throughout their marriage Herman had always begged Sara never to show him old letters and photographs; they depressed him too much. She pretended the album had been misplaced.

In April 1953 Herman was hospitalized. The ambulance arrived at Tower Road, and Herman was carried down on a litter. Sara stood on the balcony and watched the white-clad orderlies slide Herman into the long white car. As he lay inside, looking up at her through the ambulance window, he flashed his little two-fingered salute. "I knew that was the last time," says Sara. "I knew he'd never come back."

In the hospital Herman had visits from Johanna, but she would sit impatiently on the edge of the bed and say, "How much longer are we staying?" Sara had told her he was merely there for more tests. On one visit Herman was thrilled when Johanna told him she had been nominated for student body president. He exulted. How wonderful; certainly she would win. When he finished, she told him, "I just turned it down." He was crestfallen.

The entire story was made up. He had reacted to one more assertion of her independence. "I wanted to prove to him that achievements—being best—didn't mean so much," said Johanna. "Needless to say, that is not my most cherished memory."

Herman's edema became so extreme that a forest of needles was inserted into his legs and arms to siphon off the fluid. His swollen heart constricted his breathing, and more and more he lived inside an oxygen tent. Sara retained an eminent heart physician as a consultant. The doctor's opinion was delivered in front of the hospital on the sidewalk. He told Sara and Herman's regular doctors, "I cannot suggest anything that could be done." Sara, furious, considered the statement cold-blooded and heartless, just what you would expect, she told herself, from a non-Jewish doctor. "I wanted to kill them all," says Sara.

She went back to see Herman, who was with his secretary, working out a movie idea he hoped to sell. Then she went off to Elizabeth Arden for her therapy of a facial massage and broke down weeping. When she returned to the hospital, Herman was quiet and peaceful. Sara bent over to kiss him, and suddenly they were in a frenzy of kisses, pressing them on each other's face and neck and arms.

Mattie sat with Herman the next morning. He was in the oxygen tent. When he summoned the nurse to open it up so he could smoke, the woman insisted, "That's the worst thing you can do, Mr. Mankiewicz. You shouldn't be smoking."

"I'm dying," said Herman incredulously, "and she's trying to break me of the cigarette habit."

With much amusement Herman told Mattie he had asked the night nurse if she thought he would get well. "How would I know?" answered the nurse.

Herman began to doze but was afraid he might never wake up. He asked Mattie to move her chair to where he would see her the instant he opened his eyes. When Sara arrived and bent over him, he said, "Hey, that was some love scene we put on in public." His chest pains had abated, and the oxygen tent was opened up. The room was filled with family and light joking talk. Somebody asked about Erna Mankiewicz, who was famous in the family for always knowing what other people should do. Erna was living in Italy, and Joe said he had arranged a job for her coaching Roman actors. "Coaching them in what?" asked Sara.

"Italian, of course," Herman said.

Frank arrived from San Francisco in a best blue suit. "That's a very bad sign," Herman said. "Your suit is much too black and absolutely appropriate for a funeral." Herman began seeing people alone, settling up his affairs. When Johanna came, still unknowing, he told her, "Be a good girl, Miss J." When Frank emerged from the room, he stood sobbing in the hallway. Herman had apologized for being a bad father.

Don was there from New York. To him Herman gave instructions for the funeral. "Put in the paper a notice that says, 'No flowers,'" Herman commanded. "Then you put, 'In lieu of flowers, contributions may be given to plant trees in the Arab section of Palestine.'" Don had to promise there would be no religious garb of any kind.

"Assuming that this ceremony will be held indoors," Herman continued, "hats will not be worn. You won't have any trouble, except that Dore Schary will wear his hat. You are to go up to Dore Schary and tap him on the shoulder and say, 'Dore, I have a message for you from the deceased: Take off your hat, you're in the house.'"

Herman, part of him still hoping, telephoned his secretary, Miss Linden, who had worked for him at Paramount, and they discussed the next day's work schedule at the hospital. When a rabbi entered the room, Herman sent him scurrying: "Get the hell out of here. I never had any use for you when I was living, and I've got no use for you now!"

Late in the afternoon Herman and Joe had their private talk. Herman was sitting up in bed, its back cranked high. On the wall hung a picture which Johanna had painted specially for the room. Herman's voice was controlled, weak, peaceful. His face was shrunken, a sad version of the plump, successful

Joe, the survivor. The family attachments, the jealousies, were reduced to the pinpoint of this moment. "I came closer to loving Herman than at any time in my life," Joe says. "It was the first time I ever felt he was listening to me and that he approved of what I was saying." Joe told him that he would get well. And then they talked about Johanna's future. Joe, who had been Herman's comaker on so many Morris Plan loans, promised to put her through college. Then as his brother left the room, Herman said his last words, a rueful joke.

"Well," said Herman, "that finishes everything I've got to take care of before I go to meet my maker." He paused for a lopsided smile and added, "Or in my case, should I say comaker?"

Soon afterward the nurse hurried to Sara and told her that Herman was in a coma. Sara rushed to the room, confident that she could rouse him. His breath was loud and shallow in his throat. She called to him against his ear, "Herman!" With a cloth she wiped his face. Suddenly, from the depths of his coma, he pushed her away with abrupt strength. "Whatever he was doing or thinking or wherever he was going," says Sara, "he did not want to be interrupted."

HERMAN J. MANKIEWICZ FILMOGRAPHY

The Road to Mandalay. MGM, 1926. Director, Tod Browning. Story, Tod Browning and Herman J. Mankiewicz. Script, Elliott Clawson. Players, Lon Chaney, Lois Moran, Henry B. Walthall, Owen Moore, Sojin.

Stranded in Paris. Paramount, 1926. Director, Herbert Arthur Rosson. Adapted from play, *Jennie's Escape*, authored by Hans Bachwitz and Fritz Jakobstetter. Film adaptation, Herman J. Mankiewicz and John McDermott. Script, Ethel Doherty and Louise Long. Players, Bebe Daniels, James Hall, Ford Sterling.

Fashions for Women. Paramount, 1927. Director, Dorothy Arzner. Adapted from play, *The Girl of the Hour*, by Gladys B. Unger, based on a story by French authors Paul Armont and Leopold Marchand. Film adaptation, Herman J. Mankiewicz and Jules Furthman. Script, Percy Heath. Players, Esther Ralston, Raymond Hatton, Einar Hanson.

A Gentleman of Paris. Paramount, 1927. Director, Harry d'Abbadie d'Arrast. Adapted from play, *Bellamy the Magnificent*, by Ray Horniman. Film adaptation, Benjamin Glazer. Script, Chandler Sprague. Titles, Herman J. Mankiewicz. Players, Adolphe Menjou, Shirley O'Hare, Arlette Marchal.

Figures Don't Lie. Paramount, 1927. Director, Edward Sutherland. Script, Ethel Doherty and Louise Long. Titles, Herman J. Mankiewicz. Players, Esther Ralston, Richard Arlen, Ford Sterling.

The Spotlight. Paramount, 1927. Director, Frank Tuttle. Adapted from story, "Footlights," authored by Rita Weidman. Script, Hope Loring. Titles, Herman J. Mankiewicz. Players, Esther Ralston, Neil Hamilton.

The City Gone Wild. Paramount, 1927. Director, James Cruze. Script, Charles and Jules Furthman. Titles, Herman J. Mankiewicz. Players, Louise Brooks, Marietta Millner, Thomas Meighan.

The Gay Defender. Paramount, 1927. Director, Gregory La Cava. Original story, Ray Harris and Sam Mintz. Script, Kenneth Raisback. Titles, George Marion, Jr., and Herman J. Mankiewicz. Players, Richard Dix, Thelma Todd.

Honeymoon Hate. Paramount, 1927. Director, Luther Reed. Adapted from an original story authored by Alice M. Williamson. Adaptation, Doris Anderson. Script, Ethel Doherty. Titles, George Marion, Jr., and Herman J. Mankiewicz. Players, Florence Vidor, Tullio Carminati, William Austin.

Two Flaming Youths. Paramount, 1927. Director, John Waters. Script, Percy Heath and Donald Davis. Titles, Herman J. Mankiewicz. Players, W. C. Fields, Chester Conklin.

Gentlemen Prefer Blondes. Paramount, 1928. Director, Mal St. Clair. From the novel by Anita Loos. Script, Anita Loos and John Emerson. Titles, Anita Loos and Herman J. Mankiewicz. Players, Alice White, Ruth Taylor, Margaret Seddon, Holmes Herbert.

The Last Command. Paramount, 1928. Director, Josef von Sternberg. Script, John F. Goodrich. Titles, Herman J. Mankiewicz. Players, Emil Jannings, William Powell, Evelyn Brent.

Love and Learn. Paramount, 1928. Director, Frank Tuttle. Script, Louise Long. Titles, Herman J. Mankiewicz. Players, Esther Ralston, Lane Chandler, Hedda Hopper.

A Night of Mystery. Paramount, 1928. Director, Lothar Mendes. Adapted from play, *Captain Ferreol*, authored by

Victorien Sardou. Script, Ernest Vajda. Titles, Herman J. Mankiewicz. Players, Adolphe Menjou, Nora Lane, Evelyn Brent, William Collier, Jr.

Take Me Home. Paramount, 1928. Director, Marshall Neilan. Script, Ethel Doherty. Titles, Herman J. Mankiewicz. Players, Bebe Daniels, Neil Hamilton, Lilyan Tashman, Joe E. Brown.

Abie's Irish Rose. Paramount, 1928. Director, Victor Fleming. Adapted from play by Anne Nichols. Script, Jules Furthman. Titles, Herman J. Mankiewicz. Players, Nancy Carroll, Jean Hersholt, Charles Rogers.

Something Always Happens. Paramount, 1928. Director, Frank Tuttle. Script, Florence Ryerson. Titles, Herman J. Mankiewicz. Players, Esther Ralston, Neil Hamilton, Roscoe Karns, Sojin.

His Tiger Lady. Paramount, 1928. Director, Hobart Henley. Adapted from play, *Super of the Gaiety*, authored by Alfred Savoir. Script, Ernest Vajda. Titles, Herman J. Mankiewicz. Players, Adolphe Menjou, Evelyn Brent, Rose Dione, Emile Chautard.

The Drag Net. Paramount, 1928. Director, Josef von Sternberg. Script, Charles and Jules Furthman. Titles, Herman J. Mankiewicz. Players, William Powell, George Bancroft, Leslie Fenton, Evelyn Brent.

The Magnificent Flirt. Paramount, 1928. Director, Harry d'Abbadie d'Arrast. Script, Harry d'Abbadie d'Arrast and Jean de Limur. Titles, Herman J. Mankiewicz. Players, Florence Vidor, Albert Conti, Loretta Young, Ned Sparks.

The Big Killing. Paramount, 1928. Director, F. Richard Jones. Script, Grover Jones and Gilbert Pratt. Titles, Herman J. Mankiewicz. Players, Wallace Beery, Raymond Hatton, Mary Brian.

The Water Hole. Paramount, 1928. Director, F. Richard Jones. From story by Zane Grey. Titles, Herman J. Mankiewicz. Players, Nancy Carroll, Jack Holt.

The Mating Call. Paramount, 1928. Director, James Cruze. From novel by Rex Beach. Script, Walter Wood. Titles, Herman J. Mankiewicz. Players, Thomas Meighan, Renee Adoree, Evelyn Brent.

Avalanche. Paramount, 1928. Director, Otto Brower. From story by Zane Grey. Script, Herman J. Mankiewicz, J. W. Rubin and Sam Mintz. Titles, Herman J. Mankiewicz. Players, Jack Holt, Olga Baclanova, Doris Hill, John Darrow.

The Barker. First National, 1928. Director, George Fitzmaurice. Script, Benjamin Glazer. Titles, Herman J. Mankiewicz. Dialogue, Joseph Jackson. Players, Milton Sills, Betty Compson, Douglas Fairbanks, Jr., Dorothy Mackaill.

Three Week Ends. Paramount, 1928. Director, Clarence Badger. Script, Louise Long, Percy Heath and Sam Mintz. Titles, Herman J. Mankiewicz and Paul Perez. Players, Clara Bow, Neil Hamilton, Julia Swayne Gordon, Harrison Ford.

What a Night! Paramount, 1928. Director, Edward Sutherland. From original story by Grover Jones and Lloyd Corrigan. Screenplay, Louise Long. Titles, Herman J. Mankiewicz. Players, Bebe Daniels and Neil Hamilton.

The Mighty. Paramount, 1929. Director, John Cromwell. From original story by Robert N. Lee. Script, Grover Jones, William Slavens McNutt, Nellie Revelle. Dialogue, Grover Jones and William Slavens McNutt. Titles, Herman J. Mankiewicz. Players, Esther Ralston, George Bancroft, Warner Oland, Raymond Hatton.

Marquis Preferred. Paramount, 1929. Director, Frank Tuttle. From novel by Frederick Arnold Kammer. Script, Ernest Vajda and Ethel Doherty. Titles, Herman J. Mankiewicz. Players, Adolphe Menjou, Nora Lane, Mischa Auer, Chester Conklin.

The Love Doctor. Paramount, 1929. Director, Melville

Brown. From play, *The Boomerang*, by Winchell Smith and Victor Mapes. Script, Guy Bolton and J. Walter Ruben. Dialogue, Guy Bolton. Titles, Herman J. Mankiewicz. Players, Richard Dix and June Collyer.

The Canary Murder Case. Paramount, 1929. Director, Mal St. Clair. From novel by S. S. Van Dine. Script, Florence Ryerson and Albert S. LeVino. Dialogue, S. S. Van Dine. Titles, Herman J. Mankiewicz. Players, William Powell, Louise Brooks, Jean Arthur, James Hall.

The Dummy. Paramount, 1929. Director, Robert Milton. From play by Harvey J. O'Higgins and Harriet Ford. Script and dialogue, Herman J. Mankiewicz. Players, Ruth Chatterton, Fredric March, Zasu Pitts, Jack Oakie, Mickey Bennett.

The Man I Love. Paramount, 1929. Director, William Wellman. Original story, Herman J. Mankiewicz. Script, Percy Heath. Dialogue, Herman J. Mankiewicz. Titles, Joseph L. Mankiewicz. Players, Richard Arlen, Mary Brian, Olga Baclanova, Pat O'Malley, Howard Green.

Thunderbolt. Paramount, 1929. Director, Josef von Sternberg. From original story by Charles and Jules Furthman. Script, Jules Furthman. Dialogue, Herman J. Mankiewicz. Titles, Joseph L. Mankiewicz. Players, Fay Wray, George Bancroft, Richard Arlen, Tully Marshall.

Men Are Like That. Paramount, 1929. Director, Frank Tuttle. From play, *The Show-Off*, by George Kelly. Script, Herman J. Mankiewicz and Marion Dix. Dialogue, Herman J. Mankiewicz. Players, Hal Skelly, Charles Sellon, Doris Hill, Helene Chadwick.

Ladies Love Brutes. Paramount, 1930. Director, Rowland V. Lee. From play, *Pardon My Glove*, by Zoe Akins. Script and dialogue, Herman J. Mankiewicz and Waldemar Young. Players, Mary Astor, George Bancroft, Fredric March.

Honey. Paramount, 1930. Director, Wesley Ruggles. From

novel and play, *Come Out of the Kitchen*, by Alice Duer Miller and A. E. Thomas. Script and dialogue, Herman J. Mankiewicz. Music and lyrics, W. Franke Harling and Sam Coslow. Players, Nancy Carroll, Stanley Smith, Lillian Roth, Skeets Gallagher, Zasu Pitts, Mitzi Green, Jobyna Howland.

Laughter. Paramount, 1930. Director, Harry d'Abbadie d'Arrast. Script, Harry d'Abbadie d'Arrast and Douglas Doty. Dialogue, Donald Ogden Stewart. Producer, Herman J. Mankiewicz. Players, Fredric March, Nancy Carroll, Frank Morgan, Diane Ellis, Glenn Anders.

Love Among the Millionaires. Paramount, 1930. Director, Frank Tuttle. From original story by Keene Thompson. Script, Grover Jones and William Conselman. Dialogue, Herman J. Mankiewicz. Players, Clara Bow, Stanley Smith, Mitzi Green, Skeets Gallagher, Stuart Erwin.

The Royal Family of Broadway. Paramount, 1930. Director, George Cukor, with Cyril Gardner. Based on play, *The Royal Family*, by Edna Ferber and George S. Kaufman. Script, Herman J. Mankiewicz with Gertrude Purcell. Players, Fredric March, Ina Claire, Henrietta Crosman.

The Vagabond King. Paramount, 1930. Director, Ludwig Berger. From play, *If I Were King*, by Justin Huntly McCarthy, and from operetta, *The Vagabond King*, by William H. Post, Brian Hooker and Rudolph Friml. Screen adaptation, Herman J. Mankiewicz, including some additional dialogue. Players, Dennis King, Jeanette MacDonald, Lillian Roth, O. P. Heggie, Warner Oland.

True to the Navy. Paramount, 1930. Director, Frank Tuttle. Script, Doris Anderson and Keene Thompson. Dialogue, Herman J. Mankiewicz. Players, Clara Bow, Fredric March, Harry Green, Sam Hardy.

Ladies Man. Paramount, 1931. Director, Lothar Mendes. From original story by Rupert Hughes. Script and dialogue,

Herman J. Mankiewicz. Players, William Powell, Kay
Francis, Carole Lombard, Gilbert Emery.

Man of the World. Paramount, 1931. Director, Richard Wal-
lace. Original story and script by Herman J. Mankiewicz.
Players, William Powell, Carole Lombard, Guy Kibbee,
Wynne Gibson, Lawrence Gray.

Monkey Business. Paramount, 1931. Director, Norman Mc-
Leod. Associate Producer, Herman J. Mankiewicz. Orig-
inal story and script, S. J. Perelman with Will B. Johnstone.
Additional dialogue, Arthur Sheekman. Players, Groucho
Marx, Harpo Marx, Chico Marx, Zeppo Marx, Thelma
Todd, Tom Kennedy.

Horse Feathers. Paramount, 1932. Director, Norman McLeod.
Script, Bert Kalmar, Harry Ruby, S. J. Perelman and Will
B. Johnstone. Music and lyrics, Bert Kalmar and Harry
Ruby. Associate Producer, Herman J. Mankiewicz. Players,
Groucho Marx, Harpo Marx, Chico Marx, Zeppo Marx,
Thelma Todd, Nat Pendleton, David Landau.

Dancers in the Dark. Paramount, 1932. Director, David Bur-
ton. From play, *The Jazz King*, by James Ashmore Creel-
man. Adaptation, Brian Marlow and Howard Emmett
Rogers. Screenplay, Herman J. Mankiewicz. Players,
Miriam Hopkins, Jack Oakie, William Collier, Jr., Lyda
Roberti, Eugene Pallette.

Girl Crazy. RKO, 1932. Director, William A. Seiter. From
musical comedy by John McGowan and Guy Bolton. Music
and lyrics, George Gershwin and Ira Gershwin. Script, Herman J. Mankiewicz and Tim Whelan. Dialogue, Tim
Whelan, Herman J. Mankiewicz, Edward Welch and Walter
DeLeon. Players, Bert Wheeler, Robert Woolsey, Mitzi
Green, Eddie Quillan, Arline Judge, Kitty Kelly.

The Lost Squadron. RKO, 1932. Director, George Archain-
baud. Script, Wallace Smith. Original story, Dick Grace.
Dialogue, Wallace Smith and Herman J. Mankiewicz.

Players, Richard Dix, Mary Astor, Erich von Stroheim, Joel McCrea, Hugh Herbert, Dorothy Jordan.

Million Dollar Legs. Paramount, 1932. Director, Edward Cline. Producer, Herman J. Mankiewicz. Script, Joseph L. Mankiewicz. Players, Jack Oakie, W. C. Fields, Lyda Roberti, Ben Turpin, Susan Fleming, Andy Clyde, Hugh Herbert, George Barbier, Dickie Moore, Billy Gilbert, Hank Mann, Teddy Hart.

Another Language. MGM, 1933. Director, Edward H. Griffith. From play by Rose Franken. Script, Herman J. Mankiewicz with Gertrude Purcell. Dialogue, Herman J. Mankiewicz and Donald Ogden Stewart. Players, Helen Hayes, Robert Montgomery, Louise Closser Hale, John Beal, Henry Travers, Margaret Hamilton.

Dinner at Eight. MGM, 1933. Director, George Cukor. From play by Edna Ferber and George S. Kaufman. Screenplay, Frances Marion with Herman J. Mankiewicz. Additional dialogue, Donald Ogden Stewart. Players, Jean Harlow, Marie Dressler, Wallace Beery, John Barrymore, Lionel Barrymore, Lee Tracy, Billie Burke.

Meet the Baron. MGM, 1933. Director, Walter Lang. Original story, Herman J. Mankiewicz and Norman Krasna. Script, Allen Rivkin and P. J. Wolfson. Dialogue, Arthur Kober and William K. Wells. Players, Jack Pearl, Jimmy Durante, Zasu Pitts, Edna May Oliver, Ted Healy.

The Show-Off. MGM, 1934. Director, Charles F. Reisner. From play by George Kelly. Script, Herman J. Mankiewicz. Players, Spencer Tracy, Madge Evans, Lois Wilson, Grant Mitchell.

Stamboul Quest. MGM, 1934. Director, Sam Wood. From original story by Leo Mirinski. Script, Herman J. Mankiewicz. Players, Myrna Loy, George Brent, C. Henry Gordon, Lionel Atwill, Mischa Auer.

After Office Hours. MGM, 1935. Director, Robert Z. Leonard. From original story by Laurence Stallings and Dale

Van Every. Script, Herman J. Mankiewicz. Players, Clark Gable, Constance Bennett, Billie Burke, Stuart Erwin, Harvey Stephens.

Escapade. MGM, 1935. Director, Robert Z. Leonard. From German-language film, *Maskerade*, by Walter Reisch. Script, Herman J. Mankiewicz. Players, William Powell, Luise Rainer, Virginia Bruce, Frank Morgan, Mady Christians, Reginald Owen, Laura Hope Crews.

It's In the Air. MGM, 1935. Director, Charles F. Reisner. Script, Byron Morgan and Lew Lipton. Players, Jack Benny, Una Merkel, Mary Carlisle, Nat Pendleton, Ted Healy. (Note: Screen Writers Guild credits Herman J. Mankiewicz with having worked on this film. His name does not appear in screen credits.)

John Meade's Woman. Paramount, 1937. Director, Richard Wallace. From original story by John Bright and Robert Trasker. Script, Vincent Lawrence and Herman J. Mankiewicz. Players, Edward Arnold, Francine Larrimore, Gail Patrick, John Trent, George Bancroft, Sidney Blackmer, Aileen Pringle.

My Dear Miss Aldrich. MGM, 1937. Director, George B. Seitz. Original story and script, Herman J. Mankiewicz. Players, Edna May Oliver, Maureen O'Sullivan, Walter Pidgeon.

The Emperor's Candlesticks. MGM, 1937. Director, George Fitzmaurice. From novel by Baroness Orczy. Script, Monckton Hoffe and Harold Goldman. Players, William Powell, Luise Rainer, Maureen O'Sullivan, Robert Young, Frank Morgan. (Note: Screen Writers Guild credits Herman J. Mankiewicz with having worked on this film. His name does not appear in screen credits.)

It's a Wonderful World. MGM, 1939. Director, W. S. Van Dyke II. From original story by Ben Hecht and Herman J. Mankiewicz. Script, Ben Hecht. Players, James Stewart, Claudette Colbert, Nat Pendleton, Guy Kibbee.

Keeping Company. MGM, 1941. Director, S. Sylvan Simon. From original story by Herman J. Mankiewicz. Script, Harry Ruskin, James H. Hill and Adrian Scott. Players, Ann Rutherford, Irene Rich, Virginia Weidler, Frank Morgan, John Shelton, Gene Lockhart.

Citizen Kane. RKO, 1941. Director, Orson Welles. Original screenplay, Herman J. Mankiewicz and Orson Welles. Players, Orson Welles, Joseph Cotten, Dorothy Comingore, Everett Sloane, Ruth Warrick, Paul Stewart, Agnes Moorehead, William Alland, George Coulouris, Ray Collins, Erskine Sanford, Harry Shannon, Buddy Swan, Sonny Bupp.

The Wild Man of Borneo. MGM, 1941. Director, Robert B. Sinclair. From play by Marc Connelly and Herman J. Mankiewicz. Script, Waldo Salt and John McClain. Producer, Joseph J. Mankiewicz. Players, Frank Morgan, Mary Howard, Donald Meek, Billie Burke, Bonita Granville, Marjorie Main.

Rise and Shine. Twentieth Century-Fox, 1941. Director, Allan Dwan. Story idea from the book, *My Life and Hard Times*, by James Thurber. Script, Herman J. Mankiewicz. Players, Jack Oakie, George Murphy, Linda Darnell, Walter Brennan.

Pride of the Yankees. RKO, 1942. Director, Sam Wood. From original story by Paul Gallico. Script, Jo Swerling and Herman J. Mankiewicz. Players, Gary Cooper, Teresa Wright, Babe Ruth, Dan Duryea, Walter Brennan.

Stand By for Action. MGM, 1942. Director, Robert Z. Leonard. Story idea from the story, "A Cargo of Innocence," by Laurence Kirk. Original story, Captain Harvey Haislip and R. C. Sherriff. Script, George Bruce, John L. Balderston, and Herman J. Mankiewicz. Players, Robert Taylor, Charles Laughton, Brian Donlevy, Marilyn Maxwell, Walter Brennan.

This Time for Keeps. MGM, 1941. Director, Charles F. Reisner. The characters created by Herman J. Mankiewicz in his original story, "Keeping Company," were used in the film. Script, Muriel Roy Boulton, Rian James and Harry Ruskin. Players, Ann Rutherford, Robert Sterling, Irene Rich, Guy Kibbee, Virginia Weidler.

The Good Fellows. Paramount, 1943. Director, Jo Graham. From play by George S. Kaufman and Herman J. Mankiewicz. Script, Hugh Wedlock, Jr., and Howard Snyder. Players, Helen Walker, Cecil Kellaway, James Brown.

Christmas Holiday. Universal, 1944. Director, Robert Siodmak. From novel by Somerset Maugham. Script, Herman J. Mankiewicz. Players, Deanna Durbin, Gene Kelly, Gladys George, Richard Whorf.

The Enchanted Cottage. RKO, 1945. Director, John Cromwell. Adapted from the play, *The Enchanted Cottage*, by Sir Arthur Wing Pinero. Script, DeWitt Bodeen and Herman J. Mankiewicz. Players, Dorothy McGuire, Robert Young, Mildred Natwick, Spring Byington, Herbert Marshall, Hillary Brooke.

The Spanish Main. RKO, 1945. Director, Frank Borzage. From original story by Aeneas MacKenzie. Script, George Worthing Yates and Herman J. Mankiewicz. Players, Maureen O'Hara, Paul Henreid, Binnie Barnes, Walter Slezak.

A Woman's Secret. RKO, 1949. Director, Nicholas Ray. From the novel *Mortgage on Life*, by Vicki Baum. Script, Herman J. Mankiewicz. Producer, Herman J. Mankicwicz. Players, Maureen O'Hara, Melvyn Douglas, Gloria Graham, Victor Jory, Bill Williams.

The Pride of St. Louis. Twentieth Century-Fox, 1952. Director, Harmon Jones. From original story by Guy Trosper. Script, Herman J. Mankiewicz. Players, Dan Dailey, Joanne Dru, Richard Crenna.

BIBLIOGRAPHY

Adams, Franklin P., *The Diary of Our Own Samuel Pepys*, Simon and Schuster, New York, 1935.

Adams, Samuel Hopkins, *Alexander Woollcott: His Life and His World*, Reynal & Hitchcock, New York, 1945.

Adamson, Joe, *Groucho, Harpo, Chico & Sometimes Zeppo: A Celebration of the Marx Brothers*, Simon and Schuster, Inc., New York, 1973.

Allen, Frederick Lewis, *Only Yesterday: An Informal History of the 1920's*, Harper & Brothers, New York, 1931.

Benchley, Nathaniel, *Robert Benchley, A Biography*, Mc-Graw-Hill, New York, 1955.

Ehrenburg, Ilya, *Memoires 1921–1941*, The World Publishing Co., Cleveland, 1964.

Friedrich, Otto, *Before the Deluge: A Portrait of Berlin in the 1920's*, Harper & Row, New York, 1972.

Gottesman, Ronald: Editor, *Focus on Citizen Kane*, Prentice-Hall, Inc., New York, 1971.

Graham, Steven, *New York Nights*, George H. Doran Co., New York, 1927.

Grosz, George, *A Little Yes and a Big No: The Autobiography of George Grosz*, Dial Press, New York, 1946.

Harmetz, Aljean, *The Making of the Wizard of Oz*, Alfred A. Knopf, New York, 1977.

Hayes, Helen, *On Reflection: An Autobiography*, M. Evans and Company, Inc., New York, 1968.

Hecht, Ben, *A Child of the Century: The Autobiography of Ben Hecht*, Simon and Schuster, Inc., New York, 1954.

Hecht, Ben, *Charlie: The Improbable Life and Times of Charles MacArthur*, Harper & Brothers, New York, 1957.

Higham, Charles, *The Films of Orson Welles*, University of California Press, Berkeley, California, 1970.

Houseman, John, *Run-through: A Memoir*, Simon and Schuster, Inc., New York, 1972.

Irwin, William, *Highlights of Manhattan*, Century Co., New York, 1927.

Kahn, E. J., Jr., *The World of Swope: A Biography of Herbert Bayard Swope*, Simon and Schuster, Inc., New York, 1965.

Keats, John, *You Might As Well Live: The Life and Times of Dorothy Parker*, Simon and Schuster, Inc., New York, 1970.

Kramer, Dale, *Heywood Broun: A Biographical Portrait*, Current Books, Inc., New York, 1949.

Kramer, Dale, *Ross and the New Yorker*, Doubleday & Co., Inc., New York, 1951.

Marx, Groucho and Anobile, Richard, *The Marx Bros. Scrapbook*, Grosset & Dunlap, New York, 1973.

McBride, Joseph, *Orson Welles: The Illustrated History of the Movies*, Jove Publications, Inc., New York, 1977.

Meredith, Scott, *George S. Kaufman and His Friends: A Biography*, Doubleday & Co., Inc., New York, 1947.

Parkman, Francis, *The Oregon Trail*, Little, Brown, and Company, Boston, 1872.

Rosmond, Babette, *Robert Benchley: His Life and Good Times*, Doubleday & Co., Inc., New York, 1970.

Rosten, Leo C., *Hollywood: The Movie Colony, The Movie Makers*, Harcourt, Brace & Co., Inc., 1941.

Seroff, Victor, *The Real Isadora: A Biography*, The Dial Press, New York, 1971.

Swanberg, W. A., *Citizen Hearst*, Charles Scribner's Sons, New York, 1961.

Teichmann, Howard, *George S. Kaufman: An Intimate Portrait*, Atheneum, New York, 1972.

Thurber, James, *The Years With Ross*, Grosset & Dunlap, Inc., New York, 1957.

Wilson, Edmund, *The Twenties*, Farrar, Straus and Giroux, New York, 1975.

Zierold, Norman, *The Moguls*, Coward-McCann, Inc., New York, 1969.

Zuckmayer, Carl, *A Part of Myself: A Portrait of an Epoch*, Harcourt Brace Jovanovich, Inc., New York, 1970.

INDEX

Aaronson, Emanuel, 310
Aaronson, Estherlea, see Silverman, Estherlea Aaronson
Aaronson, Mattie, see Fox, Mattie Aaronson
Aaronson, Naomi, 34–35, 41, 60, 310
Aaronson, Olga, 36–37, 41, 272
Aaronson, Reuben, 35, 36–37, 42
Aaronson, Ruth, see Chase, Ruth Aaronson
Aaronson, Shulamith Sara, see Mankiewicz, Shulamith Sara Aaronson
Adams, Franklin P., 71–72, 97, 99, 115–118, 153
Adlon Hotel (Berlin), 51, 60, 65
After Office Hours, 152
Alexander, Rita, 19, 249, 255, 263, 264, 278
Algonquin Hotel Round Table, 18, 68, 70, 74, 84, 90, 92–99, 115–122, 123, 145, 153, 250, 281, 286, 315
All About Eve (Joseph Mankiewicz), 176, 312
Allen, Kelcey, 85
Ambassador Hotel (Hollywood), 206
American Jewish Chronicle, 33, 34
Anderson, Maxwell, 86
Androcles and the Lion, 306
Animal Crackers, 114
Anna, Tante, 48, 57
Another Language, 150
Arlen, Michael, 76, 91, 307
Arlen, Richard, 140
Arnold, Edward, 174
Atkinson, Brooks, 73, 132, 126–127

Barnes, Howard, 270
Barr, Richard, 252, 258, 264
Barrymore, John, 211
Bautzer, Greg, 314
Beach, Sylvia, 44

Benchley, Nathaniel, 229
Benchley, Robert, 76, 85, 92, 97, 98, 99, 114, 115, 116, 118, 127, 152, 172, 288, 316–317
Berkeley, Busby, 145
Berlin, Germany, in the 1920's, 48–60
Berlin, Irving, 137
Bibesco, Prince, 87
Birchall, Frederick, 78
Blumenau, Johanna, see Mankiewicz, Johanna Blumenau
Boardman, Eleanor, 211, 228
Bodenheim, Maxwell, 87
Bogart, Humphrey, 206
Bogdanovich, Peter, 265
Bolitho, William, 76
Boni, Albert, 52
Boni, Charles, 52
Boni and Liveright, 52, 78, 80
Bow, Clara, 138, 140
Brandon, Mary, 115
Breen, Joseph, 313
Brisbane, Arthur, 213, 230
Broadway in the 1920's, 73, 74
Broderick, John, 288
Broun, Heywood, 71, 85, 92, 97, 98, 100, 118, 276, 288
Brown, John Mason, 92
Brown Derby (Hollywood), 141, 166, 190, 244
Butter-and-Egg Man, The, 86

cabaret life in Berlin, 58–59
Caesar and Cleopatra, 99
Cain, James M., 140, 141
Campbell, Alan, 115
Campbell Ranch, Victorville, California, 249–275
Cantor, Eddie, 147, 286
Carnival (Welles), 272
Carroll, Nancy, 140, 163
Case, Frank, 116, 120

Cerf, Bennett, 314
Chaney, Lon, 124
Chaplin, Charles, 127, 148
Chase, Ruth Aaronson (Mrs. William), 61, 310
Chasen, Dave, 194
Chasen's (Hollywood), 141, 194, 263
Chevigny, Hector, 313
Chicago *Daily News,* 59
Chicago *Tribune,* 20, 50–55
Chimes at Midnight (Welles), 271
Christian Endeavor Church and Temperance, 114
Christmas Holiday, 19, 279, 281, 282
Citizen Kane, 11, 18, 19, 86, 139, 177, 227, 235, 237, 243, 262, 275, 279, 282, 286, 313, 314
  American Academy of Motion Picture Arts and Sciences award, 271
  attempted suppression of, 267–270
  conception of, 246–248
  controversy over credits, 237, 238, 246–248, 251–266, 270, 272–273
  cost of production, 270
  critical praise of, 236
  filming of, 262, 266
  Geraldine Fitzgerald and, 246
  Hearst and, 266–270
  John Houseman on, 238, 254, 255
  Pauline Kael on, 236–238, 265, 272
  Don Mankiewicz on, 247
  Louella Parsons and, 266–270
  narrative of film, 19–20, 238
  precursors of, 172, 174
  Rashomon and, 247
  Andrew Sarris on, 238
  source of characters in, 72, 77–79, 174, 247, 248, 251, 260–261
  theme of, 238
  Orson Welles on, 247, 248, 251–252, 271, 273, 275
  Thornton Wilder and, 258
  writing script of, 19, 249–275
Claire, Ina, 140, 157
Clover Club (Hollywood), 134
Cocoanuts, The, 74
Cohan, George M., 150
Cohn, Harry, 14, 155
Colony Club (Hollywood), 134
Columbia Pictures, 14, 142, 155
Columbia *Spectator,* 29
Comingore, Dorothy, 262
Comrade X, 160
Connelly, Madeline, 70

Connelly, Marc, 70, 85–88, 92, 98, 99, 100, 114, 121, 126, 132
"Conning Tower, The," 71, 117–118
Cooper, Gary, 206, 272, 278
Cornell, Katherine, 244
Cotten, Joseph, 79, 207, 259, 274, 287
Coughlan, Robert, 312
Cowley, Malcolm, 97
Crawford, Joan, 128
Creelman, Eileen, 271
Crocker, Harry, 228
Cukor, George, 157, 201
cummings, e. e., 80
Curley, William, 282
Custer, Dr. Robert, 186

Dancers in the Dark, 146
D'Arrast, Harry, 234
Davies, Marion, 18, 144, 160, 208, 211, 212, 213, 228–231, 247, 266, 282
Davis, Frank, 176, 287
Davis, Isabelle, 317
Davis, Johanna Mankiewicz, 14, 318–320
  birth of, 199–203
  childhood and adolescence of, 290–292, 304–305
  death of, 11
  parents of, *see* Mankiewicz, Herman Jacob; Mankiewicz, Shulamith Sara Aaronson
  perceptions of father, 292, 311, 314, 319
  sister of, *see* Mankiewicz, Donald Martin; Mankiewicz, Frank
Dean, Dizzy, 141, 314
De Mille, Cecil B., 214
Dempsey, Jack, 62, 66
di Frasso, Countess, 206
Dillinger, John, 167, 172, 246
Dinner at Eight, 150
Disney, Sharon, 305
Dodsworth, 242
Dorsey, Tommy, 307
Drucker, Rebecca, 53
Duck Soup, 148, 150
Duncan, Isadora, 18, 62–63
Dunning, Decla, 164, 165, 166
Durbin, Deanna, 278

Ehrenburg, Ilya, 59
Einstein, Albert, 30–31
Eldridge, Florence, 231–232
Emerson, John, 85
Emperor's Candlesticks, The, 174

Enchanted Cottage, The, 278
Escapade, 152
Essenin, Sergei, 62–63
Evans, Ross, 119
Everson, William, 278–279

Fast Company, 143
Famous Players-Lasky Corporation, 127
Faulkner, William, 80, 97, 155–156
Ferber, Edna, 60–61, 118, 140, 150
Fields, W. C., 74, 128, 206
Fighting Father Dunne, 287
Firebrand, The, 86
Fitzgerald, F. Scott, 81, 95, 156, 201, 206, 317
Fitzgerald, Geraldine, 14, 194, 202, 231, 242, 246, 307
Fitzgerald, Zelda, 206
Fitzmaurice, George, 214
Flynn, Errol, 165
Fox, Mattie Aaronson (Mrs. Saul), 41, 167, 235, 272, 318, 320
Fox, Dr. Saul, 283
Francis, Kay, 140, 206
Freud, Sigmund, 80, 119
Front Page, The, 81, 139

Gable, Clark, 160, 162
Gaige, Crosby, 135
gambling in Hollywood, 134, 135
Garbo, Greta, 18, 128, 206–207, 209–211
Gay Defender, The (Parsons), 286
Gehrig, Lou, 278
Geisler, Jerry, 283
Gershwin, George, 198, 282
Gershwin, Ira, 282, 283
Gershwin, Lee, 282, 283, 284
Gilbert, John, 127, 209–212
Girl Crazy, 140, 146
Goldwyn, Samuel, 134, 137, 183, 279
Good Fellow, The, 116, 132, 172
Granet, Bert, 159
Green Hat, The, 91
Green Pastures, The, 121
Gribble, Harry Wagstaff, 172
Gunther, John, 283

Hacker, Dr. Fred, 135, 144, 177, 278
Hale, Ruth, 115
Hammerstein, Dorothy, 182, 201
Hammerstein, Oscar II, 28, 75, 182, 201
Harris, Jed, 113, 286, 307

Hart, Lorenz, 28, 29, 85
Hart, Moss, 198, 201, 272, 289
Hayes, Helen, 13, 81–82, 119, 162, 210, 289, 317
Hayward, Brooke, 305
Hayward, Leland, 169
Hayworth, Rita, 253–254
Hearst, Bill, 267
Hearst, William Randolph, 17, 53, 72, 88, 206, 212–214, 227–231, 261, 264, 266–270, 282–283
Heart of Darkness (Welles), 242
Hecht, Ben, 11, 12, 13, 59, 76, 81–82, 87–88, 117, 130, 133, 134, 137, 150–151, 160, 165, 189, 264, 272, 289, 312
Hecht, Rose, 272, 312
Held, Anna, 75, 76
Hemingway, Ernest, 80, 97, 117
Herbert, Victor, 85
Hergesheimer, Joseph, 127
Hermann, Bernie, 253
Hoffenstein, Sam, 34, 87
Hollywood Reporter, The, 131, 134, 153, 201, 271
Hopkins, Arthur, 86
Hopkins, Miriam, 140, 146, 163, 164
Hopper, Hedda, 266, 267, 313
Hornblow, Arthur, Jr., 14, 210
Horse Feathers, 146
Houseman, A. E., 309
Houseman, John, 11, 154, 159, 174, 236, 240, 241–242, 243, 248, 249, 250, 254–255, 256, 257, 259, 262, 264–265, 279, 286
Howard, Sidney, 153
Huckleberry Finn, 242
Hyman, Bernie, 152, 161, 168

Imperial Hearst (Lundberg), 256
Income Tax Wife, 163
Ingersoll, Ralph, 125
Insull, Samuel, 77, 248

Jackson, Felix, 279, 281, 282
Jaffe, Judy, 291, 305
Jaffe, Mildred, 208, 209
Jaffe, Sam, 139, 144, 171–172, 191, 208, 235, 239, 309
Jessel, George, 11, 201
Jester, The, 31
John Meade's Woman, 174
Johnson, Nunnally, 123, 133, 136, 139, 145, 156, 176, 232, 264, 266, 286, 307

Johnson, Will, 145
Johnstone, Justine, 37

Kael, Pauline, 139, 236–238, 265, 272
Kahn, Dorothy (Waring), 32, 96
Kahn, Otto, 86
Kalmar, Bert, 146, 150
Kaufman, Beatrice, 94, 96, 99, 281
Kaufman, George S., 11, 18, 34, 58, 65, 68, 70, 72–73, 76–77, 78–79, 84–89, 92, 96, 99, 100, 113, 116, 117, 122, 123, 140, 150, 160, 239, 276, 281, 289, 317
Kaufman, S. Jay, 84–85
King, Alexander, 317
Knopf, Edwin, 189, 193, 311, 314
Knopf, Mildred, 96

Lardner, Ring, 95, 118
Last Command, The, 131, 143
Laughter, 140
Lederer, Charles, 144, 160, 192, 206, 208, 212, 314, 317
LeRoy, Mervyn, 161
Letter to Three Wives, A (Joseph Mankiewicz), 176, 312
Levant, Oscar, 68, 204
Lindbergh, Charles, 66, 234
Linden, Rachel, 130, 321
Lindsay, Howard, 132
Little Shows, 86
Liveright, Horace, 78, 80, 86, 153
Lockhart, Gene, 245
Lombard, Carole, 140, 206
Long Christmas Dinner (Wilder), 258
Love 'Em and Leave 'Em, 84
Love in Exile, 231
Love Parade, The, 149
Lowe, Edmund, 210
Loy, Myrna, 152, 162
Lubitsch, Ernst, 129, 201, 235
Lundberg, Ferdinand, 256

MacArthur, Charles, 13, 81–82, 87, 118, 119, 122, 160, 210, 317
McAniff, Phil, 26–27
McCarey, Leo, 149
McGuinness, James, 144
McGuire, Dorothy, 278
McPherson, Aimee Semple, 313
McPherson, Roberta, 314
Mad Dog of Europe, The, 233
Maibaum, Richard, 279

Man with Red Hair, The, 161
Mankiewicz, Donald Martin, 65, 70, 136, 142, 150, 183, 202, 203, 247
  birth of, 61
  novelist and TV scriptwriter, 184–185
  parents of, see Mankiewicz, Herman Jacob; Mankiewicz, Shulamith Sara Aaronson
  siblings of, see Davis, Johanna Mankiewicz; Mankiewicz, Frank
Mankiewicz, Erna, see Stenbuck, Erna Mankiewicz
Mankiewicz, Frank, 142, 151, 180, 183, 190, 291, 321
  birth of, 115
  law school, 318
  parents of, see Mankiewicz, Herman Jacob; Mankiewicz, Shulamith Sara Aaronson
  siblings of, see Davis, Johanna Mankiewicz; Mankiewicz, Donald Martin
Mankiewicz, Franz, 20–27, 29, 52, 60, 95, 138, 148–149, 199, 201
  ambitions of, 22, 27–28
  attitudes toward wife, 21, 23, 30
  birth and boyhood in Berlin, 21
  children of, see Mankiewicz, Herman Jacob; Mankiewicz, Joseph Leo; Stenbuck, Erna Mankiewicz
  death of, 280–281
  education of, 21, 30
  journalist and teacher, 21–22, 23, 24, 25, 28, 30, 31
  letters from Herman, 39, 128, 167
  letters to Herman, 154, 167, 240
  rivalry with Herman, 29, 53–54, 98, 139
  wife of, see Mankiewicz, Johanna Blumenau
Mankiewicz, Herman Jacob
  Academy Award, 272
  Franklin P. Adams and, 71, 97–99, 115–117, 153
  Algonquin Hotel Round Table and, 89–122
  boyhood of, 17–27
  as Broadway producer, 84–86
  brother of, see Mankiewicz, Joseph Leo
  career aspirations, 13, 54, 86, 95, 96, 123, 124, 126, 127, 132, 133, 146, 147, 171–174, 318
  children of, see Davis, Johanna

Mankiewicz; Mankiewicz, Donald; Mankiewicz, Frank
Citizen Kane and, 17, 53, 139, 177, 235–275, 276
collaborations, 84–89, 116, 126, 132, 140, 158, 235–275, 276, 286
controversy over Citizen Kane, 236–273
courtship and marriage, 34–46
death of, 11–12, 322
drinking habits of, 29, 31, 48, 77, 87–88, 95, 115, 127, 149, 156, 166–167, 192–193, 195–198, 231, 249, 263, 278, 279, 280, 281–282, 312, 318
Isadora Duncan and, 62–64
erudition, 13, 15, 16, 17, 25, 26, 86, 124, 179, 204, 226, 230, 276, 279
father of, see Mankiewicz, Franz
gambling, 16, 31, 32, 56, 60–61, 115, 124, 135–137, 141, 186, 199, 250, 259, 286, 306, 318
Helen Hayes and, 289; on, 13, 162
William Randolph Hearst and, 17, 72, 88, 212–214, 227–231; on, 230, 247–248, 261, 264, 267–268
Ben Hecht and, 81–82, 87, 88, 133, 137, 273, 312; on, 12, 130, 165
John Houseman and, 248, 249, 250, 254–265, 286; on, 154, 159, 174, 236–238, 240–241, 255
Sam Jaffe and, 139, 144, 171–172, 191, 208, 235, 239; on, 315
Nunnally Johnson on, 133, 136, 145, 307
journalism and, 18, 26, 28, 41, 50–54, 57, 65, 73, 77–79, 213, 260, 276, 284–285
George S. Kaufman and, 18, 34, 58, 65, 68, 70, 72–73, 76–79, 84–89, 116, 132, 136–137, 158, 281; on, 73
Charles MacArthur and, 13, 81–82, 87–88, 119, 289
Marx Brothers and, 145–150
Louis B. Mayer and, 169–170, 236; on, 170
H. L. Mencken and, 289
at MGM, 127, 150–174, 235–236
mother of, see Mankiewicz, Johanna Blumenau
at Paramount, 130–150

as playwright, 85–89, 126, 132, 133, 172, 173
political interests of, 16, 29, 53, 72, 86, 98, 126, 139, 191, 230–236, 247, 276, 304
popularity of, 165, 207, 242
as producer (Hollywood), 140, 145, 146, 148
psychoanalysis, 198–199
as radio scriptwriter, 242, 245, 307
at RKO, 248–275, 286–288, 306
Harold Ross and, 18, 89–91, 92, 115, 117, 121, 124–125, 147, 152–153, 179, 261
Dore Schary and, 142, 287, 288; on Dore Schary, 321
B. P. (Ben) Schulberg and, 130–133, 137, 140, 142–143, 146, 149, 168, 174
as scriptwriter in Hollywood, 127, 130–131, 137, 140, 142, 146, 150–162, 167–169, 170–171, 174–175, 245–275, 278–280
David O. Selznick and, 92, 140, 157, 168
sister of, see Stenbuck, Erna Mankiewicz
as theater critic, 72–79, 89–91, 124
Twentieth Century-Fox and, 152, 183, 278, 314–315, 334, 335
unfinished early play on Hearst, 88
in U.S. Marines, 38, 95
at Universal, 281–282
vaudeville influences, 26, 27, 316
Orson Welles and, 17, 236–275, 283; on, 18, 158, 165, 236, 241, 248, 251, 252, 253, 258, 273–274, 275
on Orson Welles, 252, 261–263, 275
wife of, see Mankiewicz, Shulamith Sara Aaronson
wit, humor, irony of, 13, 14, 17, 24, 27, 29, 32, 39, 71, 72, 74–75, 87, 97, 120, 130, 132–133, 134, 142, 148, 149, 153, 157–158, 165, 167, 186, 207, 242, 263, 271, 283, 284–285, 315, 319
Alexander Woollcott and, 16, 34, 58, 60, 71, 79, 92–97, 100, 119, 281; on, 95, 114–119, 255, 267–268, 281
Mankiewicz, Holly Jolly, 187, 188, 318
husband of, see Mankiewicz, Frank

Mankiewicz, Ilene Korsen, 186
  husband of, see Mankiewicz, Donald Martin
Mankiewicz, Johanna, see Davis,
  Johanna Mankiewicz
Mankiewicz, Johanna Blumenau, 21,
  23, 30, 42–43, 60, 66, 83, 281
  attitudes to Herman, 24
  children of, see Mankiewicz, Herman Jacob; Mankiewicz, Joseph
  Leo; Stenbuck, Erna Mankiewicz
  death of, 281
  husband of, see Mankiewicz,
  Franz
Mankiewicz, Joseph Leo, 22–24, 28,
  60, 74, 83, 142–143, 152, 176–
  178, 239, 280, 309, 312, 313
  attitudes to Herman, 22–23, 24,
  83, 142–143, 175, 321–322
  early years, 21, 41, 177
  siblings of, see Mankiewicz, Herman Jacob; Stenbuck, Erna
  Mankiewicz
Mankiewicz, Shulamith Sara Aaronson, 60–61, 70, 83–88, 115, 127,
  163–169, 179, 188–189, 190,
  193, 195–197, 242, 251, 264,
  272, 320, 322
  on brother-in-law Joe, 176–177
  children of, see Davis, Johanna
  Mankiewicz; Mankiewicz, Donald Martin; Mankiewicz, Frank
  on Citizen Kane, 259, 263
  correspondence, 11, 35–36, 41–42,
  44, 63, 69, 148, 173, 189, 312–
  313
  courtship and marriage, 34–46
  family background, 34–37, 43–44,
  311
  family life in Hollywood, 180–186
  on Hearst and San Simeon, 214,
  227–230
  husband of, see Mankiewicz, Herman Jacob
  parents of, see Aaronson, Olga;
  Aaronson, Reuben
  "Poor Sara," 136, 166–167, 192,
  196, 213, 259, 284, 308–309,
  312
  siblings of, see Aaronson, Emanuel; Aaronson, Naomi; Chase,
  Ruth Aaronson; Fox, Mattie
  Aaronson; Silverman, Estherlea
  Aaronson
  as a wife, 168, 310–312
Mankiewicz, Tom, 189

Mann, Thomas, 156
Mannix, Eddy, 137
March, Fredric, 140
Marriage Mask, The, 157
Marshman, D. M., 316
Marx Brothers, the, 74, 114, 145–
  150, 206
Marx, Chico, 146, 147, 148
Marx, Groucho, 18, 74, 86, 114,
  145–146, 147
Marx, Harpo, 76, 145, 148, 150, 201,
  209
Marx, Sam, 153
Marx, Zeppo, 137
Mason, Pamela, 175, 178, 187
Mayer, Edwin Justus "Eddie," 86,
  129
Mayer, Louis B., 130, 135, 159, 160,
  169, 170, 201, 206, 211, 236
Meal Ticket, The, 172
Meet the Baron, 157
Mencken, H. L., 92, 97, 281, 289
Mercury Theatre, 241, 253, 255
Merrily We Roll Along, 289
Messenger, Lillie, 18
Metro-Goldwyn-Mayer (MGM), 123
  127, 142, 150, 209, 212, 235–
  236, 242, 269, 282, 324, 332,
  334
Metropole Cabaret, 60
Miller, Alice Duer, 94
Million Dollar Legs, 140, 176
Miracle, The, 84, 86
Monkey Business, 145–146, 148
Mr. Arkadin (Welles), 275
Murder of Roger Ackroyd, 242
My Dear Miss Aldrich, 174
Myers, Henry, 146, 176

New York American, The, 69
New York City during Prohibition,
  17, 66
New York Herald Tribune, 270
New York Journal American, 282
New York Sun, 69, 271
New York Telegraph, 84
New York Times, The, 18, 26, 57,
  73, 97, 114, 126, 233
New York Tribune, 33, 41, 53, 69
New York World, 66, 68–73, 86, 98
New York World-Telegram, 271
New Yorker, The, 18, 89–91, 116,
  123, 124, 125, 139, 176, 180,
  236, 265, 284–285
"News of the Berlin Stage," 57
"News on the Rialto," 73

newspapermen and Hollywood, 13, 138, 139, 152, 174, 260
Number, The, 314

Oakie, Jack, 130, 140, 143, 146
"Off Hour, The," 28–29, 32
"On Approaching Forty," 179
Oppenheimer, George, 100–101, 163, 200, 284
Orsatti, Frank, 270

Paramount Pictures, 127, 129, 130, 133, 137, 139, 142, 143, 146, 148–149, 174, 324, 326, 327, 328, 329, 330, 331, 332, 333, 335
Parker, Dorothy, 66, 85, 92, 96, 98, 99, 100, 115, 116, 118, 121, 244, 289, 317
Parsons, Louella, 131, 140, 266–270, 286
parties and other Hollywood customs, 206–230
Pascal, Gabriel, 306
Peace Pirate, The, 128
Pegler, Westbrook, 68, 276
Pemberton, Brock, 74
Pemberton, Murdock, 94, 116
Perelman, S. J., 145
Perkins, Bertram, 56
Perkins, Ray, 28
Perrin, Nat, 148
Phantom President, The, 150
Phipps, Tommy, 239
Pierson, Frank, 265
Pirosch, Robert, 176
Pitts, Zasu, 138, 140
Pride of St. Louis, The (Harmon Jones), 314
Pride of the Yankees (Sam Wood), 278, 279
Pringle, Aileen, 210, 214
Puncheon Club (New York), 138

Rabwin, Marcella, 141
Rainer, Luise, 152, 174
Rapf, Harry, 160, 167
Rathbone, Basil and Ouida, 206
Reinhardt, Gottfried, 207
Reinhardt, Max, 57, 84, 207
Revnes, Maurice, 162
Rifkin, Alan, 157
Rip Van Winkle, 242
Rise and Shine, 278
RKO Pictures, 140, 183, 244, 263, 264, 268, 269, 270, 287, 289
Road to Mandalay, The, 124

Robson, Mark, 253
Rockefeller, John D., 269
Rockefeller, Nelson, 269
Rodgers and Hart, 85
Romanische Cafe, 58
Romanoff, Mike, 164
Romanoff's, 153, 164–166, 282, 284, 312
Roper, Jack, 163
Rose Room at Algonquin, 92, 94
Rose, Billy, 289
"rosebud," 17, 19, 20, 21, 250, 271, 286
Rosenberg, Julian, 31
Ross, Arthur, 191
Ross, Harold, 18, 89–91, 92, 115, 117, 121, 122, 123–126, 147, 152–153, 191, 261, 284–285, 289
Round Table, The, see Algonquin Hotel Round Table
Round the Town, 84–85, 86
"Round the Town," 84
Royal Family of Broadway, The, 140
Ruby, Harry, 146, 149
Ryskind, Morrie, 31

San Simeon, 214, 227–230
Sandburg, Carl, 209
Sarnoff, David, 269
Sarris, Andrew, 238
Saturday Review of Literature, 285
Schaefer, George, 262, 267, 269, 270, 272
Schary, Dore, 142, 169, 287, 288, 306
Schary, Jill, 305
Schenk, Joe, 137
Schenk, Nicholas, 269
School for Sweethearts, 146
Schulberg, B. P. "Ben," 130, 131, 132, 133, 134, 137, 140, 142, 143, 146, 149, 174, 201, 206, 272, 308
Schulberg, Stuart, 134, 137
Schultz, Sigrid, 53, 55, 56
Screen Playwrights (studio union), 171
Screen Writers Guild, 170, 171, 264
Seaton, George, 157
Seldes, George, 51
Selznick, Danny, 169
Selznick, David O., 11, 135, 140, 141, 143, 150, 157, 168
Selznick, Irene, 159, 160, 168, 199–200, 201, 272, 310

Selznick, Myron, 143
Shaw, George Bernard, 99, 306
Sheean, Mr. and Mrs. Vincent, 118
Sheekman, Arthur, 86, 147
Sherwood, Robert, 11, 85, 92, 97, 115, 316
Show-Off, The, 152
Silverman, Estherlea Aaronson (Mrs. Murray), 116, 310
Simmel, Dr. Ernst, 198
Skippy, 143, 149
Sleeper Jump, 281
Smiler With a Knife (Welles and Mankiewicz), 245
Society Sphere, 33
Spanish Main, The, 287
Spitzer, Marion, 32, 89, 143, 189
Stallings, Laurence, 86, 120, 137
Stamboul Quest, 152
Stenbuck, Erna Mankiewicz, 21, 60, 142, 178, 199, 239, 280, 281
  brothers of, see Mankiewicz, Herman Jacob; Mankiewicz, Joseph Leo
Stevens, Ashton, 247
Stewart, Donald Ogden, 100, 121, 127, 135, 156, 159, 233
Stewart, James, 252–253
Stewart, Paul, 253
Sullavan, Margaret, 12, 163, 169, 184, 189, 208, 240, 284, 310
Swerling, Jo, 280
Swope, Herbert Bayard, 68, 289

Take Me Home, 131
Talmadge, Constance, 214
Talmadge, Norma (Mrs. George Jessel), 201, 214
Tashman, Lilyan, 210
Tasker, Martin, 286
Taylor, Deems, 116, 118, 286
Taylor, Dwight, 282
Taylor, Laurette, 282
Templar, Irma May, 319
Thalberg, Irving, 212, 213
Thanatopsis and Inside Straight Club, 95
Thau, Bennie, 205
"Theatrical Notes," 73
Three Week Ends, 131
Thunderbolt, 131
Thurber, James, 92
Toland, Gregg, 286
Toohey, John Peter, 90, 120
Tracy, Spencer, 152, 162
Tree Will Grow, The, 172, 246
Trosper, Katherine, 262

Truax, Mrs. Hawley, 113
Tucker's People, 286
Twentieth Century-Fox Studio, 152, 183, 278, 314, 319

Underworld, 134
Universal Studios, 163, 282

Vagabond King, The, 140
Valentino, Rudolph, 128
Vanity Fair (magazine), 97
Vanity Fair, 242
Variety, 136, 142, 149, 153
Vidor, King, 145, 210, 228
von Sternberg, Josef, 137
von Wiegand, Karl, 53, 56

Wallace, David, 119
Wallis, Gladys, 77, 248
Walpole, Hugh, 161
Wanger, Walter, 127, 133
Warner Brothers, 268, 270
War and Peace (ballet), 85
"War of the Worlds, The" (Welles), 243
We the People, 87, 88
Weaver, John V. A., 76, 84
Weber and Fields, 26
Weissberger, Arnold, 270
Weisenkorn, Louis, 319
Welles, Orson, 17, 175, 237, 238, 240–249, 251–267, 270–275, 314
  Richard Barr on, 252, 258, 264
  Citizen Kane and, 236–275
  Joseph Cotten on, 274
  education of, 243
  family of, 243
  Geraldine Fitzgerald on, 242
  as a Hollywood outcast, 244, 245, 271
  John Houseman on, 238, 254, 255, 256, 257, 259
  letters to and from Mankiewicz, 271, 273
  Mankiewicz and, 17, 18, 158, 165, 168, 236–275, 283
  on Mankiewicz, 18, 158, 165, 168, 236, 241, 248, 251, 252, 253, 258, 260–261, 273–274, 283
  "March of Time" and, 244, 246–247
  Mercury Theatre and, 241
  Louella Parsons and, 266, 270
  Ashton Stevens and, 247
  James Stewart on, 252–253
Wellman, William, 10
White, Katherine (Mrs. E. B.), 125

Whitney, John Hay, 172
Whitney, Richard, 260, 285
Whoopee, 47
Wild Man of Borneo, The, 126, 132, 172
Wilder, Thornton, 97, 258
Wilson, Edmund, 97
Wilson, Richard, 252, 264
Winchell, Walter, 230
Wirth, Chancellor Josef, 55
Wise, Robert, 252
Wizard of Oz, The, 174, 175
Woman on the Rock, 313, 315
Woman's Secret, A, 288
Women's Wear Daily, 55, 56, 85
Wood, Peggy, 76, 87
Wood, Sam, 279

Woollcott, Alexander, 16, 34, 58, 60, 71, 79, 92, 94–95, 97, 100, 113–114, 118, 148, 288
  letters from Mankiewicz to, 255, 267–268
Wyler, William, 313

Young, Robert, 152, 278
Young, Stark, 126

Zanuck, Darryl, 266
Ziegfeld, Florenz, 58, 75
Ziegfeld Follies, 86, 228
Zolotow, Sam, 78
Zuckmayer, Carl, 60
Zukor, Adolph, 149